HURON COUNTY LIBRARY

Date Due

W9-CIQ-456

HURON COUNTY LIBRARY

3 6492 00467644 8

Seaforth

AUG 2 1 2003

's of

BRODART   Cat. No. 23 233   Printed in U.S.A.

971.004916309034 Cam

Campey, L.
The Silver Chief ; Lord
Selkirk and the Scottish
pioneers of

PRICE: $24.95 (3559/se   )

THE SILVER CHIEF

*Lord Selkirk and the Scottish Pioneers of
Belfast, Baldoon and Red River*

LUCILLE H. CAMPEY

NATURAL HERITAGE BOOKS
TORONTO

⫴⫴ 2 3 2003

Copyright © 2003 by Lucille H. Campey

All rights reserved. No portion of this book, with the exception of brief extracts for the purpose of literary or scholarly review, may be reproduced in any form without the permission of the publisher.

Published by NATURAL HERITAGE / NATURAL HISTORY INC.
PO Box 95, Station 0, Toronto, ON, Canada M4A 2M8
www.naturalheritagebooks.com

Cover and text design by Blanche Hamill, Norton Hamill Design
Edited by Jane Gibson
Printed and bound in Canada by Hignell Book Printing, Winnipeg, Manitoba

The text in this book was set in a typeface named Granjon.

National Library of Canada Cataloguing in Publication

Campey, Lucille H.
    The Silver Chief : Lork Selkirk and the Scottish pioneers of Belfast, Baldoon and Red River / Lucille H. Campey.

Includes bibliographical references and index.
ISBN 1-896219-88-8

1. Selkirk, Thomas Douglas, Earl of, 1771–1820. 2. Scots – Canada – History – 19th century. 3. Belfast (P.E.I.) – History. 4. Baldoon (Ont.) – History. 5. Red River Settlement – History. 6. Highlands (Scotland) – Emigration and immigration – History – 19th century. 7. Canada – Emigration and immigration – History – 19th century. 8. Philanthropists – Scotland – Biography. I. Title.

FC3212.41.S44C28 2003   971'.0049163'09034   C2003-901386-3
F1063.C28 2003

ONTARIO ARTS COUNCIL
CONSEIL DES ARTS DE L'ONTARIO

THE CANADA COUNCIL | LE CONSEIL DES ARTS
FOR THE ARTS | DU CANADA
SINCE 1957 | DEPUIS 1957

Natural Heritage / Natural History Inc. acknowledges the financial support of the Canada Council for the Arts and the Ontario Arts Council for our publishing program. We acknowledge the support of the Government of Ontario through the Ontario Media Development Corporation's Ontario Book Initiative. We also acknowledge the financial support of the Government of Canada through the Book Publishing Industry Development Program (BPIDP) and the Association for the Export of Canadian Books.

CONTENTS

TABLES & FIGURES

TABLES

FIGURES

vii

ACKNOWLEDGEMENTS

I AM INDEBTED TO MANY people. First I thank Jane Penhale for having suggested the topic. I am fortunate in having Natural Heritage as my publisher. I thank Alison Fraser, archivist at the Orkney Library Archives, for helping me find my way through extensive documentation and for her warm encouragement. My trip to Kirkwall was one of life's very pleasurable experiences. I am particularly grateful to Marilyn Bell, archivist at the Prince Edward Island Public Archives and Record Office for her initial guidance on documentary sources. I wish to express my special thanks to Ian Mason manager of the Wallaceburg and District Museum for taking me to many places of interest in and near Wallaceburg and for his help in locating documentary sources and illustrations. I was thrilled when Barb Thornton sent me an original letter, written by an ancestor of hers, who was one of the Baldoon settlers.

Thanks are due to the staff at the Hudson's Bay Company Archives, Manitoba Provincial Archives, National Archives of Canada, the National Library of Scotland and the Scottish Record Office. I am grateful to the staff at the Toronto Reference Library for their patient assistance. I record my thanks to Jean Archibald, archivist, Edinburgh University Special Collections for her help in accessing Lord Selkirk's correspondence with Alexander McDonald of Dalilia and to the staff at the University of Birmingham, who helped me in my study of the Church Missionary Society papers. I am grateful for the advice given by Larry Haag and Lorraine Freeman, of the Métis Resource Centre, in Winnipeg. I would also like to record my gratitude to Dave Friesen of Hignell Printing Ltd., Winnipeg for the hospitality he provided to my husband and myself during our visit to Winnipeg.

The interlibrary loan service is one of the wonders of our modern age. I was able to read the Selkirk Papers from the proximity of my local library. I am grateful to the staff at the Salisbury Public Library for arranging loans from the National Archives of Canada for me and for their warm welcome on each of my visits.

I thank my friend Jean Lucas for her helpful comments on the initial manuscript and for permission to use her photograph of the church at Belfast, PEI. But most of all I thank my husband Geoff, for his enthusiastic support, photographic and computer skills and good sense. Without him this book would not have been possible. It is dedicated to him with much love.

PREFACE

On August 7, 1903 the people of Belfast celebrated the one hundredth anniversary of the arrival of Lord Selkirk and his 800 Scottish settlers to Prince Edward Island. A "Polly Tea" was held on the shore of Orwell Bay, near to the site where the *Polly* had landed with her many families from Skye and Wester Ross. A stone monument, commemorating Selkirk and his settlers, was erected with the proceeds raised from the anniversary picnic. This monument, standing in the grounds of St. John's Presbyterian Church, is a lasting reminder that emigration has a human dimension. The sweat and tears of pioneer life and the great pride taken in Scottish roots are expressed in a poignant inscription. And here, close to a cemetery, where large numbers of emigrant Scots are buried, Selkirk's presence can still be felt. We sense the affection and respect felt for Belfast's founder by its early settlers. Yet, many people in the outside world once viewed Selkirk quite differently.

The Manitoba scholar, George Bryce, first unearthed the many injustices which Selkirk suffered and later scholars have given sympathetic accounts of Selkirk's philanthropic motives and life's work. Although wrongs have been righted, insufficient attention has been paid to what he and his colonists actually achieved. They were in the forefront of the early exodus from Scotland to Canada. Selkirk's ideas and schemes, which offered a blueprint for colonization, greatly influenced Canada's early development. One hundred years ago, when the "Polly" monument was built, the study of history concentrated on the elite and powerful. Ordinary settlers were perceived as having little value or relevance. Selkirk's dealings, with the Colonial Office Minister of the day, and his various battles with prominent people were scrutinized in great detail; but his settlers, and the role they played, have been largely ignored. As we reach the bicentenary of the founding of Belfast, now is an appropriate time to look back at Selkirk and his settlers through modern eyes. They are the main focus of my book.

Aptly named the "Silver Chief," by the five Indian Chiefs (Moche-wheocab, Mechudewikoraie, Kayajiekebienoa, Peguis, Ouckidoat) with whom he negotiated a land treaty at Red River in the region then under the control of the Hudson's Bay Company, Selkirk spent a vast fortune on building pioneer communities. His Belfast settlers of 1803 achieved immediate success but the Baldoon venture, undertaken a year later, in Upper Canada, appeared to be a tragic failure. However, it survived and when the settlement became Wallaceburg, it thrived. Selkirk's third venture at Red River, begun in 1811, had to withstand the wrecking tactics of powerful men in the fur trade. He and his colonists persevered and created an agricultural settlement deep in Canada's North West which would have far-reaching consequences.

As my journey of discovery lengthened I became enthralled by the man. I could find fault with some of his decisions and his judgement; but his values and life's endeavours, in my view, are beyond reproach. More than anything, he had the foresight to realize that, unless more thought was given to Canada's population needs, its future would be in peril. Influenced by the thinking of the Scottish Enlightenment, he adopted progressive social ideas; his attitudes and beliefs were far better suited to our generation than his own. He was refreshingly tolerant, had strongly philanthropic motivations and fearlessly took on powerful vested interest groups for the sake of his liberal ideals. It was unheard of for Scottish Highlanders to be given the option of emigrating, rather than doing what their landlords required of them. But he gave them that option. The "trading lord," as his enemies in the fur trade called him, essentially took control of the great Hudson's Bay Company just so he could acquire land for his Red River colony. He was very much a man of the people. His settlers were not just names on a recruiting agent's list. He met them, personally supervised their settlements and even risked life and limb to rescue them.

Using Scottish archival sources, the book traces Selkirk's initial recruitment activities in the Scottish Highlands and Islands. I observed settler relocations in Canada using the Selkirk Papers. Copied on microfilm and consisting of some 20,000 pages, they are an Aladdin's cave for historians. In them, I found previously unpublished settler lists, which reveal the scale of Selkirk's undertakings and shed new light on the locations and activities of his settlers. They show how the Baldoon families were able to persevere in spite of losing around twenty per cent of their numbers. And, with the aid of Selkirk's diary, I was able to see into the intricacies of early pioneer life at Prince Edward Island. Using Orkney Island archival sources, I have investigated the important contribution made by Orcadians to Red River's early development. While the concentration is on the initial pioneers, I have also extended my study into the second half of the nineteenth century to establish their impact on later settlement trends.

On my travels I drove from Toronto to Winnipeg, stopping off at Sault Ste. Marie and Thunder Bay. In completing this daunting journey by car, I was mindful of the fact that, two hundred years ago, Selkirk had covered the same ground by canoe and horse. The scale and complexity of the problems which Selkirk and his settlers had to overcome were quite phenomenal. I hope that readers will come to share my admiration of what they achieved.

ABBREVIATIONS

DCB   *Dictionary of Canadian Biography*

DGC   *Dumfries and Galloway Courier and Herald*

EU   Edinburgh University

JC   *Inverness Courier*

IJ   *Inverness Journal*

NAC   National Archives of Canada

NLS   National Library of Scotland

OLA   Orkney Library and Archives

PAM   Public Archives of Manitoba

PANS   Public Archives of Nova Scotia

PAPEI   Public Archives of Prince Edward Island

PRO   Public Record Office

QG   *Quebec Gazette*

SA   *First Statistical Account of Scotland*

SM   *Scots Magazine*

SP   Selkirk Papers

SRO   Scottish Record Office

URSC   University of Birmingham Special Collections

THE SILVER CHIEF

Lord Selkirk and the Scottish Pioneers of Belfast, Baldoon and Red River

1. LORD SELKIRK
PHILANTHROPIST & COLONIZER

Now it is our duty to befriend these people...Let us direct their emigration and let them be led abroad to new possessions.... Give them homes under our own flag...and they will strengthen the nation.[1]

ORT DOUGLAS IS NO MORE. Founded in 1812, to support and protect the region's early Scottish settlers, its buildings once stood on the west bank of the Red River, near the forks formed by its junction with the Assiniboine River.[2] A winding path led up the riverbank to a gate set in the high wooden palisade which surrounded the fort. On Saturday, June 21, 1817, this path was to become the focal point for the large number of people who were assembling to witness the arrival of a most remarkable man. Word was out that the canoes carrying Thomas Douglas, fifth Earl of Selkirk, together with his bodyguards and soldiers were making their approach from Lake Winnipeg to Fort Douglas. A signal from the watch tower told Governor Miles MacDonell that the brigade was in sight. Months of waiting were nearly over. As the canoes came abreast of the settlement, at 9:00 PM, he gave the order for the guns of the fort to be fired. The crowd surged forward. As the tall, slender man with auburn hair, who seemed "lordly in appearance," came forward people flocked around him in such numbers that he was unable to move, "everyone striving to get hold of his hands and calling him their father."[3]

Lord Selkirk received this rapturous welcome from the local Natives. Over the next month he would negotiate a land treaty with five Indian Chiefs,[4] to reinforce his ownership of the land that he had acquired in Assiniboia from the Hudson's Bay Company. Holding him in very great esteem and being appreciative of his generosity to them, the Chiefs would award him the highest of accolades. They dubbed him "the Silver Chief," the name by which he would be known in the region for many years to come. And it was a highly appropriate title. Here was a man who was devoting much of his considerable wealth to philanthropic endeavours.

3

Lord Selkirk's sketch of Fort Douglas, 1817. Fort Douglas was situated at what is now Alexander Avenue, just north of Alexander Docks, in Winnipeg. *Photograph by Geoff Campey.*

He fostered colonization schemes. Having been shocked, as a young man, by the extreme poverty which he had witnessed during his travels in the Highlands of Scotland, he dedicated his life and substantial fortune to helping poor and dispossessed Scots relocate themselves in British North America.[5] Before getting to Red River, he had already spent huge sums on building two pioneer settlements, one at Belfast, in Prince Edward Island, and the other at Baldoon, in Upper Canada. Now his colonization efforts had taken him to his third venture, in Rupert's Land. Here, he hoped to realize his vision of an agricultural settlement, situated deep in the heart of a region dedicated solely to the fur trade.

On his arrival at Red River he would have been greeted by a few settlers and some Hudson's Bay Company workers. However, most of his colonists were absent. Having escaped an armed attack on their settlement in the previous year, many had fled to a temporary encampment at the northern end of Lake Winnipeg. After hearing the news that Selkirk was on his way, they were rushing with all possible speed to meet him. Their meeting on July 20, inspired by the presence of Lord Selkirk, would be recalled with great affection, both by the settlers and their descendants over many decades.

Yet, his image in the outside world was so very different. Selkirk was a controversial figure, who was thought, by some, to be unscrupulous and overly aggressive. In promoting emigration, he attracted considerable criticism from Scottish lairds who feared the loss of tenants from their estates.

He was accused of exploiting the weak and vulnerable for his own selfish ends, allegations which did him considerable harm. His founding of the Red River settlement contributed to a fierce power struggle between the Hudson's Bay Company and its chief rival, the North West Company. All added to his notoriety since he was accused of wilfully damaging the trade of the North West Company in the pursuit of his own interests in the fur trade war.

Selkirk's death came just three years after this visit to Red River. With his reputation badly tarnished and much of his work incomplete, he suffered a sad ending of a life dedicated to others. His beautiful and intelligent wife, Jean[6], who supported and encouraged his work, in spite of the drain on the family income was by this time managing his affairs. She sought consolation by looking to the future:

Thomas Douglas, Fifth Earl of Selkirk. Photograph from a copy, obtained by George Bryce, of a painting believed to be by Sir Henry Raeburn. At one time it was at Selkirk's ancestral home at St. Mary's Isle, Kirkcudbright, Scotland. *Courtesy of Toronto Reference Library, J. Ross Robertson Collection.*

I feel confident that, if we have patience, he will receive ample justice and when the North West Company [is] forgotten, his name and character will be revered as they ought. For this I would wish to wait, although it may be his grand-children only who are likely to feel it, only of course everything of business that concerns the success of his schemes I should as little shrink from now, as ever.[7]

She would be proven right. It would take some 60 years before the hurtful allegations made against her husband would be proved groundless and even longer for his achievements to be fully recognized.

When he arrived at Fort Douglas on June 21, Selkirk came with some papers which would one day clear his name. The payments to conspirators, the planning of brutal attacks, the spreading of malicious rumours would all come to light. The North West Company papers, which he had read during his occupation of their headquarters at Fort William, revealed their treachery and inhumanity. Yet, it would take a very long time before this evidence would change public perceptions of the man. A fixation with Red River blinded people to wider issues and concentrated minds solely on Selkirk's activities during the fur trade feud.[8] His enemies may have behaved dishonourably but he was to be condemned, as well, for his aggressive behaviour. The turning point came in, 1882, when Dr. George Bryce, a Presbyterian minister and founder of Manitoba College, undertook a major reappraisal of Selkirk's work using the Hudson's Bay Company Archives and the Selkirk family papers kept at St. Mary's Isle in Kircudbrightshire.[9] Bryce looked beyond the fur trade and saw the Selkirk who had dedicated his life to founding pioneer settlements:

> Lord Selkirk organized a colony for the good of the colonists who were in miserable circumstances in their native country; placed his colony where it would be unaffected by contact with what he considered hurtful influences; and spent time and thought, even money – even his own life being worn out in the struggle – to advance the interests of his people. Why will men attribute sordid, impure, interested motives, when pure patriotism or noble philanthropy are simple explanations, lying ready to hand?[10]

Other supportive accounts of his life have since followed, but they have focused largely on his "wild west" encounters at Red River.[11] The old tarnished image is gone, but the impact that he and his settlers made on Canada's early development has not been fully appreciated. Little notice has been taken of his Belfast and Baldoon ventures or of the part played by his steadfast settlers in the three colonization endeavours.

The August 2003 celebrations of the bicentenary of the founding of Selkirk's first colony at Belfast, Prince Edward Island, provided a fitting time to take a fresh look at his life's work. Because the Belfast settlements were launched with 800 emigrant Scots, many of whom came from the Isle of Skye, these became major bastions of Highland culture. The strong Scottish presence, still evident in the eastern Maritimes, owes a great deal to the financial backing of this one man and the catalytic effect of the Belfast settlers' early success. And after a difficult beginning, his much smaller undertaking at Baldoon, a year later, eventually transformed itself into the thriving commercial centre of Wallaceburg, thus establishing a major enclave of Argyll Scots in this then remote corner of Upper Canada. But it was his Red River colony which would have the most far-reaching consequences. Eventually succeeding beyond Selkirk's wildest dreams, it concentrated many Sutherland and Orcadian settlers in what would become the province of Manitoba at a crucial point in Canada's history.

Selkirk was well ahead of his time and in many respects would have been far better suited to our present era. A "hands on" aristocrat, with liberal views and a passion to establish successful pioneer communities, he was completely out of step with the political and social climate of his day. Even those who sympathized with his aims were puzzled by his desire to devote his life and family inheritance to colonization schemes. But he had correctly anticipated the zeal for emigration from the Highlands and Islands. One of the driving forces was poverty. He could see that it was "an unavoidable result of the state of the country arising from causes above all control" and he offered people a way out.[12] He held out the prospect of a new life in British North America. Failing to win government backing for his ventures, he financed their relocation costs entirely from his own resources.[13]

Memorial, commemorating the original Fort William site located at the junction of McNaughton and McTavish streets in Thunder Bay. *Photograph by Geoff Campey.*

7

What few people appreciated at the time was that Thomas Douglas had become wedded to the new ideas on social reform, which were sweeping through Scotland, long before he became the fifth Earl of Selkirk. Although many intellectuals had been won over to the new liberal thinking, Selkirk was unique in the way he applied liberal theories to the contentious issue of Highland emigration to British North America. He believed that poor and displaced Highlanders should be assisted to emigrate on humanitarian grounds and that their relocation should be carefully planned and conducted to suit their settlement needs as well as British colonial interests. Such ideas, which seemed threatening to Scotland's ruling classes at the time, would eventually win acceptance. Selkirk would demonstrate the benefits of planned colonization although it would take many years before his and his settlers' achievements would be fully recognized.

Born in 1771 at St. Mary's Isle, near Kirkcudbright, on the southwestern coast of Scotland, Thomas Douglas was seventh in line to succeed his father, the fourth Earl.[14] Two brothers died in infancy; but with four remaining brothers, he had no realistic prospect of inheriting the title. However, all four brothers died between 1794 and 1797 (Appendix A). Thus, with his father's death in 1799, Thomas, who had always expected to make his own way in the world, suddenly found himself named the fifth Earl, when he was just 28 years of age.[15]

His exposure to the new liberal thinking of the time had begun in his childhood. His father's guest list included men like Professor Dugald Stewart, the acclaimed moral philosopher and Robert Burns, who extemporized the so-called "Selkirk Grace," on his first visit to St. Mary's Isle:

> Some hae meat, and canna eat, And
> some wad eat that want it; But we
> hae meat and we can eat, And sae
> the Lord be thankit.[16]

Entering Edinburgh University, at the age of 14, he attended classes in the humanities and law, studying under Dugald Stewart, a leading advocate of the new thinking which would become known as the Scottish Enlightenment.[17] Central to it was the belief that reason and observation should be used to formulate practical solutions to social problems. It was no longer a case of accepting the constraints, intolerance and injustices of the old feudal society. Intellectual effort was to be directed at improving all aspects of life, not just for a chosen few, but for the betterment of everyone.[18] These philosophical ideas, which would ultimately be the foundation of our modern-day political thinking and the social sciences, were to have a profound effect on the young Thomas.

Keenly interested in humanitarian principles, he, together with his classmates who included Walter Scott, founded a literary society known as "The Club," which met monthly in rooms in Carruber's Close, off the High Street. While his enquiring mind found an outlet, his shyness and reserve prevented him from playing an active part in its activities. The French Revolution also had an impact on him and he went to France to study it at first hand. But, while he supported liberal ideals and good causes, he had little sense of direction in his life. It would be his tour of the Highlands in 1792 that made a huge impression on him.[19]

He perceived that the agricultural changes being introduced in the Highlands, to make way for sheep farms, had left many crofters homeless and despairing. The move towards larger more productive farms had occurred with little protest in the Lowlands, since people affected by the agricultural changes generally had little difficulty in finding alternatives. But the Highlands were totally different. With limited natural resources and low productivity, the region suffered high levels of poverty. The forces of commercialism, which came to the Highlands from the late eighteenth century, brought deep social unrest. Landlords did extremely very well out of the changes but many of their tenantry were to experience evictions.[20] Selkirk estimated that the value of the landlord estates increased by nearly seven fold between 1745 and 1805, and yet people perished from hunger and lived in dire poverty.[21] In these circumstances, emigration, which held out the prospect of land ownership and the ability to preserve a traditional way of life, was seen by many as preferable to a factory job in the manufacturing Lowlands or the uncertainties of staying put.

Though he was not then in a position to offer practical help, Thomas began now to develop his view that emigration was an inevitable outcome of the changes and that it was a movement which needed to be given firm direction. He learned that many hundreds of people had already left Scotland for the New World but "were dispersing to a variety of situations, in a foreign land" where they were lost to their native country. He recommended that, in future, emigrant Scots should be encouraged to go to the British colonies rather than the United States. This would help Britain to maintain her control over her colonies and the emigrants to maintain their culture and way of life:

I thought, however, that a portion of the ancient spirit might be preserved among the Highlanders of the New World – that the emigrants
might be brought together in some part of their own colonies, where
they would be of national utility and no motives of general policy would
militate (as they certainly may at home) against the preservation of all
those peculiarities of customs and language, which they themselves are
so reluctant to give up, and which are perhaps intimately connected
with many of their most striking and characteristic virtues.[22]

On his return from the Highlands, his education was further broad-
ened by a grand tour of Europe. Then, with the deaths of two brothers
in 1794 and a third in 1796,[23] Thomas' circumstances changed rapidly.
Possibly anticipating that he would soon take over the family estate, he
took up farming. Purchasing a small farm from his father, he put his farming theories into practice and worked on it as if he were a tenant:

> It was the wonder of the countryside, and long afterwards the natives
> liked to point out a field that Tom Douglas had broken to the plough,
> driving the clumsy implement with his own slender hands.[24]

John, Lord Daer, the eldest surviving son died a year later.[25] Thomas,
the youngest of the seven sons, became Lord Daer and, in 1799, with the
death of his father, he inherited the title. Five years before this he had
few prospects and now he was the fifth Earl. It must have seemed to him
that the hand of fate had intervened. From then on he applied his fortune to his colonization theories. Following a rebellion in Ireland, in 1798,
sparked off by starvation and extortionate rents, Selkirk spent some
months there to view conditions for himself. He submitted proposals in
the winter of 1801-02 to the Colonial Office, advocating the establishment
of an Irish colony in the Red River Valley, within the distant interior of
British America; however, he failed to win any support. He fared better
when he proposed the emigration of Highlanders.[26]

In a year's time he would be heading off to Prince Edward Island with
hundreds of Highlanders to launch his first venture. In 1806, he would
become one of sixteen elected Scottish Peers to go to the House of Lords
and in the year following would marry Jean Wedderburn-Colvile. The
marriage would bring him additional Hudson's Bay Company shares at
a crucial time in his negotiations to gain a controlling influence in the
company.[27] But this was no marriage of convenience. Jean was to be a
tower of strength to him, the great love of his life and the source of most

of his future happiness. When on his way to Red River in the Spring of 1817, he had "only one misfortune to lament since leaving Fort William, the loss of a precious memorial of my dearest, the brooch that I have worn on my breast for these nine years and odds." Having slept in the open in his clothes he had woken up to find "the pin was broke and the brooch gone. I think someone will send to get a new one made but it will not make up for the loss of that which has so often been pressed to my lips."[28]

This was a side of him which few people saw. His settlers were always struck by his boundless energy, seriousness and attention to detail. His note book was always on hand to record facts and observations. He would engage people in lengthy discussions on farming and building methods. A sketch pad was often close by to give pictorial illustrations to landscapes and buildings. Yet this shy and earnest intellectual was also a man of action. He showed strong leadership ability in the founding of his settlements and great courage in his battles with the North West Company. He had incredible determination but he was too highly principled ever to use unscrupulous methods. This put him at a considerable disadvantage with the North West Company partners, who, history has shown, were masters of deceit and treachery.

The legendary figure who stepped out of his canoe onto the west bank of the Red River at Fort Douglas, on June 21, 1817, was about to make history. Selkirk's land treaty was the first entered into between a British subject and the Natives of Rupert's Land and would pave the way for the acquisition of the region, by Canada, a half century later. His settlers did not know it at the time but their descendants would eventually found the City of Winnipeg. And his prophecy that the region "might afford ample means of subsistence for thirty millions of British subjects" would be proved right.[29] He was the first person ever to recognize Manitoba's immense agricultural potential as an important wheat producer. But before Red River, his colonizing achievements would take place in Prince Edward Island and Upper Canada. In the face of heated opposition from his many critics, he had set out in 1802 to locate willing recruits in the Highlands and Islands of Scotland.

2. EMIGRATION FRENZY IN THE HIGHLANDS & ISLANDS

We may venture to say that 9,700 have migrated to Carolina, Canada and Nova Scotia since the Peace [1784]; and I can assure you that all the Islands from the butt of the Lewis to Barra Head are in a ferment; every measure has been taken by the tacksmen to avert the spirit of emigration, but it appears to have too deep a root.[1]

D R. WILLIAM PORTER, WHO SUPERVISED one of the British Fisheries Society's fishing villages at Lochbay on Skye, was appalled that so many people had left the Highlands and Islands for a new life in North America.[2] He was one of many commentators who wrote of their alarm over the growing exodus from the Highlands and Islands in the winter of 1802-03. To make matters worse, Lord Selkirk had actually been to see him in the autumn of 1802 to ask him to use his "good offices" to find Skye recruits for his colonization venture in Upper Canada. But Porter was certainly not inclined to help. As far as Porter was concerned, emigrants had to be saved from the scurrilous men who would entice them with forged letters "from emigrants in America" and with a little "beating up with a bag-pipe and flag" mixed with "vast quantities of spirits" would whisk them away, to the detriment of themselves and Scotland.[3]

Porter was on the side of those who wanted the government to take action to stop the exodus. He wanted the villages of the British Fisheries Society to have "certain immunities" to encourage Highlanders to move to them rather than adding "strength to other nations by leaving this kingdom."[4] Feeling this to be a "matter of great national importance" he was certain that emigrants were being duped:

The nation may not feel it, but the people themselves, they who emigrate know not when or where they are going. America is not now what it was when best known to Highlanders. I mean before the Civil

War of 1774 – they found it then a paradise where they had nought to do but pluck and eat; now they shall find it as the land of Egypt in the days of the plagues of Pharaoh.[5]

Growing rapidly from the late eighteenth century, the exodus had been fuelled by adverse economic and social factors within Scotland and the favourable reports which were filtering back from the New World. The introduction of larger farms and commercial sheep farming in the Highlands and Islands had displaced many people and left many others wondering about their future.[6] But the opposite trend was happening in the kelping districts in the Hebrides and on the west coast, where land was being sub-divided into ever smaller lots. Here the population was growing with the rising demand for burnt kelp.[7] While this proved extremely profitable for landlords it was not so good for their tenantry who became dissatisfied with their payments and conditions.[8] Kelp making was, according to Robert Brown, factor of Clanranald's Uist estates, "a dirty and disagreeable employment" which required a man "to go out at the ebb of the sea to his middle in salt water" to cut seaweed, then to go "up to his neck in that element" to drag it ashore on the incoming tide.[9]

And at Lord MacDonald's estates in Skye and North Uist and at the Clanranald estate in South Uist, where kelp manufacture was booming, tenants felt particularly aggrieved by their poor prospects and increasing rents. In 1802, the zeal to emigrate attracted support from "nearly six parishes in Skye and North Uist" and 300 were expected to leave from South Uist.[10] Few had the option available to Lowlanders, in the more fertile regions of the country, of finding alternative agricultural or manufacturing work in their immediate area.[11] In these conditions even vague fears of what lay ahead rather than actual experience of destitution were enough to propel people into taking drastic remedies.

The late eighteenth century exodus had been largely organized by disgruntled tacksmen, who, having lost their earlier role of supplying military services to their lairds, found themselves with much higher rents to pay. Many emigrated taking, with them, large sections of the tenantry from their former estates. Creating several important Highland settlement foci in British North America, even before the end of the American Rebellion, they were soon followed by further waves of Highlanders.[12] The fact that so many followed in the footsteps of these earlier migrations demonstrates an outright rejection of other alternatives available in Scotland. This was a conscious decision to seek the preservation of a traditional way of life and the independence which comes from owning land. For them emigration was preferable to the bleak uncertainties of remaining at home.

While most prominent Scots lamented this state of affairs and tried to thwart the rising tide of emigration, Lord Selkirk grasped its inevitability and personally sought to direct pioneer settlements. Shocked by what he had seen of the poor and destitute during his travels to the Highlands and in Ireland, Selkirk advanced arguments in favour of emigration as a means of helping dispossessed people and strengthening British interests overseas.

In contrast, Highland landlords saw no inconsistency in making their tenants redundant, while at the same time hampering their attempts to emigrate. Emigration was a runaway force which had to be contained and stopped where possible. They supported employment schemes which they hoped would deter emigration by offering better employment prospects at home. They preferred to see their displaced tenants re-employed in some public works scheme as fishermen, road builders or canal diggers. Emigration was not an option even to be considered. They never asked whether their tenants actually wanted to do these jobs or were particularly well suited to them.

Selkirk did ask, and he concluded that emigration offered Highlanders the best way out of their intolerable economic situation and he made it his life's work to assist them in their relocation to British North America.

Selkirk had good reason to speak to William Porter, in 1802, about the prospects of finding willing recruits in Skye. Sheep farming had made some inroads in Skye, but a more significant factor was the earlier exodus of people from Skye to North Carolina. Outraged over sudden and large increases in their rents, first introduced in 1769, large numbers had opted for a new life in North Carolina.[13] According to "a gentleman of very considerable property" the emigrants who left the Western Isles between 1768 and 1772 took with them "at least £10,000 in specie."[14] Some 370 people, including "people of property who intend making purchases of land in America," went from Skye to North Carolina in 1771 followed by a further 450 in the following year.[15] A group led by James MacDonald of Portree and Norman MacLeod of Sleat had petitioned for 40,000 acres of land in North Carolina in 1771 but were refused in 1772, on the grounds that "the emigration of the inhabitants of Great Britain and Ireland to the American colonies is a circumstance...which cannot fail to...prejudice the landed interest and manufactures of these Kingdoms."[16] But in spite of this discouraging response, the exodus to North Carolina continued.

During his visit to Skye in 1773, Dr. Samuel Johnson heard songs in "words which I did not understand. I inquired the subjects of the songs, and was told of one...composed by one of the Islanders that was going in this epidemical fury of emigration to seek his fortune in America."[17] He later saw the *Nestor* in Portree harbour "waiting to dispeople Skye by carrying the natives away to America," one of two ships which took nearly 400 people to North Carolina in that year.[18] And in 1790, when he recalled the exodus which had taken place since 1771, the Reverend William Bethune, Minister of Duirinish, would tell of the eight ships "which have sailed from this Island [Skye] with emigrants...at very moderate computation carried away...2,400 souls and £24,000 sterling, ship freights included."[19]

Understandably there had been growing alarm throughout Scotland over the scale of the exodus to North America. By 1773 Stornoway and Stromness had become major collecting points for ships which were taking many hundreds from the north of Scotland to the United States.[20] George Dempster, having "made a little excursion to the counties where the spirit of emigration seems the strongest...from Fort William to Tain by Inverness," reported that 3,000 people had left those counties in the summer of 1783.[21] Writing in 1791, the Secretary of the Society for Propagating Christian Knowledge reported that, since 1772, "no less than sixteen vessels full of emigrants have sailed from the western parts of the counties of Inverness and Ross alone...carrying with them, in specie, at least £38,400 sterling."[22] And further north, clergymen in the Orkney Islands were expressing concern over the loss of Orcadian men to the Hudson's Bay Company:

> Nothing however contributes so much to the hurt of this place as the resort of the Hudson's Bay Company's ships to Stromness and their engaging lads from this country. A few lads returning with money make excellent recruits for the Company's service.... Young men who have learned any of the trades needed there have good wages and often come home with considerable sums of money.[23]

By January 1802, there was a general state of panic. Three ships had sailed for Pictou from the west coast in the previous year. One sailed from Ullapool in Loch Broom with 130 passengers and two from Fort William with 565 passengers; "but there is reason to believe that several people followed the vessels after their clearance and went on board on the passage to the Sound of Mull. It is suggested that no fewer than 700 people

View of Stromness Harbour, photographed c.1900. Hudson's Bay Company workers, recruited in the Orkney Islands were collected regularly from Stromness from as early as the mid-eighteenth century. *Courtesy of Aberdeen University Library, George Washington Wilson Photographic Archive A1765.*

were conveyed in two vessels from Fort William."[24] Not only was this a very large loss of people from one part of the Highlands, but these crossings had been undertaken in appalling conditions of severe overcrowding. Arming itself with ship tonnage statistics and passenger numbers, the Highland Society of Edinburgh had proof that emigrants were being packed like sardines in some ships. Its devastating critique of extreme overcrowding, likened to conditions on slave ships, had electrifying consequences. One was the introduction of tougher passenger legislation in 1803. The government set new legal limits on the minimum space and food to be allocated to passengers in ocean-going vessels and in doing so greatly increased the cost of transatlantic travel for emigrants.[25]

An immediate effect of the 1803 Act was to cause fares to more than double.[26] This considerably dampened down "the spirit of emigration" as did the Napoleonic Wars, which lasted from 1803 to 1815. But in December 1802, when Selkirk had his meeting with William Porter, the Highlands and Islands were buzzing with reports of emigrants who had left or were about to leave. Advertisements were being "publicly stuck up on the Church doors of some parishes and some of the Catholic

16

Chapels" tempting emigrants "by the payment of a reduced demand for their passage."[27] In June 1802, four ships were due to sail from Greenock and Port Glasgow with 1,032 emigrants and a further three ships were being fitted with passenger berths at Saltcoats before going on to Fort William to collect even more emigrants.[28] Such reports led the Highland Society to conclude that "20,000 will go in the summer" of 1803 and predict that large swathes of the Highlands would soon be depopulated. Of course this was more fluster than fact.[29] But alarm bells were ringing, and in such circumstances Selkirk had to choose his words carefully. He also had to abide by new instructions.

Worried by the loss of so many people to North America, Scottish landlords had convinced the government of the need to limit Selkirk's recruitment activities. Selkirk had been told to restrict himself to those emigrants who would otherwise be lost to the United States and to find such people without increasing "the general spirit of emigration."[30] Clearly obeying these terms, Selkirk told Porter, he "would accept of none but those who already had engaged to emigrate" to North Carolina.[31] Although Porter seemed to think Selkirk's efforts in Skye would fail, hundreds came forward that year from Lord MacDonald's estate on the east side of the Island. Before he left Skye, Selkirk also told Porter about "the Roman Catholics of Uist" who "have sent him a deputation." An agent was already hard at work and here, too, there were special reasons why Selkirk's endeavours would be fruitful.[32]

Unlike Skye, which had lost its people to the United States, South Uist had been, since 1772, a supplier of "vast numbers...to the Island of St. John, Nova Scotia and Canada."[33] The exodus had its origins in rising rents and in the ill-feeling which had been created within the estates of MacDonald of Clanranald, when the Roman Catholic tenantry had been put under pressure to convert to Presbyterianism. Alarmed by this situation and feeling aggrieved by his own prospects in the Clanranald estates, John MacDonald of Glenaladale, a prominent tacksman, decided to emigrate, taking some two hundred Roman Catholics from South Uist with him.[34] Settling in 1772 at Scotchfort, on the east side of Prince Edward Island, they were followed by many more South Uist emigrants in the early 1790s.[35] According to Robert Brown, Clanranald's factor,[36] some 277 people emigrated from South Uist in 1802 while, in 1803, "nearly as many more" were due to sail with Lord Selkirk.[37]

Thus, by the time Selkirk met Porter he knew that he could find the recruits he was looking for in Skye and South Uist. Their long-standing links with North America would absolve him from any suggestion that he was facilitating emigration for its own sake. At this stage it had been Selkirk's intention to locate the people who enlisted with him at the Falls of St. Mary (later Sault Ste. Marie) in Upper Canada. Selkirk had told Porter:

> that settling the banks of the Lake Huron...with Highlanders would form a valuable barrier to Canada against the French which occupy Louisiana...the land on which the people were to be settled was not actually his but he was to have a grant for them from the Crown, provided he could settle them.[38]

However, the land was not going to be his. Selkirk fell victim to the continuing campaigns being waged by landlords to halt the alarming loss of people from their estates. Alexander Irvine, a Rannoch clergyman had entered into the fray in 1802 by writing a book entitled *An Inquiry into the Causes and Effects of Emigration from the Highlands and Western Isles of Scotland, with Observations on the Means to be Employed for Preventing It*. Defending the Highland lairds, Irvine argued that emigrants were not suffering from "the oppression, exactions or harsh treatment of superiors"; any discontent they felt arose "from the perturbation of their own mind." It was their "avarice, or the love of money" which drove them to emigrate and because people were motivated by self-interest, they were susceptible to the false promises of the "interested persons, who promote the ferment of the people and go about recruiting." The prompters of emigration could thus be held largely responsible for the "mania." Once "their exaggerations and fictions" were used on people they worked "like a talisman's wand or an electric shock." Seen as the most prominent of the emigration promoters, Selkirk, by universal agreement, had to be stopped.[39] Bowing to the force of public opinion, Lord Hobart, Secretary of State for the Colonies, withdrew his offer to Selkirk, early in 1803, of a land grant in Upper Canada.[40] But the government was prepared to give favourable consideration to settlements which Selkirk might establish in Prince Edward Island.[41]

The Island's failure to attract settlers was causing the government grave concern. It was suggested to Selkirk that if he approached the various proprietors who owned large tracts on the Island, then lying empty, he could purchase the land he needed for his settlements easily and relatively cheaply.[42] This Selkirk agreed to do. Of course, he had first to persuade those he had already enlisted from Skye and South Uist to transfer their destinations to Prince Edward Island. They were unhappy with the change at first, but eventually acquiesced. The turning point came when Selkirk promised to get them out before the 1803 Passenger Act came into force. By going with Selkirk they could escape the much higher fares which would come in later in the year.

The irony is that far from dampening down Selkirk's sphere of operation, the transfer of location from Upper Canada to Prince Edward Island greatly increased it. Because it was not engaged directly in granting land to Selkirk, the government could give him guarded support without courting unfavourable publicity. Both the government and Selkirk had a shared wish that he should succeed. And because he was encouraged to think beyond his original purchases, in the knowledge that the government would look kindly on his further efforts to acquire land for colonization, Selkirk had the prospect of enlisting even larger numbers. Acquiring 60,000 acres through his purchase of lots 10, 57 and 58 in Prince Edward Island he was ready to proceed.[43] He had the land but needed to complete his search for the settlers. Once again he turned his attention to the Highlands and Islands.

Selkirk would later disclose that in addition to finding many settlers for the Island in Skye and South Uist, he had also enlisted "a few others from Ross-shire, from the north part of Argyllshire and from some interior districts of Inverness-shire, all of whose connections lay in some part of the United States."[44] Tombstone inscriptions and death notices for Prince Edward Island Scots would later reveal that Selkirk's initial group had also included people from Perthshire and Sutherland. And both of these counties had "connections" with the United States, as well, in the sense of having lost people to it from as early as the 1770s.

Argyll and Perthshire were in the forefront of the new farming methods being introduced in the late eighteenth century, having extensive sheep farms by the 1770s.[45] In 1772, forty-two poor families from Sutherland said that they had decided to emigrate because of the "want of the means of livelihood at home through the opulent grafters ingrossing the farms and turning them into pasture."[46] And Ross-shire and Inverness-shire also experienced a steady growth in sheep farming, primarily from the late 1780s, while sheep farms had advanced into large swathes of Sutherland by the turn of the century. As more of the Highlands was given over to sheep, many of the people who became uprooted, or feared they would be, chose emigration. Most of the emigrants who left from these counties in the early 1770s went to either New York, North Carolina or Philadelphia. However, the exodus was halted in its tracks in 1775 with the outbreak of the American War of Independence. Resuming again in

1784, when the war was over, British North America, not the United States, became the major recipient of the later waves of emigrants from these regions.

As the first settlers established their footholds, they often attracted successive waves of people from their Scottish homeland. The pull of compatriots, who had established themselves much earlier in Highland communities abroad, was a very powerful force. Reports home gave people valuable insights into pioneer life and information on the opportunities to be had. This in itself stimulated further emigration. Thus, those areas which had shown an early desire to emigrate to the United States were often the districts which continued to experience an outflow of people to North America in later decades. If these areas were also continuing to experience major disruptive changes such as the continuing spread of yet more sheep farms, the incentive to emigrate was all the greater. So Selkirk would have been only too pleased to confine his recruitment activities to regions which had lost people to the United States. Far from hindering him, as had been hoped, he was being encouraged to look in the very districts where the desire to emigrate was strongest and his chance of getting recruits was greatest. His biggest problem was in convincing people to break their ties with the past:

> In whatever Colony the emigrants from any particular district happen first to settle, those who have since left the same quarter have gone to the same [place] from the habit and the desire of settling near their former friends and relations; the emigrants from a great proportion of the Highlands still resort to North Carolina and New York.[47]

Requiring "no small labour to overcome the prejudices respecting the climate and other disadvantages of Canada which are entertained by the people," Selkirk had, by the end of 1802, persuaded "at least 100 families who will otherwise emigrate to Carolina" to come with him to British America.[48]

When Selkirk began his search for settlers "the whole west coast from Oban to Loch Broom," including "the greater part of Mull" was said to be "under sheep."[49] Fears were being expressed in March 1803, that Lord Gower's intentions to "adopt the sheep farming system" in the "extensive portion" of Sutherland, which he owned, would "cause a numerous emigration of the present and old inhabitants."[50] John MacNeill of Gigha was especially concerned at the very high prevalence of emigration from Argyll, particularly in North Knapdale – "I see it is going on very fast,

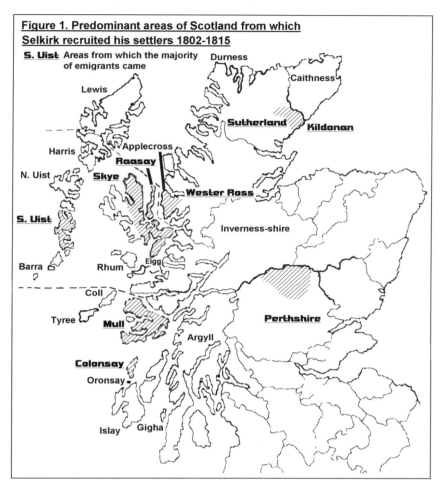

Figure 1. Predominant areas of Scotland from which Selkirk recruited his settlers 1802-1815

S. Uist Areas from which the majority of emigrants came

Durness

Caithness

Lewis

Sutherland

Kildonan

Harris

Applecross

Raasay

N. Uist

Skye

Wester Ross

S. Uist

Inverness-shire

Barra

Rhum

Eigg

Coll

Tyree

Mull

Perthshire

Argyll

Colonsay

Oronsay

Islay

Gigha

and several ships are freighted to carry the emigrants away," while a group of Mull people were trying to find a ship that would take them to Pictou.[51] By 1803 huge swathes of west Inverness-shire, from Moidart north to Glenelg and east to Strathglass, were losing people to the advancing sheep and contributing large numbers to the emigration totals.[52] Many of these areas would provide people for Selkirk's Prince Edward Island venture (Figure 1).

To the dismay of most lairds, clergymen and the general Scottish establishment many hundreds left the Highlands and Islands in June 1803, for Orwell Bay. Edward Fraser of Reelig, the customs collector at Inverness, was sure that Selkirk was preparing to send four ships with 1,200 emigrants to Prince Edward Island, adding that he expected him to "elude the [Passenger] Act and the Customs Houses."[53] Selkirk actually had three ships and a group of 800 — but even so, this number would have given little cheer to his critics. And for the many lairds who were alarmed by the steady outflow of tenantry from their estates, worse news was yet to come. As would become clear later, Selkirk's ambitions extended far beyond his 1803 activities.

Selkirk's approach had been to involve as many regions as he could in his recruitment campaigns. This was far more difficult and time-consuming than just getting his agents to sign up people irrespective of where they lived. He believed that in "the interests of establishing an extensive local connection…people should be taken from a variety of districts rather than from one in particular."[54] His logic was quite simple. Successful pioneer settlements attracted follow-on emigration from the part of Scotland from which the initial colonizers had originated. Thus, by involving many districts across the entire Highlands and Islands, Selkirk created a multiplicity of channels through which subsequent emigration would be pulled.

So Selkirk would build on the success of his Skye and South Uist recruits as well as the "few others" from Argyll, Perthshire, Inverness-shire, Ross-shire and Sutherland. While they would be the initial colonizers of his land, they would also attract others to follow. In enlisting John and William MacLeod from Durness, in Sutherland, Selkirk created opportunities which were taken up by the other Durness families who followed in 1806.[55] Selkirk's venture had clearly attracted "the spirited tribes of MacRaes" from Ross-shire, who in March 1803, were thought to be considering "warfare or emigration." They were almost certainly the "strong party of Ross-shire people" from Applecross who gave Selkirk such a difficult time in August of that year when he and they argued over land allocations at Point Prim in Prince Edward Island. Attracting further settlers from Ross-shire, many members of the Applecross contingent would later colonize the Middle River area of Cape Breton.[56] But it was from the Argyll Islands of Mull and Colonsay and Perthshire that Selkirk had his greatest success in promoting further emigration. Between 1805 and 1810 hundreds of emigrants would come on ships which had been secured through Selkirk's contacts on the Island and in the Highlands of Scotland.[57]

Although the three ships carrying Selkirk's 800 settlers had left at roughly the same time in June 1803, the *Dykes*, which carried Selkirk, was the first to arrive. Prince Edward Island's south shore came into view on Monday, August 8, 1803. Approaching Cape Bear, the *Dykes* tacked from side to side, as her sails caught the prevailing winds. Slowly she progressed along the south coast, past Wood Islands then, on the following day, "with a favourable breeze" was finally steered into Hillsborough Bay. On passing Point Prim, Selkirk could see a ship already anchored in Orwell Bay lying "just at the situation" which had been specified for the *Polly*. It was the *Polly*. The *Oughton* would take another 19 days to reach the Island.[58] The arrival was a moment to savour. A long sea journey had ended. But as the *Dykes'* passengers got ever nearer and the vast wilderness of trees opened up before them, relief turned to fear and bewilderment:

> There cannot be a more extreme contrast to any country that has been long under cultivation, or a scene more totally new to a native of these kingdoms than the boundless forests of America. An emigrant set down in such a scene feels almost the helplessness of a child.[59]

Of course they would not be helpless, at least not for the month of August when Selkirk would use his energy, money and organizational skills to direct their every move. Immediately engrossing himself in the many practical problems and difficulties which had to be overcome, Selkirk supervised the land clearance work and house building with military precision.

Selkirk's colonization venture in Prince Edward Island was on a scale never before seen in North America. His was the earliest systematic attempt to settle large numbers of emigrants in North America. When he returned to the Island briefly in October of the following year, it was already clear that his settlers were quickly adapting themselves to their new and difficult surroundings. He now had solid proof that his colonization ideas were workable. And his settlers could look forward to the rewards of the flourishing settlements which would follow.

3. SUCCESS AT BELFAST, PRINCE EDWARD ISLAND

It is a proof of great exertion, taking the settlement in the aggregate...
for it must be observed that the most part of the colony came from the
country where Dr. Johnson did not see a tree older or larger than himself;
it cannot therefore be supposed that they were expert at handing an axe
on their arrival.[1]

JAMES WILLIAMS, SELKIRK'S AGENT IN Prince Edward Island, was
full of admiration for the people from Skye who had first impressed
Samuel Johnson some thirty years earlier. When Dr. Johnson had
observed their preparations to emigrate, in 1773, they were heading for
North Carolina. But, by 1803, Prince Edward Island had become the
favoured destination of most Skye emigrants. Although totally unfamiliar
with the sight of large trees, their first task, when they arrived on the
Island, was to hack their way through huge dense forests. However daunting this must have been at the time, they succeeded. They, together with
a smaller number from Wester Ross, became the initial settlers of Belfast.
Within eight months of landing at Orwell Bay, some sixty-three Skye
families were planting crops on newly cleared land.[2] James Williams
described it as "proof of great exertion." But it was far more than this.
For people with little or no experience of the tree felling, farming and
building methods required of them in Prince Edward Island, their ulti-
mate success as pioneer settlers was a great and heroic achievement.

Thanks to Selkirk's highly organized approach we can follow events
on the Island as they unfold. From the moment he first saw the south
coast of Prince Edward Island on August 8, 1803, he kept a diary, recording his observations of life on the Island and the progress being made by
his settlers in adapting to their new conditions. The disembarkation of
the emigrants from their ships is described, as are the early phases of land
clearance, and the inevitable squabbling over who would get the most
prized settlement locations. More of an *aide-memoire* than a chronicle of

his innermost thoughts and feelings, the diary gives us a unique, on-the-spot account of early pioneer life.[3] Selkirk paints a remarkable picture of events, people and places during his one month stay on the Island, commenting, one minute, on the state of the roads, techniques for clearing forests and methods of house building, then describing his encounters with various individuals.

While he was highly systematic in approach, Selkirk was not stuffy or autocratic. He had an easy, relaxed style. There was "a hearty shaking of hands" when he and his settlers first met.[4] Although he had worked out, in principle, how he was going to proceed he had first to convince his colonists that his plans were workable. That was always going to be difficult. Having been thrust into unfamiliar territory, they were fearful, restless and confused. He won them over gradually but it was a fraught and difficult process. Combining a managerial flair with a convivial style he was in his element directing the settlers in their various tasks. While he employed Dr. Angus MacAulay as his agent to help supervise activities initially, Selkirk was careful to maintain a direct line of contact with his settlers at all times.[5] He had a warmth about him which put people at their ease and an ability to sum up situations and people very quickly. He appreciated both the value and pleasure of being in a situation where he could speak "his best Gaelic," and share his dinner with "four fine Ross-shire lads."[6]

When the *Dykes* first neared the Island on the 8th of August, Selkirk's impatience had got the better of him. As they approached Wood Islands, Selkirk jumped into a small boat with "Mr. Shaw, Cameron and the two MacDonalds" hoping to get back on board, soon after; "but, she did not come back on her expected tack."[7] Night came and:

> despairing of finding the ship we made for the shore in order to kindle a fire and show where we were. Just as we were about to land we heard a gun and took again to the oars; after that the guns continued at half hour intervals until we reached the ship, past midnight. It surprised us to learn that the guns had been firing for some hours...also lights, hung out, which we several times were looking out for and thought we perceived but could not fix them distinctly. Yet the distance could not have been above 6 or 8 miles and the sea dead smooth.[8]

However, this was Selkirk just being curious and seeking a pleasurable diversion. Now that he had arrived at Belfast his serious and well-organized side took over.[9] Intending that the *Dykes* would reach the Island before the *Polly,* he had hoped to have sufficient time to provide

25

the *Polly*'s passengers with "some kind of barracks." But he arrived after the *Polly,* and by the time he came on the scene, on the August 9, the *Polly* passengers were "hutting themselves in wigwams."[10] To make matters worse, Dr. MacAulay, his agent, had misunderstood his instructions and "was proceeding to fix the people in two or three large villages instead of ten or twelve small ones."[11] That mistake had to be rectified immediately as did the problem with the squatters on his land. They had to be removed before they caused trouble:

> These are people who have set themselves down on the lands under the idea they would revert to the Crown and then they would have a claim of preference by their occupancy…they are now sour at finding themselves to be turned out and would gladly disgust the new comers."[12]

Selkirk reached the harbour at Hillsborough Bay, next morning. He had planned "to row up to the town" but was greeted by Major Holland, who appeared in a small boat. Being met by the son of Captain Samuel Holland, the late Surveyor of the Island, was the best possible beginning Selkirk could have had. He accepted his invitation to go into Charlottetown where he met Colonel Edmund Fanning, the Lieutenant-Governor of the Island, who invited him to stay at his house. Charlottetown would be his base for the next few days.

Dr. MacAulay arrived that evening, at the Fanning residence, having received Selkirk's message. He was to organize the disembarkation of the *Dykes'* passengers the following day. Unlike the *Polly*, which had been anchored further south at Orwell Bay, the *Dykes* was berthed at Charlottetown harbour. "An old windmill, now used as a Signal Tower," had been purchased by Selkirk so that the *Dykes'* passengers could have some temporary accommodation. When they came ashore, they were met by "several Highland settlers of the town and neighbourhood…who came down to the shore and seemed to behave kindly to the women and children, though quite strangers and of a different quarter of the Highlands."[13]

There were already three Highland communities on the Island. Close by, to the north of Charlottetown, was Stanhope (lot 34), founded in 1770 by Perthshire emigrants.[14] A second group of emigrants from Argyll had established a settlement at Malpeque Bay (lot 18) that same year. But being situated on the east side of the Island, it was much further away.[15] Then there were the Gaelic-speaking, Roman Catholics who lived at Scotchfort (lot 36). Originating from South Uist and west Inverness-shire they

Painting of Charlottetown Harbour in 1839, by Alexander Cavalie
Mercer (1783–1868). *Courtesy of National Archives of Canada,
C-013788.*

had come in large numbers from 1772 to establish their settlement; it too
was near the main harbour.[16] Roman Catholics would no doubt have
seemed "quite strangers" to the staunch Presbyterians who had sailed on
the *Dykes,* but almost certainly they were the welcoming party.

The *Dykes* passengers would soon learn that Catholic Highlanders were
in fact the dominant ethnic group on the Island. So much so that there
was "great jealousy and bitterness" felt over their presence on the Island
"among the government people." As was the case in Britain, prejudices
ran very deep. Catholics on the Island were not permitted to hold land
until the 1780s, nor could they be counted as settlers in terms of fulfilling
proprietor settlement obligations. And even though they represented two-
thirds of the inhabitants of Prince Edward Island, "the Catholic can neither
can hold any office nor vote for the election of members of the Assembly." Thus Highlanders, being mainly Catholics, were "no favourites."[17]

Selkirk accepted the Governor's invitation "to stay all night" and
allowed himself to be pressed into staying a second night, "which I
thoughtlessly yielded to and this interfered considerably with business."
Although he found the "bonhomme's politeness" to be "rather burden-
some," the evening was an entree "to most of the principal people of
Charlottetown." In addition to Major Holland, these people included
Thomas DesBrisay, a former Lieutenant-Governor of the Island, and "old
Mr. Stewart, father of John and Charles, who was Chief Justice for about

20 year, but resigned a few years ago on account of his age."[18] And like him, these men owned large tracts of land on the Island. DesBrisay held lots 14, 31 and 33, Holland lot 28, while the Stewart family held a half share in lot 18.[19] The following night Selkirk established him in "comfortable lodgings" at John Cambridge's new home. A prominent merchant, John Cambridge owned lots 63 and 64, situated only a short distance to the southeast of Belfast.[20]

Selkirk had found it relatively easy to acquire land. There had been a lottery in 1767 when the entire Island had been surveyed and granted out in a single day. Various proprietors, irrespective of their suitability or motives had obtained large tracts of land. Few attempted to meet their quit rent payments or locate the required number of settlers on their land.[21] Thus there were any number of original grantees or their successors, who were only too happy to sell their land to Selkirk for a cash payment. Having little time for the proprietors who "keep up the impracticable idea of getting a tenantry like that of Europe" he would not offer leaseholds. Apparently, John MacDonald of Glenaladale, the organizer of the Scotchfort settlement, would not even give his tenants leases; they had to make do with "a bare verbal promise of a lease!"[22] Selkirk would always try to sell land to settlers.

When he arrived on the Island in 1803, Selkirk already owned lot 10 on the west side of the Island, lots 57 and 58 at Belfast, a one-half share of lot 60 at Flat River and a third share of lot 53 at Three Rivers. By the following year he had acquired lot 62 at Wood Islands and, by 1805, he owned the remainder of lot 60, a one-half share of lot 12 (near lot 10) and a one-third share of lot 59, which bordered on lot 57. His purchase of lot 31 in 1806 brought the total acreage under his control to some 143,000 acres (Figure 2).[23] Although Selkirk was liable for arrears in quit rent owed on the land he had purchased, his liability had been greatly reduced by the advantageous terms granted to him by the government. This had been a major factor in his decision to extend his land ownership and colonization activities on the Island.[24]

Returning to Orwell Bay on 13th August, Selkirk found that the *Polly* passengers had scattered along the shore:

I set off for the settlement at the old French Village called Belfast... and went on board the *Polly*, from which everybody was landed, but there was still some baggage on board. It was difficult to keep order among so great a number — two hundred and eighty full passengers and nearly four hundred souls.[25]

TABLE I: THE 1803 INFLUX FROM SCOTLAND TO PRINCE EDWARD ISLAND

Name	Year died	Age at death	Scottish Origins	PEI Location	Lot Number
Beaton, Malcolm [Came on the *Polly*]	1877	79	Skye	Flat River	60
Bollum, Elizabeth [Wife of Peter Bollum, daughter of Roderick McKenzie of Applecross]	1866	N/K	Applecross, Ross-shire		49
Buchannan, John	1864	80	Skye	Belfast	58
Buchannan, Malcolm	1877	76	Skye		57
Cameron, Allen	1870	87	Ardnamurchan, Argyll	Augustine Cove	28
Campbell, Angus [Came on the *Polly*]	1888	97	Western Isles	N/K	
Campbell, Angus [Arrived in 1803; Nova Scotia in 1812 where died at Middle River.]	1901	106	N/K	N/K	
Campbell, Roderick	1888	91	N/K		58
Docherty, Angus	1827	73	Skye		58
Docherty, Donald [Came on the *Polly* with his wife Sarah]	1881	92	N/K		50
Docherty, Finley [Wife, Mary, also from Skye, came 1803]	1854	69	Skye		58
Enman, Margaret [Widow of Jeremiah Enman]	1864	77	Inverness	Vernon River	49
Fraser, Donald [Came with Christiana, his wife, also from Inverness]	1873	86	Inverness		58
Furness, Ann [Came on the *Polly*]	1877	91	Skye (Kilmuir)		N/K
Gilles, Donald	1858	71	Ross-shire		58
Gillis, Donald [Came on the *Polly*]	1874	78	N/K		N/K
Gillis, John	1851	82	Ross-shire		58
Gillis, John [Came on the *Polly*]	1886	83	Ross-shire	Flat River	N/K

Name	Year died	Age at death	Scottish Origins	PEI Location	Lot Number
Gordon, Donald [Came with wife Christina MacLaren also from Fincastle.]	1819	57	Fincastle, Perthshire	Brudenell	53
Lamont, Alexander [Came with his wife Eunice Currie]	1845	84	Skye		58
MacAulay, John	1881	96	Uist	N/K	34
MacAuly, Angus M.D.	1827	67	N/K	Belfast	58
MacDonald, Ann	1889	90	Long Island	N/K	47
MacDonald, Donald R. [Came on the *Polly*]	1891	68	N/K	Eldon	57
MacDonald, John [Served in Ireland in 1798 rebellion as Lieutenant in Glengarry Fencibles.]	1836	64	N/K	N/K	N/K
MacDonald, John [Came on the *Polly*]	1884	82	Skye	Orwell Cove	57
MacDonald, John	1871	80	Skye	Pinette	58
MacDonald, Margaret [Came on the *Polly*, widow of Donald MacDonald]	1881	84	N/K	Orwell	50
MacDonald, Ronald	1877	77	Skye	N/K	N/K
MacDougall, Donald [Came on the *Polly*]	1875	86	Skye	Belle Creek	62
MacEachern, Margaret [Came on the *Polly*, widow of Charles MacEachern]	1884	92	Inverness	N/K	66
MacFarlane, Janet	1867	90	N/K	N/K	N/K
MacInnis, John	1887	89	N/K	Gallas Point	50
MacKay, John	1848	76	N/K	St Peter's Bay	41
MacKenzie, Elizabeth [Widow of Alexander, daughter of Duncan MacDonald]	1873	79	Fort Augustus	Flat River	60
MacKinnon, Charles	N/K	N/K	Skye	N/K	58
MacLaren, James	1871	87	Blair Atholl, Perthshire	N/K	N/K
MacLaren, Mrs. John [Came on the *Polly*]	1881	87	N/K	Charlottetown	33
MacLean, Sarah [Came on the *Polly*]	1891	95	Mull	N/K	16
MacLeod, Alexander	1838	66	Skye	N/K	58

Name	Year died	Age at death	Scottish Origins	PEI Location	Lot Number
MacLeod, Angus	1885	88	N/K	Belfast	58
MacLeod, John	1838	77	Durness, Sutherland	Yankee Hill	21
[Came with wife Mary McPherson on the *Polly*]					
MacLeod, John [Came with wife Flora]	1864	91	Skye	N/K	58
MacLeod, Malcolm [Came on the *Polly*.]	1844	98	Skye	Pinette	59
MacLeod, Mary [Came on the *Polly*]	1892	92	N/K	Point Prim	57
MacLeod, William	1860	76	Durness, Sutherland	Park Corner	20
MacNeill, John	1884	83	N/K	North River	32
MacRae, Donald	1844	69	N/K	Point Prim	57
MacRae, Donald	1852	68	N/K	N/K	58
MacRae, Duncan	1872	87	Applecross, Ross-shire	N/K	58
MacRae, Finlay	1872	N/K	Applecross, Ross-shire	N/K	N/K
[Came on the *Polly*]					
MacRae, Finley	1862	82	N/K	N/K	58
MacRae, Margaret	1872	N/K	Applecross, Ross-shire	N/K	N/K
[Came on the *Polly*]					
MacWilliam, John [Came with his parents]	1886	86	N/K	N/K	58
Martin, Donald	1861	79	Skye	Belfast	58
Martin, Donald [Came with Lord Selkirk. May have travelled on the *Polly*.]	1848	89	Skye	Belfast	58
Martin, Samuel	1853	107	Skye	N/K	N/K
Martin, William [Came with wife Margaret Gillis, also from Skye]	1840	63	Skye	N/K	57
Master, Margery [Her father emigrated on the *Polly* in 1803.]	1886	88	Inverness	Vernon River	49
Murchison, Alex'r	1865	64	Skye	Point Prim	57
Murchison, Donald [Came with wife Ann, also from Skye.]	1831	88	Skye	Point Prim	57

Name	Year died	Age at death	Scottish Origins	PEI Location	Lot Number
Murchison, Mrs. Alexander [Came on the *Polly* with her parents Mr & Mrs J.R. MacDonald.]	1894	92	Skye	Point Prim	57
Murchison, Neil	1854	71	Skye	N/K	57
Nicholson, Charles	1864	69	Skye	Orwell Cove	57
Nicholson, Donald	1833	96	Skye	N/K	57
Nicholson, Mary [Came on the *Polly*, widow of John Nicholson]	1886	86	N/K	Orwell Cove	57
Nicholson, Samuel	1861	76	Skye (Kilmuir)	Belfast	58
Panting, Jane [Came on the *Polly*, widow of Francis]	1875	N/K	Inverness	N/K	N/K
Ross, Alexander [Came on the *Polly* with his father. Buried Lot 33.]	1878	80	Skye	Wheatly River	25
Ross, Donald [Came on the *Polly*]	1866	82	Skye	Flat River	60
Stewart, Donald [Came on the *Polly* with his parents]	1887	86	Highlands	West River	65
Weatherbie, Margaret [Came with her parents. Later moved to Lot 63.]	1886	87	N/K	N/K	49

Source: Prince Edward Island Genealogical Society; *From Scotland to Prince Edward Island: from death and obituary notices in Prince Edward Island, 1835–1910* (n.d.)

Most were "in hovels or wigwams, built oblong like the roof of one of our European Cottages and thatched in general with spruce boughs." Having had supper in Dr. MacAulay's tent, he later "went up to lodge in John MacDonald's tent," to which some of his camp beds had been taken. Quite a step down, in accommodation, compared with Charlottetown, but he was glad to be back. The camp site "had a very picturesque appearance under night. Every tent having a great fire near it illuminated the woods and each party sitting or moving around with their gypsy-like apparatus of pots and pans gave the light additional variety of play." The next morning "they came in general around me with a keenness and warmth that perhaps had a little resemblance to the old feudal times."[26]

It was now time to "explore the country in order to lay out the different lots."[27] Setting off with Mr. Shaw and Dr. MacAulay, together with Donald Nicholson and Roderick McKenzie, "the two principal men of the Skye and Ross-shire parties," they travelled up the Pinette River in "two wooden canoes."[28] However the journey was of little value. Nothing could be done until the surveyor completed his work. "He promises that in two days all that part of east of Point Prim shall be laid down," but no progress was being made, not even by August 19.[29]

"Not being able to settle the situation of the lots until the surveyor has made more progress," Selkirk decided to return to Charlottetown on August 15. "I went up Orwell Bay in a boat to the Vernon River and had a glance at the upper part of lot 57 where three or four settlers have taken the best spots." He was on his way to visit John Laird, "a Loyalist settler from Carolina who lent me a horse and agreed to show me the way to Charlottetown." Laird lived at lot 50, along the Vernon River. Journeying there with the help of the MacRae's, who hauled "the boat through the mud in the clannish style," Selkirk observed:

> ...some good settlements and considerable clearings. Along Vernon River, are a considerable number of Loyalist allotments, and their clearings joining each other give some extent of the prospect. There is a continued track of clearing in this way to near the saw mill at the head of this water.... These allotments have perhaps been more generally taken up here on account of the navigable water.[30]

Thus, having attracted British Loyalist Settlers from 1784, after the American War of Independence had ended, lot 50 was continuing to flourish.[31] Quite the opposite had happened at lots 57 and 58. A settlement founded in 1775 at lot 57 by Morayshire emigrants had failed. The Loyalists who had been offered land at lots 57 and 58 did not remain.[32] There were no traces of any previous settlements in 1803.[33] The problem was that lots 57 and 58 were "not so well situated," having less access to inland water routes than lot 50. Returning to Belfast, Selkirk had reached the stage where he wanted to see action, and quickly. The settlers had to decide on their sites, purchase their land, build their houses and begin cultivating their land well before winter set in. He asked John MacDonald to take "two of the Camerons and two others of the Mull party" to show them the "half cleared spot on Pinette Point" and to go with them to "the opposite side of the bay towards Point Prim." He was to fix the price at $1 per acre "and extra on account of any marsh or cleared land." But, Pinette Point "did not take their fancy."[34]

Trouble was brewing. Dugald Cameron had never been very keen on the Island, preferring Upper Canada. When the group returned from Pinette Point all except Hector MacDonald said they wanted to proceed to Quebec. Selkirk gave them "the money they had deposited with me and left them enquiring for passage to Quebec. In a few days however I learnt that they had taken lands from Major Holland at Tryon River (lot 28)."[35] They had been attracted by the offer of land at "6d per acre in perpetuity" and as the principal negotiator, "Cameron had got 600 acres." No offence was taken. Selkirk was certain that "there had been some talking about other situations," having been "too long in Charlottetown not to be exposed to offers. There will always be proprietors ready to pick up and tempt off settlers who are not immediately fixed." Hector MacDonald got his reward though. He got "the 200 acres he wanted at lot 57, paying only one quarter down, the rest in instalments."[36]

Selkirk was becoming increasingly annoyed that his surveyor had been wasting "his time in fiddle faddles." If they could have decided early on who got what, preferably by drawing lots, there would have been less opportunity for "whimsical objections" and less "delay in clearing the land."[37] As things were, little progress was being made. He hired a new surveyor and pressed Dr. MacAulay into action. But Dr. MacAulay would not consider the settlers' lots until his own had been determined. Being offered "a choice spot of 200 or 300 acres near Belfast" and more inland, he initially seemed satisfied and "set seriously to work among the people to collect their determination as to the extent of the land they would take."[38] However, Dr. MacAulay soon took a "liking to a part of Point Prim [lot 58] where he would have more front[age] and a more compact body of land." In the end MacAulay got his way and acquired 100 acres at Point Prim as a present as well as a further 100 acres which he was able to purchase at 5 shillings per acre.[39] Meanwhile Selkirk found much dissatisfaction amongst his settlers. More than anything, they were objecting to the prices which they were being asked to pay for land and provisions.[40] While Selkirk considered his charges to be "considerably below the current prices," they were clearly not acceptable to his settlers.[41] But always at the back of Selkirk's mind, was the constant worry that his Skye settlers, who formed the largest number, would abandon Belfast. Many of them had friends and relatives already living in North Carolina. In 1802, some 394 passengers from the parish of Sleat had sailed to Wilmington and, in 1803, a further 400 people from Sleat were preparing to leave for North Carolina.[42] Realizing that he had to make "a liberal accommodation," he halved "the price of lots being on instalments," accepted produce in place of cash and extended the period of interest-free credit.[43]

It was time to deal with the real leaders. Most of the Belfast settlers came from Skye, but there was also a vociferous and demanding group from Wester Ross. Donald Nicholson spoke for the Skye people and Roderick MacKenzie for the Ross-shire people.[44] So Selkirk treated them "with liberality and let the rest take their swing." He gave them "the two or three places where a little improvement had been made by the straggling settlers, as well as the remains of the French clearing at Pinette [which] made a few choice situations." Donald Nicholson got 300 acres at lot 57, while Roderick MacKenzie obtained 250 acres at lot 58.[45] This did the trick. "Whether it was owing to them or not, in two or three days after the rest of the people came dropping in, the majority of them agreed" to more or less take the 50 to 100 acre holdings offered to them.[46]

There was one further complication. "The MacRaes and MacGillies (a strong party of Ross-shire people) had got intelligence of a choice situation on Point Prim, where some unknown squatters had made preparations for sitting down, and had begun a little clearing." Being land which "adjoined to a fine marsh," it was far preferable than the allotment which Selkirk was offering. Judging the MacRaes to have a great deal of influence over the others, Selkirk let them have the Point Prim land at lot 58 "provided it did not interfere with the marsh." Since marshes could be used as natural water meadows to provide much-needed fodder for cattle and horses, these were particularly valuable. Selkirk's consession proved to be a wise move. "One party was fixed after another. It was necessary to chop and change the situations proposed for them, but in the course of a few days nearly everybody was satisfied."[47] Coming together as one, the Skye and Wester Ross arrivals opted for land holdings at lots 57, 58 and 60 (Table 1).

Applications "for land came in pretty generally by partnerships of three, four or five families...who clubbed together for the quantities of land each proposed to purchase." This meant that people could be settled in a "more sociable and connected manner."[48] While there were one or two disputes over land, progress was definitely being made:

The dispersing of the people to their separate lots may be considered perhaps as the decisive point – As long as they were in camp they were a mob and liable to all the sudden changes of one – separate they cannot be so easily moved. As soon as each has a little done on his own land, and has got a little into the custom of looking on it as his own, an attachment to the spot will arise, and the satisfaction of looking on an independent and permanent property – the pride of being Lairds will keep them firm.[49]

They wasted no time in building their houses. To help his settlers, Selkirk had previously sought advice from Father Angus MacEachern, who had, since his arrival on the Island in 1790, been presiding over a large congregation of Roman Catholic Highlanders. He himself "had a roomy dwelling of red sand-stone, built at Savage Harbour," from which he visited his parishioners "in all parts of the Island as well as the Magdalens, Cape Breton and parts of the Mainland."[50] Father MacEachern advised that the house should be "as small as they can do with – as the first houses that are built are seldom found to be well situated or to serve much purpose afterwards." "About 12 feet square" was the recommended size and "roofs should be covered with boards since, shingles are expensive for the first beginning, requiring many nails."[51] But crudely built and tiny though these houses were, they could be "constructed without any other materials than what the forests afford, and without the aid of any tool but the axe."[52] In 1808 the Island's "wooden houses" were much the same, being "built in general with very great dispatch but very little system ... twenty men will cut down a sufficient number of trees and build a small house in one day."[53]

As Selkirk had predicted, his Highlanders displayed a natural aptitude for pioneer life. They had "a great advantage over people who are accustomed to better accommodation, and who would have employed a great proportion of their time in building comfortable houses," thus leaving more time "to the essential object of clearing their lands."[54] He contrasted them with John Laird, the American he had met, who lived at lot 50. In just eight years Laird had cleared 50 acres. But, "if the American is best at working hard – the Highlander beats him at living hard." Not being able to "deny himself luxuries," Laird had built a far better house and had taken much longer to free himself from debt. "A Highlander beginning with a little, would be clear of the world in two years – but at the end of eight [years], he would have only 6 or 7 acres of cleared land instead of 50."[55]

The Belfast settlers "applied themselves with vigour" and by the next Spring achieved the remarkable result of having cleared their lands, ready for planting, even "though the work was of a nature so totally

Memorial at Belfast, commemorating the 800 Highlanders who arrived in August 1803. *Photograph by
Geoff Campey.*

new to them."[56] And Selkirk made sure that thought was being given
to the future. Lots were "laid out somewhat wide of each other, so that
the lands of the different parties should have some intervals between
them, which they could invite their friends to come after them and
occupy." More would follow so it was important that each settler has
"room to spread, and room for his brother or his cousin that is to follow him."[57]

Thus, a great deal of work had been completed at Belfast well before
the *Oughton* was steered into Charlottetown harbour on Saturday, August
27, 1803. Pronouncing the passengers from South Uist to be "in pretty
good health – bless God," a local commentator summed up the feelings
of all on the Island who had been anxiously awaiting the ship's arrival.[58]
Selkirk's first impression, when he went on board the ship, was that most
families were very poor, "having much too large a proportion of useless

hands." Although most had been able to pay their passage money of £4.12s, he estimated that only about ten or twelve families out of forty or fifty had enough "substance to maintain themselves the year through." Their "social clannish disposition" had made it impossible for them "to take a small number – they would not go without their friends."[59] But, having "so many friends in the Island...a considerable number dispersed" into the country.[60] For those who remained, he offered land in lot 10 on the west side of the Island:

> I did not like to mix these people with the Skye settlers both on account of the fever still among the people at Belfast – on account of the probability of religion creating differences and on account of the circumstances of these people requiring so much more to be done for them than the Skye settlers.[61]

There was immediate confusion over the terms that had been offered to them. Selkirk insisted that he had only agreed to provide them with their transport. They said that they had been promised help with their resettlement. In the end, Selkirk decided it was best "to allow them such assistance as would take away any pretext for saying that faith had not been kept with them."[62] And it soon became clear that lot 10 was not going to be acceptable. It was a remote and sparsely populated area, far removed from the main concentrations of Catholic Scots, which were much further to the east, in Kings County. Selkirk then offered them an inland position at lot 58 but:

> ...when they came to the head of the tide water, and understood that they were to go two or three miles further, they refused point blank to go a step further and returned to Charlottetown. They had lived all their lives by the sea-side, more by fishing than by farming, and did not imagine the possibility of living except on the shore.[63]

Running out of options, Selkirk had no choice but to offer lot 53, even though it was not yet in ready state to be sub-divided. With the backing of Father MacEachern, who "argued the matter with them," they accepted:

> "The men were all highly satisfied with the situation. Some large lobsters they had found soon after they reached the river overjoyed them. The creek too is full of oysters. To add to this advantage is a consider-

able tract of woods burnt a number of years ago, a part of which has burnt again this last year and remains almost ready for planting.[64]

Engaging themselves initially "in the lumber business," the South Uist emigrants made steady progress in clearing their land. By 1807 Selkirk's agent, James Williams, found them to be "upon a par with the average of the Island and that is a proof they have not been idle as they labour under the disadvantage of having no hay."[65]

Thus, by the end of August, most of the 800 emigrants who came with Selkirk had decided on their settlement locations. Except for the South Uist settlers' refusal to accept lot 10 and some minor disatisfactions which were remedied, everything had gone pretty well according to plan. The 1803-04 land sale records for Belfast (lots 57 and 58) and Flat River (lot 60) reveal that most of Lord MacDonald's former Skye tenants settled in these three lots (Table 2). Also identifiable are the Ross-shire men mentioned in Selkirk's diary.[66] So we can conclude that Belfast and Flat River were initially colonized by the Skye and Wester Ross families who had sailed on the *Polly*. Similarly, most of the South Uist emigrants who had sailed on the *Oughton* took up land at lot 53 in Three Rivers.[67] These were whole communities, being transplanted from Scotland to the Island, taking up huge, consolidated tracts of land purchased from Selkirk. However, the contingent which sailed on the *Dykes* was quite different. Originating from many parts of the Highlands and Islands, they came in small groups. And, unlike the others, they became widely dispersed on the Island, settling on land purchased from a number of proprietors including Selkirk (Table 1).[68]

After supervising the initial work that needed to be done at Prince Edward Island, Selkirk set off, in early September, for Nova Scotia where he visited Pictou, Truro and Halifax. Remaining one month, he then sailed to Boston and, from there, travelled on to New York. By mid-November he had crossed into Upper Canada and moved eastward through York and Kingston to Glengarry. Founded by west Inverness-shire Scots in 1784, Glengarry continued to attract large numbers of emigrants from the northwest Highlands particularly in the period from 1790 to 1815.[69] Having become a thriving community by the time of his visit, Glengarry provided Selkirk with considerable evidence of Highlander adaptability to pioneer conditions. They supported each other in their combined endeavours and even though their first houses were crudely built, these were far better than the hovels they had left in Scotland.[70]

Getting to Montreal in January 1804, he used his time there to speak to the many fellow Scots who were involved in the North American fur trade. In his discussions with prominent merchants, he learned something of fur trapping methods, the trade routes used and the bitter rivalries which raged within the trade. This was Selkirk's first taste of the battleground on which he would fight in later life. But now he was preoccupied with his second colonization venture at Baldoon. After another brief visit to New York City, he returned to Upper Canada in June and spent the next four months laying the foundations for the Baldoon project.[71] Then it was back to Prince Edward Island in October, for a second visit, before returning home to Scotland.

Spending one final month on the Island, Selkirk found bustling activity and much progress. He was pressed by many settlers to sell more land.[72] This he did, offering different charges and periods of credit depending on each person's circumstances. Most paid money, some bushels of wheat, but six men owed labour services, having been recruited initially as indentured servants.[73]

But Selkirk also took the opportunity provided by his second visit to identify settlers wishing to recruit further emigrants on his behalf from Scotland. He offered to pay Donald Nicholson £20 "for a free passage to Scotland," and "if he brings out settlers" to the Island, and a commission of 6 d per acre for any land purchased.[74] The Reverend Augustus MacDonald would get a free passage and his expenses for his help in locating emigrants in west Inverness-shire wishing to settle in Upper Canada, presumably at Baldoon. "He said he would go along with the emigrants to Upper Canada and see them until their arrival at the settlement (but not to remain)."[75] But Selkirk's principal agent was James Robertson. A timber merchant, based on the Island, Robertson had arrived that year with 15 or 16 families who "mostly stayed at Pictou." Next year he hoped to bring out many young men with families who would go to the Island.[76]

They probably came on the *Northern Friends,* which arrived in 1805 from Stornoway with 91 passengers. Led by Kenneth MacKenzie of Ross-shire, many settled at Flat River (lot 60).[77] All paid 9 shillings per acre except Samuel Nicholson who got a reduced rate for settling at a less desirable inland location, towards Belle Creek at lot 62.[78] Nicholson was joined by John Cameron, who obtained land free of charge at the entrance to Belle Creek, and five further families who got inland holdings at Wood Islands (lot 62), paying just 2 shillings per acre.[79] But not all of the emigrants who travelled on the *Northern Friends* settled on Selkirk's land. Many dispersed. For instance, Donald MacRae, from Glenelg, settled at lot 49, a short distance to the north of Belfast.[80]

TABLE 2: THE SELKIRK SETTLERS OF PRINCE EDWARD ISLAND AND
THEIR LAND HOLDINGS, 1803–07*

Lot No.	Purchaser†	Acreage	Cost per Acre	Total Owed‡	Sum Paid	Year Settled
			(s. d.)	(£ .s. d.)	(£. s. d.)	
31	Thomas Hide	100	9. 0	45. 0. 0		Before 1803
	Will. Clark	200	15. 0	150. 0. 0	43. 0. 0	"
	Johnson W Bearoto	150	"	120. 0. 0	24. 0. 0	"
	#Alexander Cameron &	160	10. 0**	88. 17. 9		1806
	#Donald McLaughlan					"
	#Neil Campbell	100	10. 0	55. 11. 1		"
	#John Livingston	100	"	55. 11. 1		"
	#Donald Livingston	100	"	55. 11. 1		"
	#Archibald Murray	100	"	55. 11. 1		"
	#Duncan Henderson	100	"	55. 11. 1		"
	#Duncan McLean	100	"	55. 11. 1		"
	#Archibald McLean	100	"	55. 11. 1		"
	#James McLean	100	"	55. 11. 1		"
	#Duncan Darrach (55 acres @ 15/-** £45. 16. 8 plus 210 acres @ 10/- £105. 0. 0)	265	"	150. 16. 8	11. 13. 4	1807
	#Hector McNeil	110	15. 0**	91. 13. 4		"
57	#Alexander McDonald	100	12. 6	62. 10. 0	20. 0. 0	"
	#Allan McDonald	100	"	62. 10. 0		"
	#Donald McRae	200	"	125. 0. 0	60. 0. 0	1806
	#R McDonald & bros	300	15. 0	225. 0. 0	147. 0. 0 (Partly paid in lumber)	1804
	Donald McPherson (50 acres at 2 bushells wheat per acre £25 and rest £37)	124		62. 0. 0	12. 0. 0	
	John Finlayson	75		37. 10. 0		
	#Malcolm McLeod (Lease for 5 years average rent £4)	75		4. 0. 0	2. 5. 0	
	Sarah Frazer & Sons	100	12. 6	62. 10. 0	12. 15. 0	
	John McDonald (Most of the money lodged at Portree, Scotland)	100	5. 0	25. 0. 0	25. 0. 0	
	Roderick McLeod (as above)	100	"	25. 0. 0	23. 0. 0	

Lot No.	Purchaser†	Acreage	Cost per Acre	Total Owed‡	Sum Paid	Year Settled
	Alexander McLeod (as above)	100	"	25. 0. 0	25. 0. 0	1804
	Donald McLeod (as above)	100	"	25. 0. 0	25. 0. 0	
57	John Sillers	200	5. 0	50. 0. 0	38. 17. 5	
	John McPherson	100	"	25. 0. 0	6. 15. 0	
	John Ross	100	"	25. 0. 0	10. 2. 6	
	Donald Nicholson	300	"	75. 0. 0	75. 0. 0	
	Samuel Martin	250	"	70. 0. 0	70. 0. 0	
	John & Donald Nicholson (Also received a present of 300 acres)	200	"	25. 0. 0		
	#Donald McEachern &					1806
	#Archibald McEachern &					"
	#Donald McEachern &	560	8. 0	224. 0. 0	34. 0. 0	"
	#John McEachern & (Have only a front of 22 1/2 chains and they go back nearly 2 miles which is why they pay only 8s. per acre.)					"
	Alexander McIntosh	130	7. 0	45. 10. 0		
	Duncan McDonald & (Rent last year 3 bushells wheat per 50 acres)	50	999 year lease	18. 0		
	Charles McKinnon (as above)	50	999 year lease	18. 0		
	Donald Martin (paid 2 bushells wheat per acre)	50		25. 0. 0		
	#Finlay Smith (also 50 acres for service)	50	5. 0	12. 10. 0		1807
	#William Chisholm (as above)	50	5. 0	12. 10. 0		1806
	#Donald Smith	150	4. 0	30. 0. 0	4. 0. 0	1805
	Duncan McTavish (Originally on marshland but exchanged to go at 1 1/2 miles back in the woods in 1806/7)	100	4. 0	20. 0. 0		
	Alexander Stewart (a present)	100				
	Alexander Frazer	100	5. 0	25. 0. 0		
	Samuel Nicholson (for service)	100				
	John Campbell Dr.					

Lot No.	Purchaser†	Acreage	Cost per Acre	Total Owed‡	Sum Paid	Year Settled
	Katherine Frazer	50	5. 0	12. 10. 0		
	Martin Martin &	150	8. 0	60. 0. 0		
	Donald Martin				40. 1. 1	
	Alexander Lamond	50	8. 0	20. 0. 0		
	Alexander Buchannan	112		43. 0. 0		
	(50 acres @ 5. 0 per acre is 12. 10. 0 plus 62 acres @ 2 bushells wheat/acre is 30. 10. 0)					
	John Buchannan	109		42. 0. 0		
	(50 acres @ 5. 0 per acre is 12. 10. 0 plus 59 acres @ 2 bushells wheat/acre is 29. 10. 0)					
	Donald Buchannon	114		44. 10. 0		
	(50 acres @ 5. 0 per acre is 12. 10. 0 plus 64 acres @ 2 bushells wheat/acre is 32. 0. 0)					
	Donald McLeod	50	5. 0	12. 10. 0)		
	Alexander McLeod	50	5. 0	12. 10. 0)	8. 3. 4	
	John McDonald	100	2 BW	50. 0. 0		
	#Munro McLean	113		10. 0	56. 10. 0	1806
	Donald McKinnon	209		72. 0. 0	32. 10. 0	
	(130 acres @ 5. 0 per acre is 32. 10. 0 plus 9 acres @ 10. 0 per acre is 4. 10. 0 plus 70 acres @ 2 bushells wheat/acre is 32. 0. 0)					
57	Hector McDonald	206		78. 0. 0	25. 0. 0	
	(100 acres @ 5. 0 per acre 25. 0. 0 plus 100 acres @ 2 bushells wheat/acre 50. 0. 0 plus 6 acres @ 10. 0 per acre 3. 0. 0. £12. 10. 0 of this paid to Lord Selkirk, 1803)					
	Donald Murchison &					
	John Murchison &	380	5. 0	95. 0. 0	69. 10. 6	
	Donald Murchison					
58	Dr McAulay	100	5. 0	25. 0. 0	25. 0. 0)	
	(100 in a present & 100 purchased & paid to Lord Selkirk 1803)					
	Angus McAulay			)		
	(as above)			)		

Lot No.	Purchaser†	Acreage	Cost per Acre	Total Owed‡	Sum Paid	Year Settled
	Angus McAulay Senior (paid to Lord Selkirk)	100	5. 0	25. 0. 0	25. 0. 0)	
	John McLeod	50	"	12. 10. 0		
	Donald McLeod	50	"	12. 10. 0		
	Donald McLeod, Maligar§	100	"	25. 0. 0		
	Donald O'Docherty	100	"	25. 0. 0		
	Malcolm McLeod	100	"	25. 0. 0		
	John McDonald Snr & John McDonald Jnr	200	"	50. 0. 0	13. 0. 0	
	#Muir Buchannan Jnr Malcolm Buchannan (100 acres for service)	103	12. 6	64. 7. 6	23. 18. 6	1805
	#Angus O'Docharty	100	8. 0	40. 0. 0	5. 5. 9	1806
	#Donald Nicholson (Schoolmaster) Angus McBraine (100 acres forservice) Charles McWilliam at	100	"	40. 0. 0	" " "	1806
	Saw Mill Farm	200	5. 0	50. 0. 0		1806
	Angus Frazer (50 acres for service and 50 acres purchased)	50	5. 0	12. 10. 0	" " "	1807
	Donald Ross (50 acres for service and 50 acres purchased)	50	5. 0	12. 10. 0	" " "	1806
	John McDonald Erigal‖	200	5. 0	50. 0. 0	50. 0. 0	
	#Donald McInnis & #Angus McDonald (about 330 acres)	330	10. 0**	183. 6. 8	14. 0. 0	1806
	#Allan Shaw	100	8. 0	42. 10. 0		1805
	John McLeod (Removed from his former farm)	100		34. 6. 0		
	#Alexander McPhadden (about 116 acres)	116	10. 0	58. 0. 0	14. 0. 0	1806
	John Campbell (Lease 7 years from 1805 Rent payable yearly except first year free)	100		3. 0. 0		
	Roderick McKenzie	250	5. 0	62. 10. 0	32. 18. 1	
58	#John McRae & #Donald McRae (about 200 acres)	200	11. 8	116. 13. 4	25. 4. 2	1806
	#Roderick McRae	100	10. 0	50. 0. 0	10. 0. 0	1806
60	#Pete Bolm	50	10. 0	25. 0. 0		1805
	#John McKenzie	300	7. 0	135. 0. 0	100. 0. 0	1805
	#Alexander McKenzie	100	"	45. 0. 0	10. 0. 0	"

Lot No.	Purchaser†	Acreage	Cost per Acre	Total Owed‡	Sum Paid	Year Settled
60	Angus McMillan	100	5. 0	25. 0. 0	25. 0. 0	
	#Alexander McArthur	100	15. 0	75. 0. 0		1806
	John Sillers (50 acres in 1803 @ 5. 0 per acre and 50 acres in 1805 @ 10. 0 per acre)	100	7. 6	37. 10. 0	3. 10. 0	
	Kine McKenzie (1803 5. 0 per acre 1805 10. 0 per acre)	102		38. 10. 0	15. 3. 4	
	#Dugald Ball (about)	160	12. 0	96. 0. 0	20. 0. 0	1807
	Donald McRae Snr	100	6. 0	30. 0. 0		
	#Alexander McKenzie	100	9. 0	45. 0. 0	25. 0. 0	1806
	John Nicolson	100	5. 0	25. 0. 0	15. 0. 0	
	#Kenneth McKenzie (brought 100 acres in 1805 @ 9. 0 per acre £45 and 100 acres in 1806 @ 10. 0 per acre £50)	200	9. 6	95. 0. 0	22. 10. 0	1805/6
	Angus Beaton & John Beaton & Donald Beaton & John McPherson & (50 acres for service)	250	5. 0	62. 10. 0	37. 0. 0	
	Donald Ross (Most of the money paid by these five lodged at Portree, Scotland)	100	5. 0	25. 0. 0	25. 0. 0	
	Finlay McRae (50 acres @ 5. 0 per acre £12. 10 in 1806, 50 acres @ 10. 0 per acre £25. 0)	100	7. 6	37. 10. 0	15. 0. 0	
	Duncan Mcrae (same as above)	100	7. 6	37. 10. 0	15. 0. 0	
	Peter Campbell This man had leased land originally, but afterwards made a purchase.	146	11. 8	85. 3. 4		
62	Samuel Nicholson about	300	7. 6	112. 10. 0	70. 0. 0	1806
	John Cameron (300 acres in a present at the entrance into Belle Creek and which he sold this summer and a family will be established there next Spring.)					

Lot No.	Purchaser†	Acreage	Cost per Acre	Total Owed‡	Sum Paid	Year Settled
62	#Donald McNeil	100	10. 0	50. 0. 0		1806/7
	#James Currie	100	10. 0	50. 0. 0		"
	#Malcolm McMillan	200	"	100. 0. 0		"
	#Malcolm Bell	100	"	50. 0. 0	20. 0. 0	"
	#Malcolm McNeil	100	"	50. 0. 0		"
	#Malcolm McIsaac	100	7. 6	37. 10. 0		1805
	#Roderick McLellan (200 acre @ 5. 0 per acre £50, 10 acres @ 10.0 per acre £5)	210		55. 0. 0		1804/5
	#James Munro	100	2. 0	10. 0. 0		1806/7
	#Angus Munro	100	2. 0	10. 0. 0		"
	#Malcolm Munro	100	2. 0	10. 0. 0		"
	#Neil Munro	100	2. 0	10. 0. 0		"
	#James Currie (Vire)	100	2. 0	10. 0. 0		"
53	John McFarlane (Paid 2 bushells of wheat per acre)	100		50. 0. 0		
	Duncan Robertson	100	"	50. 0. 0		
	William McLaren & Donald McLaren & James McLaren & 2 Sons in Law	466	10. 0	233. 0. 0	233. 0. 0	
	John McDonal (guard) (Paid 2 bushells wheat per acre)	62	2 BW	31. 0. 0		
	John McMillan	53	"	26. 10. 0		
	#John McDonald Junr	56	"	28. 0. 0		1805
	Angus McDonald	50	"	25. 0. 0		
	Donald McAuley	50	"	25. 0. 0		
	Donald McKennon	54	"	27. 0. 0		
	Angus Wilson	54	"	27. 0. 0		
	Donald Wilson	54	"	27. 0. 0		
	Donald Wilson Jnr	54	"	27. 0. 0		
	William Wilson	60	"	30. 0. 0		
	#Donald Campbell	100	10. 0	50. 0. 0	10. 2. 8	1805
	#Ewan & Angus McCormick	100	10. 0	50. 0. 0		1805
	Alexander McDonald (Paid 2 bushells of wheat per acre)	100	2 BW	50. 0. 0		
	Angus McDonald (Carpenter)	100	"	50. 0. 0		
	Total	**15,822**		**£6397 9. 3**	**£1744. 15. 8**	

Table 2 continued

* The list was produced by James Williams, Lord Selkirk's Agent in 1807. Source: SP (C-14) 14862-14869
† Those marked # settled after the Earl of Selkirk came to the Island in 1803/1804. The remainder were the 1803 arrivals who came on the *Polly*, *Dykes* and *Oughton*.
‡ Most of the purchases in this table were made in "Halifax Money" but some were made in sterling which was worth more. Where sterling was paid an asterisk(**) is placed next to the amount paid per acre.
§ Maligar, Skye
‖ Possibly Elgol, Skye

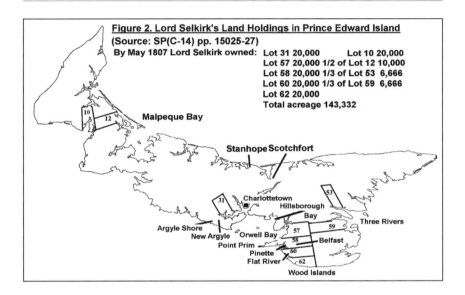

Figure 2. Lord Selkirk's Land Holdings in Prince Edward Island (Source: SP(C-14) pp. 15025-27)
By May 1807 Lord Selkirk owned:

Lot 31 20,000	Lot 10 20,000
Lot 57 20,000	1/2 of Lot 12 10,000
Lot 58 20,000	1/3 of Lot 53 6,666
Lot 60 20,000	1/3 of Lot 59 6,666
Lot 62 20,000	
Total acreage 143,332	

James Robertson was particularly active in 1806. At least 600 emigrants sailed to the Island that year on one of seven ships. But 1806 had also been "a mouse year." Mice had eaten all but a small portion of the crops on the Island and, although there was little suffering or distress, "it was discouraging to novices." And two years later "they suffered almost as much from grasshoppers, which here are called locusts."[81] But still they came. In 1808, Robertson would tell Selkirk of the "800 or 900 passengers" who were due to sail to the Island at the beginning of June:

> The majority are from Perthshire and...they will be willing to settle inland on the road from Wood Islands [lot 62]. About one third, or

St. John's Presbyterian Church at Belfast, built in 1824 by Robert Jones, on land that had been granted originally by Lord Selkirk. *Photograph courtesy of Jean Lucas.*

rather more are from Mull, who will not leave the shore, but many will settle on lot 31 or perhaps on the coast, east of Wood Islands.[82]

Robertson's activities caused considerable consternation at Blair Atholl, back in Scotland, where it was claimed that he had "carried off about 700" people to Prince Edward Island, making a handsome profit of £5 a head. Gilbert, second Earl of Minto, did not think that Lord Selkirk had "been directly implicated in this system of kidnapping." But he was involved. Robertson had been employed, all along, by Selkirk.[83]

There was of course no certainty that these new people would settle at Wood Islands but, to make this prospect more attractive, Selkirk would get their ships to land there and would incur the added expense of having a few acres cleared beforehand "in different parts along the road."[84] In the end, Robertson only brought 400 or so emigrants to the Island in 1808.[85] And they came on three ships to Charlottetown, not Wood Islands. However a good many of the Mull and Colonsay emigrants did eventually take up land at Wood Islands and some, as had been hoped, opted for lot 31, a short distance to the west of Charlottetown.[86]

Thus, Selkirk's work in encouraging emigrants from the Highlands and Islands to settle in Prince Edward Island extended well beyond the two year period in 1803-04 when he was able to deal personally with his settlers. The large influx between 1804 and 1810 had been stimulated by his efforts and by James Robertson's ability to attract recruits from Perthshire and Argyll.[87]

Soon distinct clusters emerged. Mull and Colonsay emigrants were to be found in the greatest numbers at Argyle Shore and New Argyle (lots 30 and 65), Perthshire emigrants at Beaton Point (lot 47) and the Three Rivers area (lots 52 to 54) and Sutherlanders at New London and Granville (lots 20 and 21).[88] Only a small proportion of the new arrivals ever settled on land owned by Selkirk. Some purchased land from other proprietors but a good many would have taken possession of their land by squatting.[89]

In the end, Selkirk had achieved what the Scottish lairds had most feared. He had established a successful colony at Belfast and had been the catalyst behind the major influx from the Highlands and Islands which followed. But his venture had cost him personally very dear. Large sums had been spent on a sawmill, a gristmill, a storehouse, on draining marshes, providing cattle for settlers, clearing land and in paying the agents who managed his affairs. Another heavy cost had been road building. Roads were almost non-existent. Visiting the Island in 1791, Dr. James Mac-Gregor had found that "there was not a road on the Island with the exception of the one between Charlottetown and Covehead [lot 34]."[90] When the accounts were examined in 1807, they showed a total expenditure of over £30,000. Yet only 16,000 of the 143,000 acres he had acquired on the Island had been purchased by settlers and his entire land holdings were worth, at most, only £10,000.[91] This was a staggering £20,000 deficit – roughly £1 million in today's money.[92]

Undaunted, Selkirk devoted his energy to founding a second colony at Baldoon. Seeking only fifteen families to begin with, he seemed to be esablishing a modest enough venture. But situated as it was in a distant corner of southwestern Upper Canada, there would be huge logistical problems to overcome. The site had been carefully chosen for its proximity to the United States. And unlike his relatively prosperous Prince Edward Island settlers, who could afford to pay their own passages, most of the Upper Canada recruits came from the "poorer class of emigrants only" and would need financial backing.[93]

As he sailed away from the Island back home to Scotland in October 1804, Selkirk could take much satisfaction in progress made. His Island settlers would prosper. And his second venture was already underway. During his time away from the Island, his extensive tour had included a visit to the edge of Lake St. Clair, the remote site chosen for his new settlement. Naming it Baldoon after his father's estate, he had set his agent William Burn to work planning the new buildings and preparing the way for his settlers.[94] He had even been able to meet with these families at Kingston, a remarkable feat given the uncertainties of travel at the time. Having left Kirkcudbright in May 1804, the new settlers had arrived at Lachine, Lower Canada, on July 19. Their paths crossed in August as Selkirk was heading east from Lake St. Clair and they west from Lachine. His settlers would arrive at Baldoon in September. Although they came too late in the year to grow crops, their needs would be met by the ample store of food and provisions which Selkirk had provided. However, he had not anticipated the heavy rainfall and the dangers which lay ahead. Reports that many had been stricken by a serious illness, soon after their arrival, caught up with him in Halifax, in December, just as he was preparing to return home to Britain. The news was a terrible omen of what would follow.

4. INITIAL SETBACKS AT
BALDOON, UPPER CANADA

*I am really concerned to hear such melancholy accounts of the new settle-
ment; pray would it not be advisable to remove all those that are ill up the
River St. Clair and billet them out in houses where they might be made
comfortable...I can assure you that there are people here giving out hints
unfavourable to the settlement and those that you might perhaps least expect;
if an idea of revolt was to prevail amongst the people it is uncertain whether
you would be able to compel their residence at Baldoon. This entre nous.[1]*

SELKIRK'S DECISION TO LOCATE HIS settlers along the Chenal Ecarté
River in the northern stretches of Dover township, Kent County,
brought immediate perils. The fifteen families, who arrived in September 1804, found themselves in a waterlogged location which bred
mosquitoes with a vengeance. A month later most of the people were falling
ill with malaria, and dire warnings were circulating of a possible revolt. By
November there were 16 deaths, five of them heads of families. And yet,
the site must have looked so promising to anyone seeing it for the first time.

As the flatness of the Chenal Ecarté region came into view, the settlers
would have seen a huge expanse of natural marshlands. This was a tree-
less countryside covered with lush grasslands. There were drains to lay,
but that would be cheaper and easier than chopping down woodland.[2]
Once drained, the marshlands would yield rich black soil, high in organic
matter. Of course, low-lying land bordering on rivers was not without
its hazards. Selkirk knew this. On his tour of Michigan he had seen lakes
which "were higher fourteen years ago than they have ever been since
and at that time overflowed [onto] lands at Detroit formerly cultivated
and now again dry."[3] But when Selkirk had visited the Baldoon site, the
water levels in the rivers and lakes were at an all time low, some five or
six feet lower than would be the case over the next thirty years.[4] So he
had made wrong assumptions based on what he had seen in 1804. It was

difficult enough cultivating a low-lying site, but, when the rains came and water poured onto the land, the drainage work needed was "quite beyond the power of ordinary settlers."[5] However, in spite of these adverse conditions the settlers remained at Baldoon. They located themselves, initially, on Selkirk's land in Dover township and then later moved a short distance further north to Shawnee township, afterwards known as Chatham Gore.[6] (Figure 3). Eventually, they would come together to found a settlement at "the forks" of the north and east branches of Great Bear Creek (later called Sydenham River), a place they would rename Wallaceburg to commemorate their Highland origins. Thus, these fifteen families did establish a thriving settlement, much in the way that Selkirk had always intended, although he never lived to see the final result.

And yet, at the time, Baldoon appeared to have been a terrible flop. The settlers' very survival seemed to be in doubt. How could they remain in such a remote and unsuitable place? But, they did. They colonized Selkirk's land along the Chenal Ecarté River, along Big Bear Creek and Little Bear Creek, and after a few years were enjoying their first signs of prosperity. When the British government refused to let Selkirk have the land he wanted in Shawnee township, they took matters into their own hands and acquired this better site for themselves. And, while doing this, they had to cope with the dysfunctional Alexander McDonell, Selkirk's site manager and agent. Treating his work at Baldoon as a spare time activity, he failed completely to bring any form of management or direction to the site. He had not a shred of sympathy for the settlers or their problems. Baldoon was simply a career move, for which he was completely unsuited.

Selkirk had been attracted to Baldoon because of its strategic position. He wanted to establish settlers as protectors of territory in regions, such as this, considered vulnerable to attack from the United States. This was why Upper Canada mattered so much to him. His work in Prince Edward Island had achieved much, but it had not addressed his overriding passion to see settlers, loyal to Britain, located in strategic areas. He had originally intended to move the many hundreds he took to the Island to the Falls of St. Mary (later Sault Ste. Marie) but the land he had asked for there had been refused. This quite remote location between Lakes Superior and Huron had appealed to Selkirk because of its strategic position in relation to the American border. It was also a vital point on the trade route used by the North West Company, a factor which contributed to his being denied the land.[7]

Now he was concentrating his attention on another, as yet unsettled region of Upper Canada, but this time much further south, within "the peninsula formed by Lakes Ontario, Erie, Huron and Simcoe."[8] He would spend his own money encouraging settlers to go to the key boundary area between Lakes Erie and Huron. General concerns over the vulnerability of this region had been well documented.[9] Selkirk reasoned that, to make any impact, the settlers would need to be concentrated in one large settlement instead of being spread out in small clusters. Only then could they act as a shield against "the contagion of American influences." In his view, Highlanders would be the best colonizers of such areas since their Gaelic language and distinctive culture made them less "disposed to coalesce" with any Americans. Encouragement could be given to those Highlanders who had already settled in other parts of Upper Canada and in the United States to join together to form one major settlement; and later they would attract re-inforcements from Scotland:

> The Scottish Highland emigrants are of all descriptions of people, the most proper for the purpose, since independently in their character and in other respects the very circumstance of their using a different language would tend to keep them apart from the Americans. The emigrants, who in the course of a few years must unavoidably leave Scotland, would be sufficient to form a colony of such force as would render Upper Canada safe from any attack it is likely to be exposed to and to be an effectual check on the disaffected French of the Lower Province."[10]

Selkirk's thinking was very much in line with previous government policy.[11] It had been recognized from the early days of the Conquest that loyal British emigrants could be useful to the Crown when settled in militarily strategic areas. Following the Seven Years War, which ended in 1763, many former officers and soldiers from disbanded regiments settled on free land, offered by the government, located near Quebec and Montreal as well as in the Island of St. John (later Prince Edward Island). And after the ending of the American War of Independence, in 1784, thousands of British Empire Loyalists were relocated at government expense from the United States to the Maritimes, principally around the Bay of Fundy; and many others were also moved to sites along the St. Lawrence between Cornwall and Kingston and in the Niagara Peninsula.[12] Selkirk's venture was thus an extension of this policy of creating defensive lines of settlement along major river boundaries and bays. The Baldoon site would bring loyal civilians into border territory at the southwest end of Upper Canada, just below Lake Huron, where they could "form a bulwark" against American encroachment.

Portrait of Alexander McDonell who managed Lord Selkirk's Baldoon Estate. *Courtesy of Toronto Reference Library, J. Ross Robertson Collection.*

Selkirk had first been persuaded of the importance of the Lake St. Clair region by Father Edmund Burke, a Roman Catholic priest whom he visited during his time in Halifax. After being with his Prince Edward Island settlers for the month of August, in 1803, he had left for a leisurely tour of Nova Scotia ending up in Halifax, where he remained during the last week of September and first week of October. Selkirk and Burke both shared similar concerns over the need to protect Upper Canada from American influences. Although Selkirk had some reservations over Burke's judgement, he was won over to the extent of wishing to see the region for himself.[13] Deciding to go ahead with this site, Selkirk petitioned for and later received a government grant of 1200 acres in Dover township. He would then get an additional 200 acres for each of the families he introduced into the area on proof of having regranted 50 acres to them. Having met this requirement, by 1806, for 15 families, his total land holdings were increased by a further 3000 acres.[14]

Arriving at Lake St. Clair in June 1804, with Alexander McDonell, his prospective site manager, Selkirk became directly involved in the planning and preparation work which needed to be carried out. McDonell and Selkirk had first met in York, during Selkirk's visit there towards the end of 1803. A man of some bearing and prestige, McDonell was Sheriff of the Home District and, being a Highlander himself, seemed an ideal choice.[15] He accepted Selkirk's job offer after some wavering. But, on a brief second visit to York in the summer of 1804, Selkirk would discover that General Peter Hunter, the Lieutenant-Governor of Upper Canada,[16] had misgivings about McDonell's abilities. The warning went unheeded. Although his integrity was never in any doubt, McDonell's inability to manage people and control expenditure made him a highly unsuitable choice as site manager. Known for his "obstinacy and unaccommodating temper" he repeatedly ignored Selkirk's instructions, while blaming others for the many mishaps which occurred.[17]

Selkirk had directed his agent Richard Savage, in the summer of 1802, to purchase up to 1000 sheep in the eastern United States and William

Burn had been put in charge of driving them to Queenston, which he did in the autumn of the following year.[18] In the meantime, instructions had been given, in 1803, to Lionel Johnson, a Northumbrian whom Selkirk had met that year at Albany, New York, to drive the sheep, that had been already assembled, overland from Queenston on to Baldoon. This he did with a handful of helpers, who included his eight-year-old son, James.[19] William Burn then arrived at Baldoon in April 1804, with five farm labourers and three carpenters to take charge of the preliminary building work, doing so until his death in mid-September. Alexander McDonell, who later that summer became Burn's superior, was horrified to learn that, during this time, Burns and a small number of workmen had consumed eight barrels of whisky (each containing 39 gallons).[20] But surely McDonell should never have allowed this to happen. Time and again he proved to be unreliable and negligent in his duties. And, as Selkirk would discover some years later, at Baldoon there "was waste and mismanagement carried to a pitch, almost incredible."[21]

Selkirk established a farm of around 950 acres at Baldoon. It was to become the operational centre for the colony and derive most of its income from sheep. Only the finest sheep, bred from imported, Spanish merino rams, were to be raised because they could be kept "for very little more expense than the most ordinary and produce three times the value."[22] The farm, triangular in shape, was bounded on the west by the Chenal Ecarté River, on the east by Big Bear Creek and on the north by the dividing

Site of Selkirk's former farm at Baldoon. A substantial farmhouse had been constructed but no trace of it remains. *Photograph by Geoff Campey.*

line between Dover and Shawnee townships. The settlers' lots were located along the eastern banks of the Chenal Ecarté and Big Bear Creek, as well as along Little Bear Creek.[23]

Selkirk remained at Baldoon during June and much of July directing the construction work, which included an ox stable, a storehouse, a barn and two log houses for some farm labourers who were arriving from Prince Edward Island.[24] Planning to have the necessary "ironwork" for a mill and threshing machine made in New York later that year, Selkirk also made provision for a distillery and various other sheds and workhouses.[25] He had engaged Roger Briggs of Malden township, Essex County to build his farmhouse. It was to be built "35 feet long by 18 feet wide...with a kitchen, of 16 feet by 14 feet, back of and adjoining, said house, for the sum of £220 New York currency, [equivalent to] $550." It was to have "two flights of stairs without brackets," 10 windows, 10 panel doors, 10 brass-handle locks and "70 pairs of shutter hinges."[26] A substantial house, it survived "for several generations." But, by 1882, the "one storey and a half structure" was in a ruinous state and nothing remains of it now.[27]

And yet while all of this effort was being made at Selkirk's private farm, little thought was being given to settler accommodation. Believing that his settlers would have two months of warm weather before winter set in, he intended that they should stay in temporary accommodation. However, by the time the settlers arrived in September, heavy rains had flooded the land and not even the two workmen's huts were habitable. So when McDonell finally made an appearance he was confronted by very angry settlers. He immediately agreed to have 14 log houses built, summoned up provisions and a doctor from Sandwich (later Windsor) but, by then, the malarial fever had already taken its toll.[28]

Had McDonell been more assiduous in checking conditions at Baldoon the settlers might have been spared their ordeal. But time and again he would prove to be unreliable. McDonell had agreed, in June, to move from York to Sandwich to manage the Baldoon site and to devote his full attention to it. Selkirk had, in fact, required him to relinquish his public offices as well as any ambitions he might have for government promotion. But McDonell failed to keep his side of the bargain. His marriage in 1805 and his position as Speaker of the Assembly from 1805 to 1807 required him to be based in York. Thus, he would only visit Baldoon for short periods, mainly in the summer. His regular reports back to Selkirk, which were full of unremitting gloom and despair, merely glossed over the confusion and chaos being caused by his own failings and long absences from the place.[29]

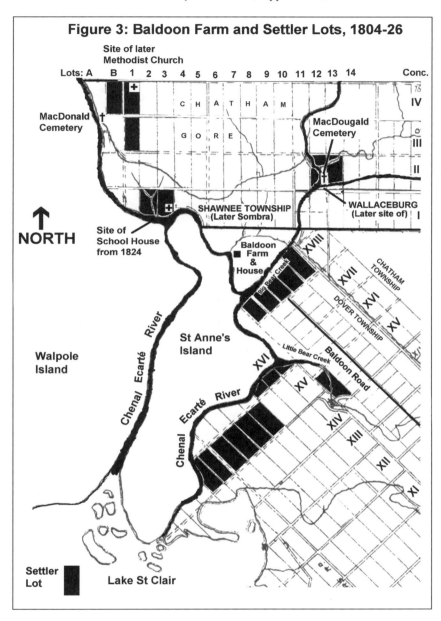

Figure 3: Baldoon Farm and Settler Lots, 1804-26

The local workmen were joined that summer by the additional men recruited by Selkirk during his tour of Upper Canada. Amongst their number were "the three Glengarry lads," who were to be offered land

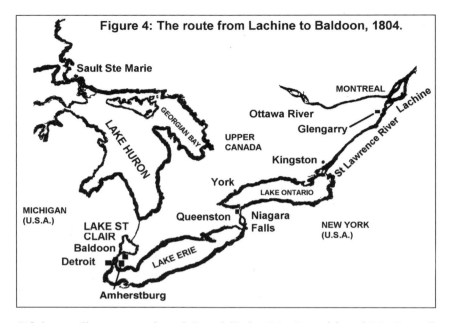

Figure 4: The route from Lachine to Baldoon, 1804.

"if they will marry and settle" and "John MacDonald and Mr. Innes" from Prince Edward Island, who "may also be encouraged to stay but will probably be more fond of the plains."[30] The latter two were probably included in the group of 15 settlers, who are known to have arrived at Quebec from Prince Edward Island, on the *Charlotte,* on June 23.[31] But the principal arrivals that year were the fifteen families from the Western Isles who, having arrived at Lachine, near Montreal, in July were making their way inland to Lake St. Clair. A total of 102 people had sailed on the *Oughton*, under Captain John Baird, the same ship and captain which had brought the South Uist settlers to Prince Edward Island the year before. Robert Buchanan, aged 10, had died on the crossing, while Hector MacDougald, aged 10 and a half, was sick on arrival (Table 3).[32] The fifteen families then travelled west in carts to a point just above the Lachine Rapids where they could board *batteaux* and be rowed up the St. Lawrence to Kingston (Figure 4).[33] There they met Selkirk on the 5th of August.[34] He dealt with their various requests for credit, food provisions, employment and land, giving them decisions on the spot, and then headed off to York for a meeting with General Hunter. Meanwhile, the settlers sailed across Lake Ontario to Queenston, a journey lasting four days. They were then taken a safe distance, by land, to a point beyond Niagara Falls where they could safely be put on *batteaux*

Painting of Kingston Dockyards and Citadel in 1816 by Francis Hall. Selkirk and his Baldoon settlers met at Kingston in August 1804. *Courtesy National Archives of Canada, C-003236.*

and rowed down the Niagara River and then on to Lake Erie. They next continued along the north shore of Lake Erie to Amherstburg where they transferred to open boats to begin the final lap of their journey northwards to Lake St. Clair, and beyond this to the Chenal Écarté River and Baldoon. They arrived on September 5, 1804.[35]

Because the fifteen families were initially collected at Tobermory, in Mull, it is likely that many originated from Mull. The passenger list completed on their arrival at Lachine, gave few details of the families apart from names and ages (Table 3). But the six MacDonald families had presented problems for the list compiler. To tell them apart he recorded some distinguishing features.[36] Thus Donald MacDonald, aged 32, the tailor from Tyree, was differentiated from the Donald MacDonald, aged 45, who came from the parish of Laggan in Inverness-shire. There was Angus MacDonald, age not given, who came from Oronsay, a small Island just to the south of Colonsay; he was thus distinguishable from the other Angus MacDonald, aged 31. In a list of family heads produced in 1806, the latter Angus MacDonald is shown as having originated from Kirkland (Dumfriesshire).[37] Alexander MacDonald, aged 35 was a piper. A letter from John MacDougald, written in 1806, indicates that the MacDougalds came from Mull, while a tombstone inscription reveals that Allan MacLean and his family had originated from Tyree. And a Gaelic Bible printed in 1777 tells us that Donald MacCallum and his family had originated from Mull.[38] Thus the group had mixed origins. Most of them probably originated from the Argyll Islands, especially Mull and Tyree, but at least two families came from the mainland (Inverness-shire and Dumfriesshire). With the exception of Allan MacDougald, aged 21, the family heads and their wives were middle-aged, with most having teenage sons and daughters.

People from the Argyll Islands had certainly shown an interest in emigrating to North America and had been doing so from as early as 1738. A great many left from the islands of Islay and Jura, in the second half of the eighteenth century, with most settling in North Carolina.[39] In the summer of 1791, it was reported that "a considerable proportion of the inhabitants [of Colonsay] had crossed the Atlantic." And "the spirit of emigration" was said to be "still powerful" in the following year, requiring "considerable alterations to extinguish it."[40] The parish of Kilfinichen and Kilvickeon, in Mull, had lost some families to North America that year while there was "some talk" that people from Tyree were preparing to emigrate. Thirty-six men, women and children had, in fact, gone to North America, that year, from the adjacent island of Coll (Figure 1).[41] And, by 1803, there were signs that tenants from Murdoch MacLean of Lochbuie's estate in Mull were intending to emigrate to Nova Scotia.[42] Thus, it is not surprising that Selkirk's agents had found willing recruits in the Argyll Islands. By the following year many Mull emigrants would be on their way to settle on Selkirk's land in Prince Edward Island and now, others would be going to Baldoon.[43]

Having intended to make the crossing in the previous year, the fifteen families had been required to spend a full year working on Selkirk's estate at St. Mary's Isle in Kirkcudbrightshire before a ship was made ready for them. Unlike most of Selkirk's recruits, they had decided to wait for an opportunity to get to Upper Canada rather than accept his offer of land in Prince Edward Island. Fearing dangers at sea during the early stages of the Napoleonic Wars, Selkirk had instructed them to delay their departure until the following year.[44] Most had agreed indenture contracts, requiring them to work on Selkirk's farm at Baldoon for a fixed number of years, in return for their free passages to the site and other benefits.[45] They would receive 50 acre lots soon after their arrival, "so that by working on them in spare time they may become attached to the place."[46] And in time they would own their own lots and acquire additional holdings.

TABLE 3: THE FIFTEEN BALDOON FAMILIES WHO ARRIVED AT
LACHINE ON THE *Oughton*, 19 JULY 1804*

Name	Age	Sex	Remarks
Peter MacDonald	42	Male	
Mary MacDonald	45	Female	
John MacDonald	13	Male	
David MacDonald	12	Male	
Peter MacDonald	5 1/2	Male	
Angus MacDonald†	31	Male	From Kirkland
Jean MacDonald	40	Female	
Angus MacDonald	3	Male	
Andrew MacDonald	6	Male	
Kath MacDonald	8	Female	
Nancy MacDonald	3 months	Female	
Donald MacCallum	50	Male	
Mary MacCallum	40	Female	
Hugh MacCallum	18	Male	
Isa MacCallum	16	Female	
Flora MacCallum	14	Female	
Amelia MacCallum	9	Female	
Peggy MacCallum	7	Female	
Ann MacCallum	4	Female	
Charles Morrison	49	Male	
Peggy Morrison	34	Female	
Flora Morrison	14	Female	
Christian Morrison	2 1/2	Female	
Fa: MacKay‡	14	Female	
James Morrison	13	Male	
John MacDougald	50	Male	Remained with a sick boy
Sarah MacDougald	47	Female	Remained with a sick boy
Angus MacDougald	17	Male	
John MacDougald	14	Male	
Hector MacDougald	10 1/2	Male	Sick
Lauchlan MacDougald	8 1/2	Male	Remained with his father
Archibald MacDougald	6	Male	
James MacDougald	2 1/2	Male	
Munly MacDougald	18	Female	
Flora MacDougald	4	Female	Remained with father
Allan MacDougald	21	Male	
Ann MacDougald	19	Female	
Mary MacDougald	5 months	Female	

Name	Age	Sex	Remarks
Angus MacPherson	49	Male	
Kirsty MacPherson	43	Female	
Alexander MacPherson	19	Male	
Donald MacPherson	17	Male	
Mary MacPherson	8	Female	
Dugald MacPherson	4	Male	
Alexander MacDonald	35	Male	A piper
Mary MacDonald	30	Female	
John MacDonald	13	Male	
Angus MacDonald	8	Male	
Neil MacDonald	3	Male	
Unice MacDonald	9	Female	
Ann MacDonald	5	Female	
Kath MacDonald	1 1/2	Female	
John McKenzie	36	Male	
Ann McKenzie	36	Female	
Keneth McKenzie	10	Male	
Donald McKenzie	8	Male	
Flora McKenzie	6	Female	
John Buchannan	42	Male	
Kath Buchannan	31	Female	
Alexander Buchannan	17	Male	
Robert Buchannan	10	Male	Died on passage from Scotland
John Buchannan	1 1/2	Male	
Marion Buchannan	19	Female	
Kath Buchannan	8	Female	
Nelly Buchannan	3 1/2	Female	
Donald Buchannan	5 1/2	Male	
Donald MacDonald	45	Male	From Laggan
Kath MacDonald	37	Female	
Chrisy MacDonald	15	Female	
Sarah MacDonald	13	Female	
Mary MacDonald	9	Female	
Kath MacDonald	7	Female	
Flora MacDonald	5	Female	
Peggy MacDonald	3	Female	
Angus MacDonald	11	Male	
Donald MacDonald	32	Male	Tiree, Taylor
Flora MacDonald	26	Female	
John MacDonald	6	Male	
Duncan MacDonald	3	Male	
Hugh MacDonald	1 1/2	Male	

Name	Age	Sex	Remarks
Donald Brown	38	Male	
Marion Brown	35	Female	
Hector Brown	7	Male	
Alexander Brown	5	Male	
Flora Brown	7	Female	
Neil Brown§	n/k	Male	
Allan MacLean	32	Male	
Mary MacLean	30	Female	
Mary McDonald	48	Female	
Kirsty MacLean	10	Female	
Mary MacLean	2 1/2	Female	
Hector MacLean	8	Male	
Effie McLean	8 months	Male	
Angus MacDonald	n/k	Male	From Oronsay
Nancy McLaughlin	n/k	Female	
Ann MacLean‖	n/k	Female	
Allan MacDonald	18	Male	
John MacDonald	16	Male	
Archibald MacDonald	n/k	Male	
Donald MacDonald	n/k	Male	
Hector MacDonald	n/k	Male	
Neil MacDonald	n/k	Male	

* Source: NAC MG24 I8 vol.4, 105–8. The names have been resequenced where necessary to keep members of the same family together in separate groups.

† Angus MacDonald is shown as originating from Kirkland (Dumfriesshire) in a later list produced by Alexander McDonell in SP (C-14) 14591.

‡ Fa: Mackay appears with the Morrison family names in the passenger list. She may have been a relative.

§ His name was added, at the end, in the original list.

‖ Ann MacLean is recorded, in the original list, with the MacDonalds who originated from the Island of Oronsay. She may have been a member of Allan MacLean's family, (listed just above) or had some connection with it.

Because of its remoteness, the land had little value. Thus, Selkirk was only able to sell it at exceptionally low prices, which would tempt the worst type of "Yankees." But those "who can scarcely by the year's labour procure the subsistence of their families would think themselves but too rich if they could have the independent possession even of a small lot of land." Thus, Selkirk sought "the poorer class of emigrants only."[47] And to lessen the risk of desertions, only families were recruited:

"They [families] will go through it with less reluctance especially if pains are taken to…give them some interest in the produce of their labour …also if young indented men come over with their parents, land may perhaps be given at once to the parents subject to the condition of their children serving faithfully."[48]

The heavy rains which greeted the settlers continued throughout October destroying most of the crops that had been sown during the summer by farm labourers already at the site. Since July there had scarcely been a day on which it had not rained.[49] The sheep driven to the site by Lionel Johnson had to be kept out of flooded areas and, being some distance away, many were killed by wolves and rattlesnakes and all suffered from "the scab."[50] And yet, in spite of these problems, McDonell left the site in November, putting Peter MacDonald in charge of the other settlers. He then returned to his home in York and resumed his various activities. While on the way to York, McDonell learned that sixteen people had died, five being heads of families, of whom one was Peter MacDonald.[51] Issuing instructions that John MacDonald, a workman from Prince Edward Island, should take charge, in place of Peter MacDonald, he travelled on to York. That was his answer to the developing crisis. He did not return to the site even though people were dying and were in desperate need of help.[52] And, there were claims that, by the end of 1804, the death toll had risen as high as forty two; however, later figures show that around twenty-two people had died.[53]

News of the deaths did not reached Selkirk, until February 1805, by which time he was back in Britain. Greatly distressed, he instructed McDonell to move the settlers immediately to higher ground either at the forks of Big Bear Creek (the later site of Wallaceburg) or along the River St. Clair.[54] This was to be a temporary move only. McDonell was instructed to have the original site drained and kept as Selkirk's personal property. Selkirk hoped, eventually to locate his settlers on higher ground in Shawnee township, to the north of his farm, but it had first to be purchased from the government.[55] In the meantime McDonell was to assign the settlers new lots in the woods along Little Bear Creek and along the projected "Baldoon Street" which would connect Baldoon with the Thames River (Figure 3). When he finally returned to Baldoon in the spring of 1805, McDonell found most people to be in better health. Disregarding Selkirk's instructions, he decided not to relocate the settlers on higher ground. But by summer the fever had returned and two more heads of family were dead.[56]

At great expense, McDonell then moved all of the Baldoon families to the town of Sandwich, where they remained throughout the summer. But even there, two more girls from the settlement died. McDonell now wanted Selkirk to withdraw his settlers from Baldoon:

> Allow me to entreat of your Lordship to turn your eyes to some more eligible part of the province for settlement, for rest assured my Lord, that not one of the present importation will ever settle at Baldoon – they declare so openly."[57]

It was November before Selkirk got McDonell's letter. Growing increasingly irritated with him, he again repeated his original instructions. McDonell was to relocate the settlers immediately. It was hoped that land would be acquired for them in the Shawnee township, but in the meantime they were to be given temporary accommodation. Now instead of being moved to Little Bear Creek and along the proposed Baldoon Street, McDonell was to purchase already cleared land on the Thames River for them, and do so immediately. McDonell was to sell the cattle, have someone look after the sheep and make sure that the buildings were kept in good repair. But once again McDonell took no notice of his instructions nor did he tell the settlers about these plans until April of the following year.[58] It was some two months later, in January 1806, before Selkirk actually found out about McDonell's lengthy absences. His patience finally snapped:

> When I learnt that you had been absent from the settlement for so long a period last winter with no better a substitute than John MacDonald to take charge, I anticipated no good, but the extravagance of which he appears to have been guilty goes beyond all bounds; and I cannot understand how you could think of leaving so unlimited a charge in the hands of a man so little capable of it."[59]

Yet, McDonell would remain the Baldoon manager for another three years. And, although he continued to neglect his duties, the settlers were beginning to make progress. So much so, that John MacDougald felt that he should write to his brother in Mull encouraging him and others to join their settlement. While there had been "a good spell of sickness since we came to this place, as no doubt you have heard," the settlers "thank God, are getting the better of it now" and are prospering:

There is not a place under the sun better than this place [Baldoon]. Any person that intends to come to this country and that can take £10 sterling to this place he may make a living of it with very little trouble.... You may tell Ronald, your brother...he would get more land than was in all Mull for about £10 Stirling.[60]

There were good opportunities for tradesmen, such as "carpenters, blacksmiths and shoemakers; they have two dollars per day and their victuals. A labouring man has from one dollar and twelve shillings per day...there is all sorts of fish in this place." In coming the hundreds of mile, "up the country" to Baldoon, he "could not see a poor man. The farther we came up the country, the better." And their friends in Morvern, on the Argyll mainland opposite Mull, should be told of Baldoon's rising prosperity:

...and especially Angus McInnes, piper, tell him that he would do a great deal better here than where he is.... You may let Hugh McPhie know if he was to come here he would make in one year what would maintain them forever and keep them in a good way.[61]

By this time the settlers were being freed of their indentures "on providing promissory notes for...the fair value of the remainder of their time or what the indentures might be sold for." And ten of the thirteen lots along Big Bear Creek and the Chenal Ecarté were "under improvement, with tolerable houses on them."[62] Allan and John, the two sons of Angus MacDonald from Oronsay, were running the ferry now established at Little Bear Creek. The incompetent John MacDonald, from Prince Edward Island, had been dismissed and Angus Macdonald, from Kirkland, now supervised the four labourers at the farm, while two shepherds, Mitchell and Lionel Johnson, were put in charge of the sheep.[63] But even so, Alexander McDonell took little cheer from these developments. He certainly did not share John MacDougald's perception of events. The settlers were to be despised for their "inordinate love of whisky and incorrigible propensity to filthiness."[64]

Hoping that his disparaging reports would cause Selkirk to come to his senses and move them out of Baldoon, McDonell's strategy was always to be negative and unaccommodating. But Selkirk was not fooled. He knew that McDonell "cherished the hope that I might fix upon another situation more within reach of the capital [York] and of his own property."[65] Always, it was McDonell's personal convenience that mattered most. The settlers' needs and Selkirk's interests in the place were only of

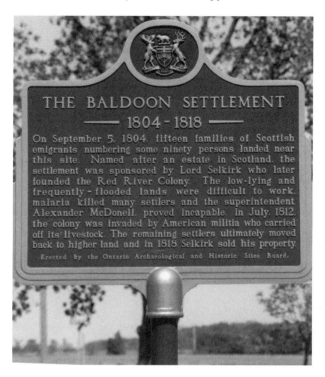

THE BALDOON SETTLEMENT
—— 1804 - 1818 ——

On September 5, 1804, fifteen families of Scottish
emigrants numbering some ninety persons landed near
this site. Named after an estate in Scotland, the
settlement was sponsored by Lord Selkirk who later
founded the Red River Colony. The low-lying and
frequently - flooded lands were difficult to work,
malaria killed many settlers and the superintendent,
Alexander McDonell, proved incapable. In July, 1812,
the colony was invaded by American militia who carried
off its livestock. The remaining settlers ultimately moved
back to higher land and in 1818 Selkirk sold his property.

Erected by the Ontario Archaeological and Historic Sites Board.

Plaque, recording the early history of the Baldoon settlement.
Originally situated at the site of the schoolhouse built in 1824
(corner of Kilbride Road and Bluewater Road), it was rescued
during later redevelopment of the site. The plaque was moved
to its present location at MacDonald Park by Bob DeKoning
and Dean MacDonald, both Wallaceburg residents. *Photograph
by Geoff Campey.*

secondary importance. But, at long last, McDonell had found the perfect
way out for himself. Believing that the position of Receiver-General for
the Province was his for the taking, he could resign from his Baldoon
job and go on to better things. Leaving Dr. John Sims in charge of Baldoon, he went off to York in August 1807, with high hopes. But they were
quickly dashed. He failed to get the appointment. On later reflection, Baldoon seemed better than nothing. Moving his family with him to Baldoon
in March 1809, he spent large sums on the Farm House. Now a country
squire, he settled in for a permanent residence.[66] And somehow, quite
miraculously, the Baldoon settlers had been transformed into the finest
"looking young men" to be found anywhere in the Province.[67]

TABLE 4: BALDOON FAMILIES AND LAND HOLDERS IN 1809*

Family Head (# denotes landholder)	Sons (# denotes landholder)	Daughters
MacDonald, Peter Mary, wife (both dead)	#John† David‡ Peter§	None
MacDonald, Alexander (piper) and wife (both dead)	#John (piper) Angus Neil	Unice Catherine
MacDonald, Donald (Laggan) and wife (both dead)	#Angus (school master)	Christy Mary Flora Peggy
MacCallum, Donald and wife (both dead)	#Hugh (school master)	Bell Peggy Nancy
MacDougald, Sarah, widow of the late John MacDougald	#John Hector Lauchlan Archibald James	Flora
MacPherson, Christy widow of the late Angus MacPherson	#Alexander‖ Donald Dougald	Mary
MacDonald, Nancy widow of the late Angus MacDonald	#John Archibald Donald Hector Neil	None
Late John Buchanan's widow married to Donald Brown	#Alexander¶ Donald John	Catherine Nelly
#MacDougald, Allan and Nancy, his wife	John	Mary Margaret

Family Head (# denotes landholder)	Sons (# denotes landholder)	Daughters
#Brown, Donald and Christine, his wife (late Mrs. Buchanan)	Neil Hector Alexander Hugh Colin	None
#Morrison, Charles and Peggy, his wife	James	Flora** Christy Bell
#McKenzie, John and Nancy, his wife	Kenneth John	None
#MacDonald, Donald (Tailor) and Flora, his wife	John Duncan Hugh Alexander	None
#MacDonald, Angus (Kirkland) and Jean, his wife	Andrew	Catherine Nancy
#MacLean, Allan and Mary, his wife	Hector	Catherine Mary Henrietta

Married in the Settlement

McDonnell, Angus John to Mary MacDougald	None	
#MacDonald, Allan lately to Bell MacKay	None	
#MacDougald, Angus lately to Flora MacCallum	None	

A total of 86 people, of whom six have left the settlement, and 80 remain.

* Source: The table lists the people living at the Baldoon settlement in 1809. (SP (C-14) 14590-1). The footnotes shown following come from this source. Data on land holdings has been taken from NAC MC24 I8 vol. 1, 145, vol. 2, 167–71, 199, vol. 5, 293, vol.13. A comparison with the 1804 *Oughton* passenger list (Table 3) reveals who died in the initial years and who were the children born to the original settlers after their arrival in Baldoon. To avoid confusion, the spelling of the surnames has been standardized (e.g. Mac not Mc) to conform to the passenger list names. Angus

Table 4 continued

MacDonell, one of the three men to be "married in the settlement," is probably McDonell, Angus John who appears, earlier in the list, as the son of Donald.
† With Innis and Grant
‡ With Mr. Allan
§ At school in York
‖ Deserted [He appears in the 1922 census; had not deserted]
¶ On board the *Camden*.
**Gone with John MacDonald to PEI; he was dismissed for incompetence.

That year Selkirk instructed McDonell to have the area along the road from Baldoon to the Thames River offered for sale to settlers. This time McDonell did what he was told and, by the following year, the land around "Baldoon Street" had been surveyed. But it would be French Canadians, particularly those who could be attracted from the United States, who would settle in this area.[68] The Scottish families remained at the original Baldoon site. By 1809 most of the settler lots were concentrated along Big Bear Creek and Little Bear Creek in the 15th, 16th and 18th Concessions (Figure 3).[69] Apart from lots 11 to 15 in the 15th Concession, which were "improvidently located" and "unfit for agricultural purposes, being constantly overflowed with water," the rest of the land was being cultivated.[70] But given the heavy loss of life, many of the lots were, by then, held by the sons of deceased fathers. In all, eight of the original fifteen heads of family had died. Now, the two sons of the late John MacDougald each had a lot as did the two sons of the late Angus MacDonald of Oronsay (Table 4). Alexander Macpherson (son of Angus), John MacDonald (son of Peter), Hugh MacCallum (son of Donald), John MacDonald, piper (son of Alexander, piper) and Angus MacDonald (son of Donald) each had lots. All together there were a total of seventeen men who had farms.[71] While only eighty of the original one hundred and two people who had arrived in 1804 had survived, additional settlers had come to join them by 1809. There were at least thirteen men who came later, one of whom was Charles Fisher, a blacksmith, who took up a lot in the 15th Concession.[72]

Selkirk's various petitions to the government for land in Shawnee township continued to be rejected. Its higher ground made it a more favourable site, but it was land that had been reserved for the Shawnee Native Peoples. Lionel Johnson, the shepherd, together with his son-in-law, James Stewart, were the first to break ranks and take matters into their own hands. Having left Baldoon over a dispute with Dr. Sims, they were living, at the time, near the Thames River. Making a private deal with the

Natives in 1809, they acquired land in the 1st Concession, at the Forks on Big Bear Creek (later, Wallaceburg). McDonell was furious. Selkirk was still trying to secure this land and they had jumped the gun. But, in the end, McDonell had a partial victory. Because their agreement was judged to be illegal, Johnson and Stewart had to move out; however, they were still able to acquire land in the 1st Concession, but it was further to the west at lots 2 and 3 (Figure 3).[73] Meanwhile the quarrels and rows continued. Try as he did to pin the blame on "the most drunken, quarrelsome, sponging, indolent of any people in Upper Canada," McDonell's time was up.[74] At the end of 1809 Selkirk finally dismissed him, although the dismissal letter did not reach him until the following year. He was then replaced by Thomas Clark of Queenston whose first task was to sell Selkirk's farm, but the outbreak of the War of 1812 prevented him from doing this. The war caused great devastation. In 1812, and again in 1814, invading American troops pillaged the settlers' homes and plundered Baldoon of its sheep and cattle.[75] Yet by 1815 Big and Little Bear Creek still had many settlers and, by 1817, a total of twenty-one families could be identified as living in the area.[76] There were seven Macdonald families, three MacDougald families, and families led by Mary MacLean (widow), John McKenzie and Margaret Morrison (widow).[77] And "the high waters which we have had in these parts" had, at long last begun to recede.[78] By the following year, some 26 families had been settled, although Selkirk had only been able to obtain land for fifteen. However, his petition for a further 2200 acres on behalf of these additional eleven families was successful. Now settlements could "be pursued with better prospects of success than hitherto, on the principles originally laid down."[79]

But his farm was another matter. McDonell had failed to let shares in the farm to tenants, as Selkirk had instructed, and the costs of running it had spiralled out of control.[80] Selkirk had mounting debts and little else to show for his efforts. Having been leased to William Jones at the end of the war, the farm was sold, in 1818, to John McNab, a Hudson's Bay Company trader. After McNab's death, two years later, it was purchased by William Jones and James Woods of Sandwich for £1281. In addition to selling his farm at Baldoon, Selkirk also put the land he had secured in other parts of western Upper Canada up for sale. In around 1806 he had acquired 578 acres, as three lots, along the Thames River, on the boundary between Dover and Chatham townships.[81] These lots were purchased by James Woods, Selkirk's solicitor. In the Township of Moulton, in Haldimand County, some 30,800 acres at the mouth of the Grand River on Lake Erie, had been acquired in 1808. Sold in 1820 to

Site of the old MacDougald Cemetery on Water Street at the corner of Park Street, Wallaceburg. *Photograph by Geoff Campey.*

William Smith, it went for only £550.[82] But his other holding of 2000 acres, somewhere "in the western districts," was considered to be very good land and was expected to get a good price.[83]

There were twenty-one families living at Little Bear Creek, in 1822, many of them the original fifteen families and their descendants. There were six McDougalds, four MacDonalds, together with Hector MacLean, John McKenzie, Widow Brown, and Daniel MacPherson. John McKenzie's family was located along "Baldoon Street" while most of the others had lots stretching in a north/south alignment from the 14th to the 18th Concessions along Little Bear and Big Bear Creeks (Figure 3).[84] But two families of MacDougalds, three MacDonalds and Alexander MacPherson's family were also to be found, much further to the north, in Chatham Gore. The former Shawnee, now Sombra township, had been surveyed and its land had become available for purchase. There were twenty families living here in 1822.[85] The first steps in moving the nucleus of the settlement further to the north had begun. Wallaceburg was the result.

Lauchlan MacDougald was Wallaceburg's first settler, taking up lot 13, at the 2nd Concession in 1822.[86] The son of John, he had been only eight-years-old when he arrived at Baldoon (Table 3). Now he was aged 26. Archibald and Hector, his younger brothers, joined him later at the 2nd Concession, taking up land on the north side of Big Bear Creek. Together they prospered, establishing a flourishing lumber business. Hector, son of Donald Brown, and aged seven on arrival, would settle at lot 1 in the 3rd Concession. Hector MacLean, who also came, settled at the 2nd Concession, as would Hugh MacCallum (lot 12). Having arrived at Baldoon as an eighteen-year-old schoolmaster, Hugh would later build a frame house on his property and continue on as a teacher. The tailor from Tyree, Donald MacDonald, together with his son John, would settle at lot B in the 4th Concession. And soon there would be a MacDonald Burying Ground near the Chenal Ecarté River.[87] But most of the "pioneers of Wallaceburg," would be buried in a cemetery on Water Street, where they have been commemorated by a stone plaque.

In the end, Selkirk suffered huge losses on Baldoon Farm, much of it attributable to Alexander McDonell. His profligacy and mismanagement probably cost Selkirk at least £5000, sterling – some £250,000 in today's money. Because of gaps in the accounts, the total cost of the Baldoon venture cannot be given with any accuracy. But it must have been at least £10,000.[88] Judged solely as a commercial undertaking, the venture was a disaster. All that money spent for thousands of acres of wilderness which, because of its remoteness at the time was virtually unsaleable. But there was another side to Baldoon. Selkirk had realized his aim of locating Highlanders in an important border area of Upper Canada, although what was achieved fell far short of the grandiose scheme that had first been envisaged. Highlanders did not flock to Baldoon in large numbers and Baldoon never became more than a small Highland community. But it was in a highly strategic border area at a time when Upper Canada was vulnerable to attack from the United States. Baldoon had been plundered twice but it had never been occupied.

Hector McLean is buried in Riverview Cemetery, Wallaceburg. The inscription on the stone reads: Hector McLean born in Tiree, Scotland, December 25, 1794, died November 21, 1877; Sophia relict of Hector McLean died June 4, 1881, aged 86 years 8 ms & 18ds. The smaller stone to the right marks the burial site of three of their children: Sophia died 1851, aged 26 years & 23 days, Damiel H. died 1852, aged 20 years, 3 months and 18 days and Caroline J. died 1847, aged 11 years, 9 months and 6 days. *Courtesy of the Wallaceburg and District Museum.*

The unsuitability of the waterlogged site was unfortunate, but Selkirk's incompetent, fractious agent was a self-inflicted problem. However,

Methodist church, Wallaceburg, built 1881–82, probably at Lot 1, 4th Concession. It replaced an earlier log church constructed in 1842 at Lot 2, 1st Concession. The timber-framed church was later moved to Whitebread where it became the Whitebread United Church. All that remains today are the steps leading up to it. *Courtesy of the Wallaceburg and District Museum, no. 995.054.24.*

replacing McDonell was no easy matter. Even when Thomas Clark took over, he only handled Baldoon's financial affairs. When it came time for Clark to leave, the farm was put under McDonell's superintendence because there was no-one else available to do the job. However, his settlers had been extremely well-chosen. Selkirk's agents never understood or appreciated them, yet the settlers were highly adaptable to extreme conditions and were thus well suited as colonizers. Poor people from remote parts of the Western Isles had "hardy habits" and were easily satisfied with the basics of life. As Selkirk predicted, rather than worry too much about the state of their houses, they would apply "themselves with vigour to the essential object of clearing their lands."[89] And he had been right to select large families with plenty of teenage sons to take over the family farm from deceased fathers. They enabled the settlement to survive and later prosper. Without them the malarial epidemic would have destroyed it. There were complaints about the rowdiness of the "very young" settlers at Baldoon. Apparently "few have visited Baldoon without either beating or being beaten." But these young men were a Godsend.[90]

This was a small group of people with mixed religions. The two school-masters, Hugh MacCallum and Angus MacDonald, may have reflected two religious affiliations. Certainly most were staunch Presbyterians, but Selkirk had also made provision for a Roman Catholic clergyman. And apparently John MacDonald's family were "strict Baptists."[91] But religion was one area where American influences proved indomitable. The Methodist preachers from the United States, who had been arriving in Upper Canada from the 1800s, found many converts. Certainly by 1824 Baldoon's principal religion was Methodism. A place of worship was established that year by Lionel Johnson at a schoolhouse built by the settlers in Sombra township (Figure 3). And nearly twenty years later a log church would be constructed on James Stewart's farm (lot 2, 1st Concession), which would in turn would be replaced, much later, by a timber framed Methodist Church. Built on land donated by William Harmon Brown (1832–1914), a descendant of Donald Brown who was one of the original family heads, it was probably situated at lot 1 in the 4th Concession of Chatham Gore.[92]

A great deal was asked of the settlers and yet they remained. Their group included tradesmen who could have easily found work in Sandwich, only a short distance away.[93] But they felt a strong sense of loyalty to Baldoon and all it stood for. When Selkirk and his settlers met in Kingston, there had been a discussion of technical issues. But much more had taken place. He had enquired how they felt about "going up country" and living away from "the sea coast." Most had lived on small Islands in the Atlantic and might have had reservations about leaving the sea. But they apparently had "little objection."[94] Three of the young men had made an impression. When he returned home, Selkirk instructed that three parcels of cotton be sent to Baldoon: one for "the school master, one for the piper, and one for Archibald MacDonald, the boy."[95] Once spun into yarn, the cotton could be used to make cloth or sold. And after hearing of Peter MacDonald's death, just a few weeks after arriving at Baldoon, he sent mittens, trousers and jackets to John, David, and Peter, his three young sons. Later on, John and David were found employment in the area while the youngest son, Peter, went to a school in York. Selkirk had almost certainly arranged this and he probably paid Peter's schooling costs for a number of years.[96] No longer just names on an agent's list, these people were now valued individuals. They would always be known as the Selkirk settlers and their descendants would take great pride in their families' associations with the Selkirk name.

Now there remained Red River. The introduction of agricultural settlers to a region dedicated solely to the North American fur trade was to
cause huge controversy. Having purchased a considerable tract of land,
five times the size of Scotland, in the Red River Valley, in what is now
Manitoba, Selkirk was ready to begin his third venture. It would be of
colossal importance and have far-reaching consequences for Canada.

5. EARLY CONFLICT AT RED RIVER

The Committee of the Hudson's Bay Company is at present a mere
machine in the hands of Lord Selkirk who appears to be so much wedded to
his schemes of colonization in the interior of North America that it will
require some time, and I fear cause much expense to us, as well as to him-
self, before he is driven to abandon the project; and yet he must be driven to
abandon it for his success would strike at the very existence of our trade.[1]

SIMON McGILLIVRAY, LONDON AGENT FOR the North West Company had tried, but failed, to prevent Lord Selkirk from acquiring
his huge tract of land in a district, known as Assiniboia, in the territories owned by the Hudson's Bay Company.[2] Through marriage and
purchase, Selkirk acquired sufficient Hudson's Bay Company shares
to dominate its policy. In 1811, he obtained from the company, a land
grant in Assiniboia of over 116,000 square miles, on condition that he
recruited 200 men annually as fur trade workers.[3] The company, which
had experienced difficulties in recruiting its workforce, believed that
Selkirk, with his "personal acquaintance and influence," in Ireland and
the Highlands of Scotland would be far more successful than it had been.
It was thus agreed that Selkirk "should undertake the management and
expense of this undertaking" and become "responsible, under a penalty,
for its success."[4]

But Selkirk's primary aim was to establish a settlement on the land he
had obtained. Choosing a site close to the junction of the Red and Assiniboine rivers, Selkirk had little difficulty in locating settlers. And the
Hudson's Bay Company also saw advantages in the venture. The Red
River settlement could supply its forts and trading posts with agricultural produce, which otherwise would have been imported from Britain.
It could also provide retired company workers, who wished to remain
in the area, with a place to settle. However, there was a major stumbling
block. A region which had always been dedicated solely to the interests

Lord Selkirk's sketch of Fort William from inside the Fort, 1816.
Courtesy of Archives of Ontario Fond F481.

of the fur trade would not want to change its ways to accommodate agricultural settlers. While the Hudson's Bay Company supported Selkirk's venture, the North West Company, the HBC's principal rival certainly did not. From the time it first learned that a colony was to be founded, it mounted a vigorous campaign to have it stopped.[5] The two companies had long argued over their territorial rights; but Selkirk's plan to introduce agricultural settlers into the region propelled their feuding into a major clash for overall control of the North American fur trade. The North West Company had trading posts and supply routes in Assiniboia. A successful settlement would dominate the vital communication links between the Athabaska and St. Lawrence waterways. From it, Selkirk would be able to control communications between the North West Company's western posts and their headquarters at Fort William, on Lake Superior (Figure 5). He had threatened their interests once before with his unsuccessful endeavours, in 1802, to colonize the Falls of St. Mary (Sault Ste. Marie). It too straddled the North West Company's supply routes.[6] Little wonder then that Simon McGillivray warned the wintering partners of the North West Company that the Red River colonists would have to be driven out.[7]

However, Selkirk denied all along that his real aim was to destroy the North West Company. He realized that colonization could only be achieved in the region if it had the backing of one of the two great fur trade companies. Otherwise, settlers would be caught up in the crossfire between the warring companies and be vulnerable to attacks from either side. Although he had little stomach for the fur trade, he recognized that he had to work within it rather than around it:

It is a business [fur trade] that I hate from the bottom of my heart, but in this country there is no possibility of going on without, either trading, or being in concert or connection, with those who do.[8]

By the time he came to this conclusion, the Hudson's Bay Company was nearly insolvent. The Napoleonic Wars had played havoc with its European markets. Loss of sales led to greatly reduced share values. By 1808 the market value of it stock had fallen from £250 to less than £60 a share. This was the perfect time to purchase shares. Selkirk had become a shareholder in the previous year by marriage and, by 1811, having invested £35,000 in it, acquired a controlling interest in the company.[9] Gaining control over the North West Company would have been impossible at the time. Thus, it was through his dominance of the Hudson's Bay Company that Selkirk had obtained Assiniboia and was now able to plan his settlement. One of his first moves was to appoint Colin Robertson, a former North West Company employee, as a recruiting agent.[10] He would play an even more vital role in the years ahead.

Fur traders had been careful to keep silent about the fertile lands and agricultural opportunities to be had in the regions west of the Great Lakes. Upon arrival at Red River, Miles MacDonell, Selkirk's principal agent, wrote of "the fertility of the soil in the highest terms"; and there seemed little doubt "of the practicability of raising good crops even at

Reproduction of the Hudson's Bay Company Coat of Arms at Lower Fort Garry. Its 1670 charter gave the Company control of all the land which drained into Hudson Bay.
Photograph by Geoff Campey.

York Factory," on Hudson Bay.[11] Thus more was at stake than the conflicting interests of the fur trade. Long before the Red River area became Manitoba, Selkirk had appreciated that its land would yield far greater riches in crops than it ever would from the fur trade:

> It is a very moderate calculation to say that if these regions [Assiniboia] were occupied by an industrious population, they might afford ample means of subsistence for thirty millions of British subjects.[12]

This was a truly staggering prophecy and would, in time, be proved right. The region would become one of the great bread baskets of the world. While none around him appreciated its agricultural potential, Selkirk had the foresight to secure it by introducing Scottish and Irish colonizers. And he was concerned also with "the important question whether extensive and fertile regions in British North America are ... to be inhabited by civilized society."[13] Of course, by this Selkirk meant that the British concept of a settled, agriculturally-based society should be introduced. "Civilizing" influences would create stable communities and bring improved living conditions and economic prosperity. And, in time, British values and methods would supplant the culture and way of life of the Native and mixed race peoples, who formed the local population. Not a workable proposition in today's multicultural era, but in Selkirk's time this represented enlightened thinking. He was spending vast sums of money, not to make any profit for himself but, to secure this region's immense agricultural potential for the British Crown and give farming opportunities to the emigrant Scots who would colonize it.

In his "Prospectus" he stated that his millions of acres were to be "sold extremely cheap, on account of the situation, which is remote from present establishments."[14] Religion was not to be the "grounds for any disqualification"; Protestants and Catholics emigrants would have equal access to opportunities and provision would be made for the support of clergymen. He would offer favourable terms for their passages to Red River and give credit of up to £40.[15] And certain "respectable tacksmen" were to be offered townships free of charge as "they might be the means of animating those people who are already well disposed towards the cause and perhaps might also gain friends to it."[16]

Initially, the settlement went from crisis to crisis. The people who came to live at Red River were attacked and driven out on two occasions, the second attack involving bloodshed. The loss of most of its initial settlers meant that it would be the later arrivals from the County of Sutherland

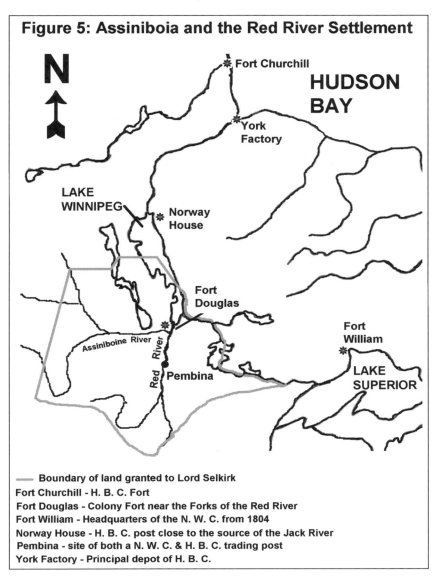

Figure 5: Assiniboia and the Red River Settlement

N

HUDSON BAY

Fort Churchill

York Factory

LAKE WINNIPEG

Norway House

Fort Douglas

Fort William

Assiniboine River

Red River

Pembina

LAKE SUPERIOR

—— Boundary of land granted to Lord Selkirk
Fort Churchill - H. B. C. Fort
Fort Douglas - Colony Fort near the Forks of the Red River
Fort William - Headquarters of the N. W. C. from 1804
Norway House - H. B. C. post close to the source of the Jack River
Pembina - site of both a N. W. C. & H. B. C. trading post
York Factory - Principal depot of H. B. C.

who would form the nucleus of the settlement. However, they would not attract any followers. The attacks, harsh climate and remoteness of the place deferred most Sutherlanders who chose instead to go to the Maritimes or Upper Canada. Gradually these Sutherlanders would, in later years, be joined by men from the Orkney Islands who came to the settlement with Native wives. The Orcadians were recruited initially as fur trade workers and later they became settlers. They, together with other mixed-blood (or Métis) settlers, would transform Red River into a multi-ethnic settlement.[17] Thus the fur trade interests, which initially brought destruction, later gave Red River the means to augment its British population. It was not what Selkirk had envisaged; but it was an outcome that he would have relished.

An extremely costly undertaking, the Red River colony had depleted most of his family's fortune by the time of Selkirk's death in 1820. And all along it looked as if the settlement was going to fail. Selkirk would know only the battles for survival and nothing of the later successes. It was a miracle that it did survive. The resilience and courage of his settlers were quite extraordinary. Equally important was Selkirk's ability to attract fresh contingents, despite hostile publicity from newspapers and the on-going sabotaging activities of the North West Company. The worsening economic situation in Scotland and Ireland worked to his advantage in encouraging people to contemplate emigration. For the people in the Highlands and Islands who faced an uncertain future as advancing sheep farms displaced them from their lands, the prospect of a better life in Red River was an option well worth considering. Although people did not come forward in 1811 and 1812 as much as he would have liked, Selkirk was able to recruit sufficient numbers to launch a settlement and, by 1813, had far more wishing to go to Red River than could be accommodated in the available Hudson's Bay Company ships.

Selkirk first met Captain Miles MacDonell, his choice as superintendent of the Red River colony, in Glengarry during his 1804 tour of Upper Canada. Like his brother-in-law, Alexander McDonell, the man put in charge of Baldoon, Miles MacDonell was a Highlander with a commanding presence.[18] A successful local farmer who looked "very much a gentleman in manners and sentiment," he seemed ideal.[19] But as was the case with Alexander, Miles was an incompetent manager. His judgement was not always good, he could be overbearing and he did not keep very good accounts. But he was courageous and would prove to be extremely effective in the battles which lay ahead.

The first group which left in July 1811, had been assembled in great haste. Selkirk's agents had wasted no time in issuing advertisements across Scotland and Ireland for men needed to go to Hudson's Bay. Those recruited were taken to a collecting point at Stornoway:

All the men are to sign contracts in the usual form whether intended for the Red River settlement or the Company's commercial establishments

Painting of ships meeting in the North Atlantic by Peter Rindisbacher, July 16, 1821. The *Prince of Wales* and *Eddystone*, two
Hudson's Bay Company ships, being met by *Hecla* and *Griper*,
two Royal Navy vessels. *Courtesy of National Archives of Canada,
C-001908.*

and these contracts will be for 3 years at the stipulated wages .... Of the
Irish 12 or 15 may be sufficient, including the tradesmen, the rest may
be Highlanders. All the married men should of course be taken and the
more elderly of the unmarried, both as being most likely to be steady and
also less fitted for the Company's commercial business.[20]

Roderick McDonald, Selkirk's agent in Glasgow, located 32 men while
Charles McLean, his Western Isles agent, recruited 20 men, 14 of whom
were from Lewis.[21] Miles MacDonell, a Roman Catholic, who had been
sent to Ireland to persuade Irish Catholics to go to Red River instead of
the United States, signed up a further 14 men. But the largest numbers
came from the Orkney Islands, the area of Scotland which, for many years,
had been the Hudson's Bay Company's major source of employees.[22] Arriving in the *Prince of Wales,* some 59 Orcadians arrived from Stromness to
join the others, bringing the overall total to one hundred and twenty five.[23]

This recruitment had gone ahead against the backdrop of a vicious
newspaper campaign organized by the North West Company. Chal-
lenging Selkirk's advertisement in the *Inverness Journal,* which extolled
Red River's "good climate, favourable soil and situation," prospective emigrants were warned of "the dangers and distresses which they are
ignorantly going to encounter." They would be "surrounded by war-like

savages, who subsist by the chase" and be saddled with land which was "totally unfit for cultivation in consequence of the sterility of the soil as well as the severity of the climate."[24] As this edition of the *Inverness Journal* circulated in Stornoway, a furious Miles MacDonell found copies being handed to his recruits, people "who were not in the habit of receiving newspapers" and in some cases "could not read them." And all of this was happening just when he was trying to organize the final departure arrangements for the ships.[25]

Leaving Stornoway in late July, the men sailed on three Hudson's Bay Company ships: the *Prince of Wales, Eddystone* and *Edward and Ann.*[26] There was confusion over the numbers who actually sailed on each ship and considerable delay in setting sail.[27] Failing to record, accurately, the numbers who had actually left Stornoway, MacDonell had to later reduce his total from 125 to 105 to allow for the 20 men who had withdrawn their names and left their ships. For some unexplained reason, he accommodated most of the men on the worst ship, the *Edward and Ann.* By his own reckoning she had "old sails [and] ropes," was "very weakly manned," with a crew of only 16, and "ill fitted for a northern voyage."[28] By contrast the *Prince of Wales,* with a crew of 32, carried around 25 men, while the *Eddystone,* took the same number with a crew of 20.[29] Because of their late departure and a longer than normal sea crossings the three ships did not get to York Factory until 24th September.[30] Because winter would soon be closing in, this made it too late to attempt the onward journey of 728 miles to Red River. Thus, the advance party of thirty six men, who were to have built houses and planted crops, had to remain behind in York Factory until the following summer.[31]

Food shortages were a problem, scurvy broke out and there was an armed mutiny.[32] But order was eventually restored by men from the Hudson's Bay Company. In July 1812, Miles MacDonell led a much depleted group of only eighteen men from York Factory to the Forks of the Red and Assiniboine rivers. Eight were Irish, four were Orcadian, four came from Lewis, one was from Ayr and one from Argyll.[33] Choosing a site two miles north of Fort Gibraltar, a North West Company post situated at the Forks, MacDonell led his group to "an extensive point of land [later called Point Douglas] through which fire had run and destroyed the wood, there being only burnt wood and weeds left."[34] The settlement would develop here and in due course would acquire the colony fort of Fort Douglas. Eventually a palisade would be "built of standing wood, the lower ends driven into the ground, and composed of good-sized logs, twelve or fifteen feet high." The fort would have "a store inside of it, also a forge, a carpenter's shop, the master's house and a great many other buildings."[35] Having just arrived, the men were immediately set to work to build a storehouse and prepare the site for the second contingent who would be arriving in two months time. MacDonell's task in leading the expedition was thus completed. He now became the colony's first Governor.

Because of the scarcity of food, they had to move south for the winter to Pembina (now in Minnesota), where both the North West and Hudson's Bay companies had trading posts. The large numbers of grazing buffalo in the area provided much needed food and, having built living quarters there, the men were able to survive their second winter. It was not long before they were joined by the second group of emigrants who had sailed in June 1812 from Sligo in Ireland. And, as it did the year before, the North West Company continued to give "his Lordship some annoyance through the medium of the press." Simon McGillivray even boasted that his letters in the name of "a Highlander" would "in a great measure, prevent him from getting servants or emigrants from the Highlands of Scotland."[36] This did not happen; but he was having an effect:

Tombstone, Kildonan Cemetery, in Kildonan, now a suburb of Winnipeg, for John Polson, "one of the first Selkirk settlers, born in Sutherlandshire Scotland," He died 3rd Feb. 1890, aged 80. *Photograph by Geoff Campey.*

> Our adversaries have been very busy in the Highlands and have succeeded for the present in narrowing our supply of men from that quarter. The Highlander continued his lucubrations in the *Inverness Journal* with more and more personality…. These calumnies…made a great impression and deterred many from engaging in the service.[37]

However, Selkirk had access to a very favourable report written by Archibald Mason, a Highlander who had recently returned from the Assiniboia region. His report, written in February 1812 went beyond Selkirk's "expectations as to the fertility of the soil and the favourable climate" and was just what he needed to refute the North West Company's claims:

The heavy groans of the poor have reached the ears of God in these oppressed places – the relief many of them got by going to the Earl of Selkirk's lands and settlement, although very disagreeable at first, would give all the world to get back – but, in a little time after, would not exchange their situations with the first lord in Scotland – all they wish is to have their countrymen to join them.[38]

Sending "young MacDonald" to Fort Augustus "to enquire quietly what the people there think of Mason and how much weight would be given to his report," Selkirk learned that Mason's good name was being deprecated by his opponents.[39] Once again, the North West Company had got the upper hand in the propaganda war.

Seventy-one people sailed from Sligo in the summer of 1812 on the *Robert Taylor,* "a very good ship" which Selkirk had chartered "on account of the settlement to carry out the people." She was a much better prospect than the *Edward and Ann* and was properly manned.[40] A second ship, the *King George,* sailed with her to carry the large consignment of goods, which included Spanish merino sheep purchased by Selkirk.[41] Those who sailed on the *Robert Taylor* included ten families from Mull and Islay as well as company workers who originated from Ireland and the Orkney Islands. The families had been recruited by Charles McLean and were thought by Selkirk to have "been well selected having scarcely any children below 8 years old and a number of lads and lassies fully or nearly grown and without the parents not super annuated." Alexander McLean's family had attracted special attention. McLean, a former tacksman with "the rank of a gentleman," was just the sort of settler whom Selkirk wished to attract. He gave him a township of 10,000 acres along with twelve merino sheep and a subsistence allowance for his family and servants during their first year at Red River. And to ensure that all went smoothly Selkirk went to Sligo "to be ready to act according to circumstances."[42] Dining with the captain and his officers on board the ship, on June 24, he remained on the *Robert Taylor* until she cleared Sligo Bay and then watched the ships put to sea.

Leading the 1812 expedition of settlers, was Owen Keveny, a brutal Irishman who dealt with disputes by putting men in irons and having them run the gauntlet between lines of their fellow settlers armed with clubs. The crew nearly mutinied but quick action by the captain brought matters under control. As the *Robert Taylor* entered Hudson Bay on August 24, she was buffeted by a tremendous storm lasting three days. In the midst of the terror and confusion Mrs. McLean, from Mull gave birth to a daughter. The

Painting by Peter Rindisbacher. A Hudson's Bay Company ship arrives at its anchorage in York Factory, 1821. *Courtesy of National Archives of Canada, C-001916.*

ship survived the storm and a day later was met by a schooner from York Factory. The second group had arrived safely and in good time.[43] They would get to Red River that year, arriving in October. But a shortage of food supplies meant that they too had to spend their first winter at the newly built encampment of Fort Daer at Pembina.[44]

In June 1813, Selkirk had found "a most interesting body of emigrants from a quarter not hitherto, in our contemplation, but extremely promising in every respect." In the Scottish parishes of Clyne and Kildonan "one great sheep farm has led this year to the displacing of more than 100 families." Failing to get their landlord to reconsider his actions, the people were determined to emigrate, having told Selkirk they were "at a loss how to proceed when I stepped in and they have with joy accepted my proposal of settling in Red River."[45] Selkirk could hardly contain his excitement:

If they [Sutherland emigrants] do well and are satisfied with the situation, they will be the means of attracting a great body of their friends and others from the same County, who must emigrate in the course of a few years. People of a superior description than any we have yet had to do with. The Sutherland men seem to me, both in person and moral character a fine race of men. There are great numbers among them who have prosperity enough to pay their passage and settle themselves with very little assistance and many capable of paying in cash for their land.[46]

His initial intention had been to recruit Kildonan men for a Canadian Regiment. The American declaration of War against Britain in 1812 created a need for more armies and what better solution than to "raise a corps for service in America…with a stipulation that at the conclusion of their service the men should be settled [at Red River] and their families brought over at the expense of the government."[47] With the help of William Mac-Donald, a retired sergeant of the Sutherland Highlanders (93rd), Selkirk claimed to have found 580 men willing to sign up for his proposed regiment.[48] By early May, the list had grown to "1,300 men, women and children," causing Selkirk to conclude that his "sergeant has overdone the business tremendously!"[49] But Lady Stafford was highly sceptical, believing that her tenants would never leave their families behind.[50] And in the end the government got cold feet. Selkirk's proposal was rejected leaving him to carry the cost of the venture himself.[51]

Now instead of the hundreds he was seeking earlier for a Regiment he wanted only "40 or 50 of the young men of Kildonan" who "might be taken into the Company's service…and about 80 more who might go as settlers on their own account were recruited." William Young, Lady Stafford's Estate Manager, thought that Selkirk had "brought himself to an awful scrape" and the estate "to a world of trouble, for what can the people now do for themselves without proper aid from the government?" But Selkirk persevered and soon he was "at work among the Kildonan and Clyne people."[52] Enlisting Archibald McLellan, a former Hudson's Bay Company Officer who lived at Kildonan as his agent, Selkirk went to Golspie, a coastal village in Sutherland, to take charge of the final arrangements.[53] Men did not come forward "quite as much in shoals" as McLellan's letter had lead him to think, "but perhaps enough." As "great numbers crowded in to put their names down for next year" Selkirk prepared his final list (Table 5).

Of the Kildonan people "scarcely anyone" could be regarded as "a leading man." He had "a very good account" of "the character and skill" of Samuel Lamont, the millwright from Islay. George MacDonald had "a troublesome temper" and Donald Gunn was amongst the ones he liked the least. Donald Bannerman was "well spoken of," the McBeaths were "a respectable family" and John Matheson was "very respectably connected." But George Campbell stood out from all the others because he was "more wealthy than most of them." He was "unconnected" with the other Kildonan settlers, coming from the parish of Creich, further to the south, near Ross-shire.[54] Selkirk's instincts were right. He would become a leader of sorts. He would later desert to the North West Company and work with them to foment discontent within the Red River settlement.

Left: Tombstone, Kildonan Cemetery, for John McBeath. "A native of Sutherland, he died 2 Nov. 1878, aged 86." *Photograph by Geoff Campey*. *Right*: Tombstone, Kildonan Cemetery, for John Matheson. "Elder in this Church who departed this life March 20, 1878, aged 80 years. A native of Sutherland." *Photograph by Geoff Campey*.

There were "more entire families of the Kildonan people" than he wanted. Rather than the seven or eight families he had sought, there were thirteen families and a good many single women. But he was pleased that there were forty, fit, young men and that, in addition to the families from Sutherland, he had Donald Stewart from Appin (Argyll) and four families from Islay.[55] Anticipating trouble from the "rigid Presbyterians" in the group, Selkirk's final instructions to Miles MacDonell stipulated that he should "keep as much as possible out of sight" the fact that MacDonell and many of Hudson's Bay Company officers were Roman Catholics.[56]

Finally, on the June 29, 1813, after a long delay, ninety-seven people boarded the *Prince of Wales* at Stromness.[57] Travelling in convoy, she set sail with the *Eddystone,* which carried Hudson Bay Company workers, and two other ships.[58] But soon a typhus epidemic was underway. More than two-thirds of the passengers and crew caught the disease and there were eleven deaths (Table 5). One of those who died was the group's leader, Dr. P. Laserre. And to pile on the misery, Captain Turner foolishly put into Fort Churchill rather than York Factory which had the group's food and medical supplies. Despite the advice and pleadings of the officers on his ship, he stubbornly refused to land his ship at the appointed place. As a consequence, the settlers would not get much needed medical treatment or fresh provisions and would have to wait until the following spring before they could go on to Red River.[59] Learning of the tragic loss of life in November, Selkirk was "quite in despair at this most unexpected stroke" and anticipated more dreadful publicity in the Inverness newspapers.[60] The following summer he recruited only fourteen more settlers for Red River.[61]

Young Archibald McDonald, who was now in charge of the expedition, led the settlers to a camp fifteen miles from Fort Churchill.[62] Obtaining provisions from Fort Churchill, they survived the winter of 1813-14 in "Colony Creek," the name given to their encampment. The fit members of the group, thirty-one men and twenty women, set off on April 6 for the 150 mile overland journey to York Factory, arriving there on April 19. Then, leaving on May 23, for Red River, the third group arrived on June 21 "in good health and spirits." Only a month later Archibald was able to report that the settlers "never were happier and more contented in Kildonan than they are here already."[63]

They were given land by MacDonell on "the west side of Red River …in 100 acre lots of 3 acre frontages. …Relations and connections wishing to be near their neighbours have got their different allotments adjoining each other." But his suggestion that "they should build their houses in knots of five or six families together, for material security, in the manner that your Lordship's settlers began at Prince Edward Island" did not find favour. They immediately planted crops and began to build their homes. Before the Sutherlanders had arrived there was "scarcely a person permanently established" at Red River but now, MacDonell could report that "the settlement is fairly beginning now."[64] And unlike previous years when the settlers had to move to their winter encampment at Pembina, they had sufficient supplies to be able to remain at the Forks of the Red River in the winter of 1814–15.

But these glimmers of hope were soon dashed by MacDonell's highhanded decision to prohibit the export of pemmican from Assiniboia, except under his special licence. Made of preserved buffalo meat, this was the staple food of local Natives and essential to the North West Company's brigades. MacDonell claimed his action was necessary to counter the threat of continuing food shortages in the colony. The North West Company took it to be a declaration of war. Because MacDonell could not enforce the ban, the company continued to get its pemmican supplies and the embargo had little real effect. But this provocation further angered the North West Company partners. The campaign of subversion intensified. George Campbell, their well-placed mole at Red River, spread disturbing rumours of imminent attacks by men in the employment of the North West Company. And with the attacks came the next stage. Duncan

Cameron, one of the North West Company partners, came to the settlement and held out the offer of free passages to Upper Canada and land. They were to be rescued by the nice Mr. Cameron.

Having surrendered, in the vain hope that hostilities would cease, Miles MacDonell was taken prisoner by the North West Company men and led away to Montreal. It looked like an effortless victory. But the North West Company's campaign to destroy the settlement had been hatched long before Duncan Cameron personally appeared on the scene. Clearly he had been enlisting people during the previous year. James Smith, one of those who sailed on the *Robert Taylor* in 1812, had written to Cameron in December 1814, saying that he understood: "that your honour has proposed to relieve a poor distressed people by taking them to Montreal next Spring." He hoped that Cameron would include him and his family "in the number."[65] And Hugh Bannerman, one of the Kildonan emigrants to sail on the *Prince of Wales* in 1813, knew people who "intended to leave it [Red River] as soon as they arrived." Alexander Bannerman had written to Duncan Cameron "of his own accord…after the first snow to ask for a passage," while George Bannerman claimed that he had agreed "to go to Upper Canada with Cameron before Christmas."[66] And what about the dim-wit captain who took the 1813 Sutherland contingent to Churchill instead of York Factory. Was that a mistake? Surely not. Bribery is far more likely.

It had been a cunning plan. Delaying the colonists for several months allowed time for conspiracy and hampered progress. When they finally got to Red River:

> …every insinuating art was practised to gain the good will of the settlers. They [North West Company] were extremely lavish of their wines, frequently gave balls and other diversions. They represented this country in the most horrible point of view saying that the Indians would scalp every individual, that your lordship would oppress them as slaves, that you had no right to the country and that the Hudson's Bay Charter was good for nothing.[67]

Settler fears of "being scalped in their bed's" was set against "the allurements" of Upper Canada.[68] Its land was good, and it had a far better climate. And most of all, there "they might live their lives in peace." This more than anything was what had motivated George Bannerman. His account of events retold many years later by his great-grandson, John G. Diefenbaker, the man who became Canada's thirteenth Prime Minister, reveals people at breaking point:

TABLE 5: PASSENGER LIST FOR THE *Prince of Wales* CROSSING IN 1813 FROM STROMNESS TO CHURCHILL (ARRIVED 18TH AUGUST)*

	Name	Age	Comments
1	George Campbell	25	Auchraigh Parish Creich, Sutherland
2	Helen his wife	20	
3	Bell his daughter	1	
4	John Sutherland	50	Kildonan in Parish of Kildonan, Sutherland Died 2d Septr. at C.F.† a very respectable man
5	Catherine his wife	46	
6	George his son	18	
7	Donald his son	16	
8	Alexander his son	9	
9	Jannet his daughter	14	
10	Angus McKay	24	Kildonan
11	Jean his wife		
12	Alexander Gunn	50	Kildonan
13	Christian his wife	50	Died 20th September C. F.
14	William his son	18	
15	Donald Bannerman	50	Badflinch. Died 24th September at C. F., a frank and open hearted character.
16	Christian his wife	44	
17	William his son	18	
18	Donald his son	8	C. C. dumb and epileptic.
19	Christian his daughter	16	
20	George McDonald	48	Dalvait. Died 1st September, 1813 C. F.
21	Jannet his wife	50	
22	Betty Grey	17	
23	Jean Grey	n/k	
24	Catherine Grey	23	
25	Barbara McBeath widow	45	Borobal
26	Charles her son	16	
27	Hanny her daughter	23	
28	Andrew McBeath	19	
29	Jannet his wife		
30	William Sutherland	22	Borobal
31	Margaret his wife	15	
32	Christian his sister	24	
33	Donald Gunn	65	Borobal
34	Jannet his wife transferred to Eddystone for H. B. Co. Service.	50	
35	George Gunn son to Donald	16	Borobal parish: Kildonan
36	Esther his daughter	24	
37	Katherine his daughter	20	Died 29th August 1813. C. F.

	Name	Age	Comments
38	Christian his daughter	10	
39	Angus Gunn	21	
40	Jannet his wife		
41	Robert Sutherland	17	Borobal. Brother to William Sutherland (aged 29)
42	Elizabeth Fraser aunt to Robert	30	
43	Angus Sutherland	20	Auchraich
44	Elizabeth his mother	60	
45	Betty his sister	18	Died 26th October consumption. C. C., Argyleshire.
46	Donald Stewart	n/k	Balecheulish parish Appin. Died 20th August 1813 at C. F.
47	Catherine his wife	30	
48	Margaret—daughter	8	
49	Mary—daughter	5	
50	Ann—daughter	2	
51	John Smith	n/k	Asbus parish: Kildalton (Isla)
52	Mary his wife	n/k	
53	John his son	n/k	
54	Jean his daughter	n/k	
55	Mary his daughter	n/k	
56	Alexander Gunn	58	Ascaig parish: Kildonan
57	Elizabeth McKay)	n/k	
58	Betty McKay) his nieces		
59	George Bannerman	22	Kildonan
60	John Bruce	60	Aultsmoral parish: Clyne
61	Alexander Sutherland	24	Balnavaliach parish: Kildonan
62	William his brother	19	Died
63	Katie his sister	20	
64	Hanan Sutherland	18	Kenacoil
65	Barbara his sister	20	
66	James McKay	19	Cain
67	Ann his sister	21	
68	John Matheson	22	Aultbreakachy
69	Robert Gunn: Piper	n/k	Kildonan
70	Mary his sister	n/k	
71	Hugh Bannerman	18	Dalhalmy parish: Kildonan
72	Elizabeth his sister	20	
73	Mary Bannerman	n/k	
74	Alexander Bannerman	19	Dalhalmy
75	Christian his sister	17	
76	John Bannerman	19	Duible. Died January 1814 consumption.
77	Isabella his sister	16	
78	John McPherson	16	Gailable
79	Catherine his sister	26	
80	Hector McLeod	19	Ascaig
81	George Sutherland	18	Borobal

	Name	Age	Comments
82	Adam his brother	16	
83	John Murray	21	Siesgill
84	Alexander his brother	19	
85	Helen Kennedy	n/k	Sligo—Ireland
86	Malcolm McEachern	n/k	Skibbo parish: Kilchoman, Isla
deserted			
87	Mary his wife	n/k	deserted
88	James McDonald, Blacksmith	n/k	Fort Augustus, Inverness-shire
89	Hugh McDonald, Carpenter	n/k	Fort William, Argyll; died 3 August
at sea			
90	Samuel Lamont, Millwright	n/k	Bowmore, Isla; died 3 August
91	Alexander Matheson	n/k	Keanved par.: Kildonan, Sutherland
92	John Matheson	n/k	
93	John McIntyre	n/k	Fort William; entered service of Hudson's Bay Company July 1814
94	Neil Smith son of John	n/k	Isla; entered service of Hudson's
Bay			
95	Smith of Isla above		Company July 1814
96	Edward Sheil	n/k	Ballyshannon
97	Joseph Kerrigan	n/k	Ballyshannon

Mr. P. Laserre, surgeon, died 16 Aug. at sea.

* Source: Original in NAC Miles Macdonell papers MG19 E4 vol.1 165–68; transcript in Martin, *Red River Settlement. Papers in the Canadian Archives*, 26–7.
† C.F. is Churchill Fort.

They could not have known that after all they had suffered, privations almost beyond understanding today, they would find themselves caught up in battles waged between two competing fur-trade empires.... For many this was too much to bear. What they sought was simply the chance to build anew, not to be pawns in a struggle remote from their understanding or interest. This situation prompted...them, after enduring yet another hard winter, to leave Red River for Upper Canada, where they had been promised aid in resettlement.[69]

There was not much left of the settlement after Duncan Cameron had been and gone. As Simon McGillivray put it, "The Colony had been all knocked in the head by the North West Company."[70] It lost one hundred and thirty four people, of whom, one hundred and three had been settlers and thirty-one Hudson's Bay Company workers.[71] A total of about 40 families, who collectively owed Selkirk £116 for provisions already given to them, were lost to Upper Canada.[72] Nearly all of the ninety-seven, mainly Sutherland people, who had sailed on the *Prince of Wales* in 1813 had gone. Of the two hundred and twenty-three people, who had come to the settlement in the four years from 1811 to 1814, only thirteen families and around twenty-four Hudson's Bay Company workers now remained.[73] And the company men were worried about their security and would not stay indefinitely without protection:

> Then we shall feel an interest in the improvement of our lands and make this country what your lordship intends it to be – an additional source of wealth and greatness to our native country and an asylum where the honest and industrious poor may establish their families in honourable independence.[74]

In all around sixty people had refused to go to Upper Canada. Their situation was perilous. The North West Company would not allow them to remain at Red River. But, with the help of "two Indian Chiefs and from thirty-five to forty warriors of the Saulteaux nation," who acted as mediators, they were able to secure a safe passage for themselves out of the area:

> On returning to the settlement the two Chiefs said that they and some of their young men would embark in the boats and escort us down the river, and that others of their men would go down the banks of the river to protect us. Under their escort we accordingly embarked in our boats on the 27th of June, and proceeded down the river to its entrance in Lake Winnipeg.[75]

The group then crossed the lake to Norway House, a Hudson's Bay Company fur trading post at the northern end of Lake Winnipeg, where they were able to find some temporary accommodation. Observing their departure from Red River had been John McLeod, one of four workers who had stayed behind to keep watch over the Hudson's Bay Company's property:

> Next day after our people's departure from here there came from forty to fifty men led by some of the North West Company's clerks and they set fire to all your lordship's houses…they pillaged and robbed several articles and took all of the Colony horses.[76]

TABLE 6: RED RIVER INHABITANTS WHO MOVED TEMPORARILY TO JACK
RIVER FOLLOWING THE ATTACK ON THE SETTLEMENT IN JUNE 1815

Documentary Sources*	Place of Families/Settlers	Departure Origin†	Year
I, III	Mr & Mrs McLean and 4 children‡	Mull	1812
I, III	Mr & Mrs John Pritchard & child	n/k	n/k
I, III	Pat McNaulty, wife & 2 children	Ireland	1812
I, III	Widow Stewart & 3 children§	Appin (Argyll)	1813
I	Widow McLean	n/k	n/k
I	Mrs Jordan‖	n/k	n/k
I	Miss Kennedy	Ireland	1813
II	John Smith & family	Islay (Argyll)	1813
II, III	Alexander Sutherland & sister	Kildonan (Sutherland)	1813
II, III	George and Adam Sutherland	Kildonan (Sutherland)	1813
II, III	John Bruce	Clyne (Sutherland)	1813
III	Donald Livingstone & family (3)	n/k	1812
III	John MacVicar & family (3)	n/k	1812
III	Alexander McLean & family (4)	Mull	1812
III, IV	Martin Jordan & family (2)	Ireland	1811

Hudson's Bay Company Workers

I	A. McLean	n/k	n/k
I, III, IV	Duncan McNaughton	n/k	1812
I, IV	Samuel Lamont	Islay (Argyll)	1813
I, IV	Michael Kilbride	Ireland	1812
I, IV	Pat Clabby	Ireland	1812
I	Pat Corrigan	Ireland	1811
IV	John Fowler	n/k	n/k
I, IV	Neil Muller	Norway	n/k
I, IV	Peter Dhal	Norway	n/k
I, IV	Peter Isaacson	Norway	n/k
IV	Hugh MacLean	n/k	1812
IV	Donald McMillan	n/k	1812
IV	James McIntosh	n/k	n/k
IV	Archibald Curry	n/k	n/k
IV	Colin Campbell	Islay (Argyll)	1811
IV	Donald McLean	Mull	1812
IV	John Scarth	Orkney	n/k

Documentary Sources*	Place of Families/Settlers	Departure Origin†	Year
IV	Price Holte	n/k	n/k
IV	Magnus Spence	Orkney	n/k
IV	Andrew Spence	n/k	n/k
IV	John Bourke	n/k	1812
IV	James White	n/k	n/k
IV	John McLean	Mull	1812

* Documentary Sources
  I. Colin Robertson's Journal, 7 Aug. 1815, NAC SP (C-16) 17368.
  II. Evidence of John Murray, Feb. 1816, NAC SP (C-2) 2005.
  III. Red River Settlement, Original Families, NAC MG29 C73.
  IV. Letter, Hugh MacLean to Selkirk, June, 1815, NAC SP (C-2) 1560.
† Place of Origin and Departure Year
  The year of arrival and place of origin have been taken from lists produced in 1811,
  1812 and 1813 (Table 5, Appendices B, C, D, E). According to the 1831 Red River
  Census, John Scarth and Magnus Spence originated from the Orkney Islands
‡ Mr. McLean was almost certainly Alexander McLean, a prominent Red River settler
  who originated from Mull.
§ Mr. Donald Stewart of Appin (Argyll), sailed on *Prince of Wales*, 1813.
‖ Mrs. Jordan was probably the wife of Martin Jordan who appears in III and IV.

After the invaders left John MacLeod and his three men, Hugh MacLean, Archibald Curry and James McIntosh set to work immediately to repair the damage. Crops were replanted and, by early August, MacLeod was "building a house of forty feet long, twenty feet wide and sixteen feet high" to have ready "for the people that may come up in the fall."[77] And they would return, and some would come sooner than MacLeod had anticipated.

They were a diverse group. From various eye-witness accounts we can piece together their names (Table 6).[78] John Smith and family, Alexander Sutherland and his sister, George and Adam Sutherland (brothers), "old John Bruce" and Mrs. Stewart had sailed on the *Prince of Wales* in 1813. John Smith was from Islay; Mrs. Stewart, widow of Donald, was from Appin in Argyll, while the others originated from Sutherland. Then there were the families of Mr. [Alexander] McLean (a former tacksman), John Pritchard, Donald Livingstone, John MacVicar, Pat McNaulty, Alexander McLean and Martin Jordan. Two of these families were from Ireland and two were from Mull.[79] Mrs. Stewart had no sons, only three daughters, all under the age of 10, while John Bruce was 62. Martin Jordan had come with the advance party of eighteen men who arrived at Red River in August, 1812 (Appendix C). The two McLean families and the families of Donald Livingstone, John MacVicar and Pat McNaulty, who had come with Owen Keveny on the *Robert Taylor*, had arrived soon after (Appendix E). And many of the twenty-four company workers who remained behind had also sailed with the advance party, in 1811, or in 1812. Three originated from Norway, three from Ireland, three from Mull, two from Islay and two from the Orkney Islands. Only five of the eleven families in Keveny's group had been lost to Upper Canada. In the end, it was the early arrivals who showed the greatest determination to stay.

Those on their way to Upper Canada stopped briefly at Fort William where there was great rejoicing. Duncan Cameron thought George Campbell to be "a very decent man" who had "exposed his life for the North West Company." He was to get £100 Halifax for his "very essential service in the transaction of Red River."[80] Such scenes disturbed the settlers. They could now see that the North West Company's motivation in moving them had not been driven by any humanitarian concerns. Their removal had simply been a means to an end – the destruction of the settlement. Some became disillusioned and dispirited, but those who Miles MacDonell met in the following year remained defiant:

> They all told me they did not repent of what they had done and that they were perfectly satisfied with the conduct of the North West Company towards them. Neither of them seemed to be inclined to give any information in favour of your Lordship, but on the contrary, say as much as ever against the colony.[81]

Many went to Elgin County, settling on Colonel Thomas Talbot's land in Aldborough and Dunwich townships. Arriving there in 1816, they acquired 50 acre lots on very easy terms.[82] Others went to West Gwillimbury, in Simcoe County.[83]

But at Red River, things were not as hopeless as they seemed. Colin Robertson was on his way to Red River in the summer of 1815. Now working for the Hudson's Bay Company, he was taking twenty men with him to the settlement. At Lake of the Woods he learned about its destruction. On hearing that some settlers had stayed behind, he hurried on toward Jack River, believing that they would have waited there. Finding them at Norway House, he persuaded them to return to Red River. Those of the settlers who thought "ourselves sufficiently strong to re-establish the colony" left on August 7, "for to try our fate once more."[84] They included one of the McLean families, the families of John Pritchard, Pat McNaulty and twenty-two company workers. However, some remained behind. The families of the Widow Stewart, Widow McLean, Mrs. Jordan and Miss Kennedy would delay their return "until the fall."[85] And there was another welcome development. A fifth contingent of over one hundred colonists, originating mainly from Sutherland, would be arriving at Red River later in the year.

The continuing displacement of people in Kildonan and the surrounding area, to make way for sheep farms, had led many more to contemplate emigration. Amazingly, Selkirk got about half of the total number who decided to emigrate in 1815.[86] A crucial factor in his ability to attract the eighty-four people who sailed on the *Prince of Wales* was the favourable terms he offered to families with "sons fit for the company's service." Young men could find employment as indentured servants, for an agreed period, usually three years. They would work for the Hudson's Bay Company, "pledging their wages for the payment of their parent's debt."[87] Thus, under these arrangements, poor families could get sufficient credit to finance their travel and other relocation costs. It was therefore no accident that nine of the fourteen families, in the group, had teenage sons (Table 7).[88] The boys were apparently "fine little fellows" while the girls were "generally stout and healthy" and seemed "more likely to improve the strength than the beauty of the breed of Kildonan."[89]

Led by Robert Semple, the newly appointed Governor of the Hudson's Bay Company territories, they sailed from Thurso in June.[90] A second ship, the *Hadlow*, which had collected a further 34 colonists at Stromness, some probably originating from Loch Eriboll, left at the same time.[91] Following an easy and comfortable crossing, the emigrants who sailed on *Prince of Wales,* arrived at York Factory on August 26. But because of bad weather, they did not reach Red River until the second of November. The first and very disheartening piece of news was the discovery that their compatriots had relocated to Upper Canada. But despite this, their prospects looked good. The settlement now had over 100 colonists and Colin Robertson was an adept manager. Ample crops had been harvested and stored and the settlers were busy building new houses. Red River's refounding was formally celebrated on November 4th with the firing of guns and the raising of banners.[92] However, this bravado was deceptive; the settlers remained fearful that the North West Company might instigate further attacks. Governor Semple wanted Lord Bathurst to send troops to protect the colonists but his request was turned down.[93]

TABLE 7: PASSENGER LIST FOR THE *Prince of Wales* CROSSING IN 1815
FROM THURSO TO YORK FACTORY (ARRIVED 26TH AUG.)*

No.	No. in family	Names	Age	Profession	General Remarks
1	1#†	James Sutherland	47	Weaver	Elder, authorised by Church of Scotland to baptise and marry.
2	2	Mary Polson	48		
3	3#	James Sutherland	12		Scraper and cleaner of the deck
4	4	Janet Sutherland	16		
5	5	Catherine Sutherland	14		
6	6	Isabella Sutherland	13		
7	1#	William Sutherland	54	Weaver	
8	2	Isabella Sutherland	50		
9	3	Jeremiah Sutherland	15	Scraper	
10	4#	Ebeneezer Sutherland	11	At school	
11	5	Donald Sutherland	7	At school	
12	6	Helen Sutherland	12	At school	
13	1	Widow Mathewson	60		
14	2#	John Mathewson	18	Laborer	School Master
15	3	Helen Mathewson	21		
16	1#	Angus Mathewson	30	Tailor	Steward of the Provisions & Stores
17	2	Christian Mathewson	18		
18	1#	Alexander Murray	52	Shoemaker	Cook (Brought out a pair of Mill Stones)
19	2	Elizabeth Murray	54		
20	3#	James Murray	16	Scraper	
21	4	Donald Murray	13	At school	
22	5	Catherine Murray	27		Married to George Ross 30th August at York Fort
23	6	Christian Murray	25		
24	7	Isabella Murray	18		
25	1#	George McKay	50	Weaver	
26	2	Isabella Mathewson	50		
27	3#	Roderick McKay	19	Labourer	
28	4#	Robert McKay	11	At school	
29	5	Roberty McKay	16		Married to Donald McKay 31st August 1815 at York Fort
30	1#	Donald McKay	31	Labourer	
31	2	John McKay	1		
32	3	Catherine Bruce	33		
33	1	Barbara Gunn	50		
34	2#	William Bannerman	55	Labourer	
35	3#	William Bannerman	16	Shoemaker	Scraper

No.	No. in family	Names	Age	Profession	General Remarks
37	5#	Donald Bannerman	8	At school	(father who came in 1813 died)
38	6#	George Bannerman	7	At school	
39	7	Ann Bannerman	19		
40	1#	Widow Gunn	40		
41	2#	Alexander McKay	16	Labourer	Scraper
42	3	Adam McKay	13		An Idiot
43	4#	Robert McKay	12		An Idiot
44	5	Christian McKay	19		
45	1#	John Bannerman	55	Labourer	
46	2	Catherine McKay	28		
47	3	Alexander Bannerman	1		
48	1#	Alexander McBeth	55	Labourer	Cook—Brought out a pair of Mill stones
49	2	Christian Gunn	50		
50	3#	George McBeth	16	Scraper	
51	4	Roderick McBeth	12	At school	
52	5#	Robert McBeth	10	At school	
53	6	Adam McBeth	6	At school	
54	7	Morrison McBeth	4	At school	
55	8	Margaret McBeth	18	At school	
56	9	Molly McBeth	18		
57	10	Christian McBeth	14		
58	1#	Alexander Mathewson	34	Shoemaker	Serjeant of the Passengers
59	2	Ann Mathewson	34		
60	3	Hugh Mathewson	10	At school	
61	4	Angus Mathewson	6		
62	5	John Mathewson	1		
63	6	Catherine Mathewson	2		
64	1#	Alexander Polson	36	Wheelwright	
65	2	Catherine Mathewson	30		
66	3#	Hugh Polson	10	At school	
67	4	John Polson	5	At school	
68	5	Donald Polson	1		
69	6	Ann Polson	7		
70	1#	William McKay embarked 23 June at Stromness with his family	44	Shoemaker	Brought out a pair of Mill Stones
71	2	Barbara Sutherland	35		
72	3	Betty McKay	10	At school	
73	4	Dorothy McKay	4		
74	5	Janet McKay	2		

101

No.	No. in family	Names	Age	Profession	General Remarks
75	1	Joseph Adams	25	Labourer	embarked at Gravesend
76	2	Mary Adams	23		embarked at Gravesend
77	1	Reginald Green	21	Miner	Serjeant of the Passengers, embarked at Gravesend
78	1#	George Adams	19	Labourer	embarked at Gravesend
79	1	Henry Hilliard	19	Labourer	embarked at Gravesend
80	1	Edward Simmons	20	Labourer	embarked at Gravesend
81	1	Christian Bannerman	22		Married to Robert McKay 4th September 1815 at York Fort
82	1	Jane Mathewson	22		
83	1#	Alexander Sutherland	25	Labourer	Serjeant of the Passengers
84	1	John McDonald	22	Saddler	Serjeant of the Passengers

* Source: Original in NAC SP (C-2) 1659–1661; transcript in Bumsted, *The People's Clearance*, 285–7.
† The symbol "#" designates those people whose names appear in a petition prepared by Red River inhabitants after the troubles of 1816 (Appendix F).

Meanwhile Selkirk had come to the conclusion that his colony had to be rescued. And to achieve this he needed to go to North America. On September 8, 1815, he boarded the *Pacific* at Liverpool with his wife and children and set sail for New York. He would spend the winter in Montreal with his family and then "go up the country next Spring."[94] While at New York he learned of the destruction of the Red River settlement but later, in March of the following year, he heard the wonderful news that it had been re-established. With amazing panache, Robertson had employed Jean-Baptiste Lagimonière to take this message to Selkirk's residence in Montreal. A journey of 1,800 miles, carried out in the depth of winter – it was an heroic feat. During the winter of 1816, while in Montreal, Selkirk attempted to negotiate an amicable arrangement with the North West Company in the hope that fur trade rivalries and disputes arising from the Red River settlement could be resolved peacefully. However, this proved fruitless.[95]

That winter he went to York to meet some of the former Red River settlers who had since relocated themselves north of York, in Simcoe County. There he received first-hand accounts of their ordeal at the hands of the North West Company. But they also held him partly responsible as well.[96] Much more serious criticism awaited his return to Montreal. Some of his former settlers had given evidence to Reverend Dr. John Strachan (later Bishop).[97] Implacably opposed to Selkirk's colonization schemes, he used their stories to warn "the poorer classes of his countrymen" about the plight of "these unfortunate people, the dupes of land-jobbing speculators, a class of persons well known in America, and of whom Lord Selkirk, from the magnitude of his operations, may be styled the chief."[98] Bishop or not, he had written his tawdry pamphlet, *A Letter to the Rt. Hon. Earl of Selkirk on his Settlement at the Red River near Hudson Bay,* using material given to him by his friend, William McGillivray, the head of the North West Company.[99]

Selkirk prepared to leave for Assiniboia. His wife, on whose judgement and advice he would later rely, was to remain behind in Montreal, acting as his principal agent. Although he had been supplied with soldiers from the British 37th Regiment of Foot, to act as a bodyguard, he decided that he needed more men. As it happened, men from the de Meuron and de Watteville Regiments, who had served as mercenaries for Britain during the Napoleonic Wars, were being demobilized at this time. They were now free for other service. Quick to seize the opportunity thus pre-

Memorial, erected in 1891, with financial assistance from the Countess of Selkirk, commemorating the Seven Oaks Battle of 1816. *Photograph by Geoff Campey.*

sented, he immediately signed up ninety men, mainly of Swiss origin, from these disbanded Regiments. An advance guard, under Miles MacDonell's command was sent out in May.[100] On his way to Red River, Miles heard on, June 29, of the massacre at Seven Oaks just as he and his men were approaching Lake Winnipeg.[101] At great speed he and his men turned eastwards, across Lake Superior, hoping to intercept Selkirk at St. Mary's (Sault Ste. Marie). Arriving one evening in late July, they headed straight for the home of Charles Ermatinger, a Justice of the Peace and partner in the North West Company. Selkirk and his physician, Dr. John Allan, were guests of Ermatinger and his Ojibwe wife, Charlotte, that night. Selkirk was still asleep when MacDonell arrived and, on John Allan's advice, he waited until morning before breaking the tragic news to him. It was received with what MacDonell called "a spirit becoming a Douglas."[101]

Following an attack on the settlement by the Métis on June 19, Governor Semple and twenty-one settlers had been killed. One of the dead was Alexander McLean "the head colonist" who "left behind a considerable family" – he came out with the first settlers and had been "a very active

Lord Selkirk's sketch of Fort William from the Mess Room, 1816.
Courtesy of Archives of Ontario Fond F481.

and industrious person."[102] Fort Douglas had been captured and the settlers driven away. Some of the survivors had been taken prisoner and were
being held at Fort William. Very much shocked by this news, Selkirk
immediately led his men to Fort William:

> "On the 12th of August, his Lordship came into the River Kaminis-
> tiguiâ with four canoes, attended by a number of soldiers, and by his
> guard, with whom he encamped about 800 or 900 yards above the Fort,
> on the opposite shore.
>
> Within two or three hours, eleven boats full of men, in the uniform
> of De Meuron's Regiment, came into the River, and were followed by
> one boat and two canoes loaded with arms and stores, &c. The troops
> immediately joined Lord Selkirk at his encampment. Cannon were
> landed, and drawn up, pointed to the Fort, and balls were ready piled
> beside them, as prepared for a siege and bombardment.[104]

Faced with this overwhelming display of force, the occupants of Fort
William capitulated and ceded control to Selkirk. He then obtained the
release of his imprisoned colonists and, in his capacity as a magistrate,
arrested nine of the North West Company partners.[105]

Selkirk remained at Fort William until May of the following year; but
Miles MacDonell went off, in December, with a small number of de Meu-
rons to mount the next attack. They were to recapture Fort Douglas.
Marching in deep snow and in freezing conditions they made it to Fort

The original cannons which stood at the main entrance to
Fort William. They now guard the entrance to the City Hall
in Thunder Bay. *Photograph by Geoff Campey.*

Daer, at Pembina, by December 31. Meeting little resistance they regained
the fort. Travelling on in atrocious weather for a further ten miles, they
reached Fort Douglas. Scaling the walls of the Fort in the dead of night
they captured it. "Our hardy enterprise was crowned with complete success; the North West Company, thinking themselves in perfect security
for the winter, were off their guard and consequently surprised; the country was once more in our possession."[106] On January 11, 1817, the Hudson's
Bay Company flag flew once again over Fort Douglas.

Learning that the settlers had gone to Jack River, MacDonell sent a
messenger to them. Having arrived there without any provisions, they
were in a miserable state. Had it not been for Peguis, the Saulteaux Indian
Chief, and his kinsmen they might have starved. He and his men hunted
for them and dragged food supplies to them on sleds over great distances.
MacDonell's messenger reached them in mid-March. With great joy they
learned that Selkirk had taken Fort William and was coming to Red
River. A few of the young men raced across the ice to the settlement to
prepare for the return of the others. The Silver Chief was on his way.

6. THE SILVER CHIEF ARRIVES

I shall never forget what the Great Chief, the late Earl of Selkirk, told me and recommended; he told me to take the colony under my protection. I followed his wishes by taking the Colony under my care and I shall hold it as an eagle keeps its prey in its talons.[1]

PEGUIS, THE SAULTEAUX INDIAN CHIEF, had been "a steady friend" of the Red River settlement. He and his men had helped the first arrivals to find food and had defended the settlers when they had come under attack.[2] Now in the summer of 1817 he was negotiating terms with other local Indian Chiefs which would enable Selkirk to re-establish his colony on a surer footing. A land surrender treaty signed by Selkirk and five chiefs of the Saulteaux, Assiniboine and Cree Indians would formally establish Selkirk's ownership of strips of land on each side of the Red and Assiniboine rivers. While the treaty reinforced his entitlement to land which he already claimed to own, its real importance was in the approval it won him from the assembled Chiefs. Selkirk's engaging sense of ceremony and style had greatly impressed them:

> He was tall in stature, thin and refined in appearance. He had a benignant face, his manner was easy and polite. To the Indians he was especially interesting. They caught the idea that being a man of title he was in some way closely connected with their Great Father, the King. Because of his generosity to them, they called him "The Silver Chief.[3]

Peguis, a master at diplomacy, had been the driving force behind the agreement. Short in stature, but with the voice and language skills of an orator, he had a commanding presence. Wearing, with great pride, the flag and medal presented to him by Selkirk at the treaty signing, he would, in later years, refer to himself as the "Colony Chief." And long after Selkirk's death, he held "sacred the promises" that he had made to the colony's Silver Chief.[4] Selkirk's visit was a crucial turning point in the affairs

Left: Peter Rindisbacher's portrait, believed to be of Peguis, the Salteaux Chief who was so helpful to the Red River settlers c. 1820s. *Courtesy Provincial Archives of Manitoba, N3754.*
Above: A gold medal bearing the likeness of King George III presented to Chief Peguis in 1817 by Lord Selkirk. Peguis proudly wore this medal on ceremonial occasions. *Courtesy Provincial Archives of Manitoba.*

of the settlement. When the survivors of the Seven Oaks Battle had been found at Jack River in the middle of March, the one factor which had persuaded them to return to Red River was the knowledge that he was coming to meet them. They had previously vowed never to return. But now there was "no keeping them." Sheriff Alexander MacDonnell and a few of the young men had left immediately to prepare the way for the others. Then, in early July, their ragged little fleet of boats could be seen crossing Lake Winnipeg. Racing each other across the lake, they reached Frog Plain on the evening of July 19, the day after the Silver Chief had concluded his treaty with the five Indian Chiefs. Their first meeting with him, the following morning, "excited much feeling" and would long be remembered.[5]

Selkirk had left Fort William for Red River on the May 1 with his seven bodyguards from the 37th Regiment of Foot, 37 soldiers from the former de Meuron and de Watteville regiments, as well as three Captains (F. Matthey, P. D'Orsonnens and Jean-Baptiste de Lorimière), Dr. Allan

(Royal Navy surgeon and Selkirk's medical attendant), Charles Bruce and Chauvin.[6] He had been warned about the "dark assassins" who were lying in wait for him and travelled at great personal risk.[7] He would have followed Miles MacDonell's advice "to have canoes ahead of yours for exploring" and to have "no distinction about your canoe or person different from those that are in company." The North West Company "monsters" were lurking and "your lordship's life is pointedly threatened."[8] According to Peguis, Cuthbert Grant[9] and his 116 warriors had intended "to waylay" Selkirk as he made his way to Red River. But Peguis' threat to leave his much more numerous tribe of warriors at Sturgeon Creek had the desired effect and Grant and his men had retreated.[10]

Thus Selkirk, like his colonists, was very much in debt to Peguis and the Saulteaux people. Miles MacDonell had made a particular point of "cultivating" their friendship from his "first arrival in the country."[11] Time and again they had shown themselves to be "particularly friendly to the settlers" and always "better disposed towards them than the North West Company."[12] In supporting the settlers, the Saulteaux people "had incurred the displeasure" of the fur traders. As Peguis put it, every step they took towards civilization was "like a dagger" at the fur traders' heart, "striking at the vitals of their commerce." But because he believed that "real riches was only to be found in the soil," Peguis stoutly defended and promoted the settlement. And the settlers would later attribute the "friendly reception" they got from the Native People to their "sagacity" in realizing "that our prosperity would be of permanent advantage to themselves."[13]

Miles MacDonell first learned, on June 21, of Selkirk's arrival at Fort Bas de la Rivière, Winnipeg. Selkirk's brigade had reached the fort on the previous day and was now only a day's journey away. "All our workmen and labourers were set about putting the main house in repair." The local Indian Chiefs were "highly pleased to hear that his lordship, who has been so often reported by the North West Company to have been taken prisoner, is so near"[14] The completion of a journey begun the previous year was coming to an end. As Selkirk's canoe approached Fort Douglas, later that day, the guns of the fort thundered their salute:

> His lordship arrived about 9 o'clock. Everybody was out. The Indians flocked around him in such numbers that he could not advance, everyone striving to hold of his hands and calling him their father.[15]

William Coltman, the newly appointed Commissioner to Red River, had prepared the ground, before his arrival, for the land treaty negotiations

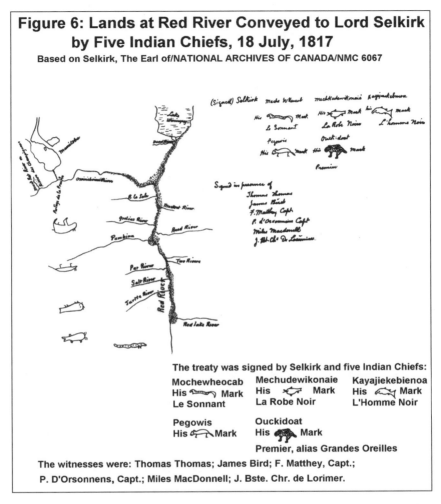

Figure 6: Lands at Red River Conveyed to Lord Selkirk by Five Indian Chiefs, 18 July, 1817

Based on Selkirk, The Earl of/NATIONAL ARCHIVES OF CANADA/NMC 6067

The treaty was signed by Selkirk and five Indian Chiefs:

Mochewheocab | Mechudewikonaie | Kayajiekebienoa
His ⟡ Mark | His ⟡ Mark | His ⟡ Mark
Le Sonnant | La Robe Noir | L'Homme Noir

Pegowis | Ouckidoat
His ⟡ Mark | His ⟡ Mark
| Premier, alias Grandes Oreilles

The witnesses were: Thomas Thomas; James Bird; F. Matthey, Capt.;
P. D'Orsonnens, Capt.; Miles MacDonell; J. Bste. Chr. de Lorimer.

which were about to begin. Although the Crees and Assiniboines were the rightful owners of the land, Peguis and the Saulteaux who had later occupied it, had the greater influence. All had to be accommodated.[16] Having established "that the Indians wish the settlement for their own advantage," Coltman concluded that they "would require scarcely any consideration for allowing to the settlers an exclusive possession of a reasonable portion of land." He recommended annual payments.[17]

The process toward an agreement began on 22nd day of June, the day after Selkirk arrived, at a meeting held in Fort Douglas:

His lordship attended by his escort under arms and all the gentlemen and the interpreters made a harangue to the Saulteaux in French, which was interpreted by Mr. [Louis] Nolin. The Chiefs, Peguis and the Premier made harangues in reply. He then addressed the Assiniboines through the Interpreter St. Maurice. Their Chief spoke in reply. Three kegs of liquor were given to the Saulteaux and one to the Assiniboines, with a proportionate quantity of tobacco.[18]

Further deliberations continued at the meeting attended by Miles MacDonell on June 29. "A pipe of peace was placed in the usual manner for grand occasions in the middle of the Lodge, supported by two forked sticks." L'Homme Noir, "a chief of the Assiniboines, who had come from a long distance," spoke of his pleasure in meeting Selkirk:

We were often harassed with solicitations to assist the Bois Brûlés in what had been done against your children, but we always refused. We are sure you must have had much trouble to come here. We have often been told you were our enemy; but we have today the happiness to hear from your own mouth the words of a true friend. We receive the present you give us with great pleasure and thankfulness.[19]

The land treaty was finally concluded on July 18 in the Mess Room, "each Chief making his mark – or distinction of his tribe which we all witnessed."[20] Each was denoted by the picture of an animal or a fish (Figure 6). In return for one hundred pounds weight of tobacco, to be paid annually to the Saulteaux and Cree tribes, the Silver Chief was to be granted land "extending in breadth to the distance of 2 English statute miles" along both banks of the Red River, from Lake Winnipeg to Grand Forks (now Minnesota). In addition he was granted a two mile strip along both sides of the Assiniboine River, from its junction with the Red River to Musk Rat Creek (or Rivière des Champignons) near present-day Portage la Prairie.[21] The two statute mile distance was "said to have been decided to be as much as could be seen by looking under the belly of a horse out upon the prairie. This was generally two miles."[22]

"About 100 persons" had apparently been living at Jack River when the news came of Selkirk's impending visit. Having heard of the miserable conditions which they had endured, he had set off from Fort William as soon as the route to Red River became navigable. But he only appreciated the full extent of their suffering when they finally met. Miles MacDonell would record only that on Sunday, July 20, "his lordship went down to Frog Plain

Memorial to Chief Peguis at St. Peter's Anglican Church,
East Selkirk "in grateful recognition of his good offices to the
early settlers." *Photograph by Geoff Campey.*

to see the settlers"; but it was a momentous happening. He would learn about
the periods of near starvation and banishment from their settlement and
the people killed in battle. But they shared his desire to move on. His generosity and wisdom greatly impressed them and continued to be spoken of
in the region for well over a century. The Silver Chief was to remain at Red
River for nearly three months. He would be in his element planning major
roadworks and building schemes and giving much needed aid and direction to the colony. For him it was the culmination of years of research,
planning and negotiation, but for the settlers it was a new beginning.

The detailed granting of plots began with the soldier-colonists from
the disbanded de Meuron and de Watteville regiments. Having been
promised good land at Red River or their transport costs back to Upper
or Lower Canada, many chose to remain. They got small tracts of land
on Point Douglas and along the Rivière la Seine, which flowed into the

111

Red River opposite the Point. It was a shrewd decision. By locating the ex-soldiers here, near Fort Douglas, they could be summoned up for action should the settlement come under attack. Then Selkirk turned his attention to the other settlers. They met "where the church and burying ground of St. John's are now found." At a great gathering held on August 10, he granted land, free of charge, "to those of the settlers who had made improvements on their lands" before being driven away in 1816. In all, he gave away 24 lots. To the others he offered land on very easy terms.[23] He also granted 100 acre lots as sites for a church and school. "Here you shall build your church" and the lot across the little stream called Parsonage Creek "is for a school." He named their settlement "Kildonan," "from their old home on the valley of Helmsdale, in Sutherland."[24]

We do not have a full list of the people met by Selkirk on August 10, 1817, but the names on a petition, produced around this time, gives us an indication of who would have been present (Appendix F). While most of those who now lived in the colony, were recent arrivals from Kildonan, in Sutherland, there were some families like the McLeans, from Mull, and men like Martin Jordan, from Ireland, who had been among the earliest arrivals to Red River. They had been at the settlement since 1812. They were in the group who had refused to go to Upper Canada and, after enduring the winter of 1815 at Jack River, had been persuaded to return by Colin Robertson. But most of those who signed the petition are to be found in the passenger list for the *Prince of Wales* crossing from Thurso, in 1815 (Table 7). At their meeting with Selkirk, some of the Kildonan settlers even recalled their first encounter in Golspie and Thurso, when he had been there to find recruits for the 1813 crossing from Thurso.[25] Thus, with its predominance of Sutherland settlers, Kildonan Parish had been aptly named.

Intending to return to Red River, but never doing so, Selkirk left in early September. Riding away on horseback from the relative safety of the settlement, he was once more a hunted man. But now, in addition to threats to his person, he faced mounting legal battles. During the autumn of 1816, while at Fort William, he had been visited by a constable, with a warrant for his arrest signed by Dr. Mitchell, Justice of the Peace at Drummond's Island (near Sault Ste. Marie). The warrant was based on evidence supplied by two North West Company clerks, who had been at the Fort during Selkirk's occupation. Given that his agent, Owen Keveny, had been brutally murdered in July, when surrendering to a North West Company warrant, Selkirk was naturally suspicious. Believing the warrant to be phony and the constable to be an impostor, he refused to accept it. Then in April, of the following year, just before he left for Red River, he had been served with another warrant, this time by Deputy Sheriff William Smith of Sandwich, who had arrived with four senior North West Company men. After examining the warrant, Selkirk declared it to be illegal. When Smith objected and later forced his way into Selkirk's room, Selkirk had him placed under an armed guard at the Fort.[26]

Thus, Selkirk had resisted arrest on two occasions. And in doing so he made a serious misjudgement. He believed himself to be in the right. He was exposing the wickedness of the North West Company and ensuring that they would stand trial for their actions. Edward Ellice, one of their London agents, had warned him that the wintering partners would do what was necessary to stop him from establishing his settlement. They were "utterly destitute of all moral principle, or the feelings of honour prevalent in civilized society" and "would not scruple to commit any crime" to achieve their aims.[27] Now there was clear evidence that they had committed criminal acts in attempting to destroy his settlement. He had seized Fort William in order to release the settlers who were being held as prisoners, to arrest the instigators of the killings at Seven Oaks and to gather evidence of this and other North West Company skulduggery. Twenty-one of his people had been killed at Seven Oaks and he was determined that those responsible should stand trial in Upper or Lower Canada. He was pursuing truth and justice. But the outside world took a completely different view. Selkirk's use of force, in taking over Fort William, attracted much criticism and, in resisting arrest, he looked as if he believed himself to be above the law.

Instructions came swiftly from Lord Bathurst, the Colonial Secretary, that Selkirk and his associates were to be bound over for trial. Bathurst issued a dispatch on February 11, 1817, ordering his arrest and appearance in a criminal court in Montreal to answer the charge of resisting arrest. Urging Bathurst on had been the Under-Secretary at the Colonial Office, Henry Goulburn, friend of Simon McGillivray and Edward Ellice, both London agents for the North West Company.[28] Jean, his wife, was livid when she received news of the further warrants. Having previously resisted them, he would first stand trial at the Assizes Court, in Sandwich, in the Spring of 1818:

> All now depends on your management with this most rascally business of the Sandwich warrants.... Come down to Sandwich, if it be necessary, so as to give these rascals the lie by your actions and we shall only rise stronger from this shameful folly of Lord Bathurst's. His injustice

is glaring and abominable.... He casts an odium on the name of Great Britain and the province is gone if they do not show that it is still the British Government that reigns.

Be firm and cheerful and keep up the spirits of those about you and all will go right. Oh that I were with you to help. I could be a thousand different things in a minute.[29]

Lady Selkirk did not yet appreciate that, through their links with Goulburn, Simon McGillivray and Edward Ellice had turned opinion within the entire British Government against Selkirk. Nor did she or her husband appreciate the extent of the power wielded by the North West Company in the Canadas. Having numerous high-ranking friends in government and in the judiciary, these men were the untouchables of their day. In spite of overwhelming evidence of their violent and unscrupulous conduct, the North West Company men would easily side-step any attempts to prosecute them. On the other hand, Selkirk would be pursued relentlessly by the Canadian courts. The North West Company would take its revenge on Selkirk and he would be denied justice.

Thus when he left Red River, in September 1817, Selkirk was only a few months away from his first court appearance. To add to his difficulties he knew that Campbell, a North West Company man, was waiting at Fort William with yet another warrant for his arrest. So, he decided to go east by way of the United States. There were other reasons for wishing to cross the border into the United States. The decision to fix the boundary between British America and the United States, at the forty-ninth parallel, had placed a large part of his Assiniboia territory in the United States (Figure 5). He wanted to negotiate the sale of his land on the American side of the boundary with the American government. And, he wished to buy American cattle and sheep for his Red River colonists. To give himself time for these activities he decided that he would remain in the United States until January of the following year. When the Red River Commissioner, William Coltman, heard the news he reacted angrily and demanded bail from Selkirk of £6,000. This very large sum was more than the total bail exacted from all of the North West Company partners who had been charged as accessories to murder. Coltman, for some unexplained reason, disapproved of Selkirk's trip to the United States. Perhaps, he had allowed the North West Company to convince him that Selkirk might be fleeing Canada for good. Realizing by now that it was counterproductive to challenge or complain, Selkirk said nothing, paid the staggering sum demanded of him and headed for the United States.

Having reached the Mississippi, Selkirk, accompanied by Captains Matthey and d'Orsonnens, as well as Dr. Allan, travelled to St. Louis by riverboat. From there they crossed through Illinois and Indiana to Ohio and went on to Kentucky, Washington, Philadelphia, New York and Albany, arriving in Montreal in January 1818. Isabella, one of his daughters, remembered seeing his approach. "He returned from this long journey, coming around the Island into Montreal Harbour, paddled by French voyageurs in swift canoes."[30] No more sleeping out in the open and in forts. He was home again with his family, living in the house that they rented from Colonel de Chambault.[31]

Attending the court at Sandwich soon after his return, Selkirk was charged with having stolen the arms of the North West Company at Fort William. But it was easy for him to show that the evidence was false and the case was dismissed. The other charges, that of resisting arrest and assault and false imprisonment were dealt with in a far more protracted manner. The court hearings for the first case were moved back and forth from Sandwich to Montreal. When the case was finally heard in Sandwich, it was thrown out by a Grand Jury. The second case, heard in Sandwich, was repeatedly postponed and only terminated, inconclusively, when Selkirk and his witnesses had scattered and left the area. All of the remaining charges made by the Crown against him were then grouped together under the heading of "conspiracy to injure or destroy the trade of the North West Company." The Grand Jury spent three days in examining forty witnesses and two in deliberation, but it failed to reach a verdict. Without assembling the Grand Jury to explain his reasons, the Chief Justice suddenly adjourned the court, *sine die.* Believing that he was about to be cleared, Selkirk lost his temper in court, accusing "the Attorney General and Prosecutor and witnesses in open court of corrupt and oppressive designs." Meanwhile the North West Company charged "his lordship of practising improperly with the grand jury," claiming "that something little different from direct bribery was used."[32] Thus nothing had been decided and Selkirk's good name remained in tatters.

The charges and counter-charges between Selkirk and the North West Company raged on. Continuing to be baffled by his enemies' influence, Selkirk made little progress in his pursuit of justice. Undermining his efforts had been the government's desire to see an end to the feuding between the two fur companies. Each was heading for bankruptcy and a merger was seen as the only way forward. It mattered little that the bloodshed and terror experienced by Selkirk's settlers at the hands of the North West Company should go unpunished. The more important aim was to find an amicable accommodation between the two factions. Thus, the government had little sympathy with Selkirk's desire to expose the shameful conduct of the North West Company. Instead it sought a cover up and looked for ways of diverting attention to Selkirk's misdemeanours.

Leaving his wife in charge of his affairs in Montreal, Selkirk sailed for Liverpool from New York on November 9, 1818. Despite deteriorating health, he was unwilling to give up in his fight to bring the North West Company to justice. Having failed to get any support from the Colonial Office he brought his case directly before the Prime Minister, Lord Liverpool.[33] He was promised that his papers would be considered, but he received no reply. His prospects improved greatly when, his brother-in-law, Sir James Montgomery, won support in the House of Commons in February 1819, for the papers on the Red River controversy to be made public.[34] Thus, it was through British political channels, not the Canadian judiciary, that the full extent of the bloodshed and violence perpetrated by the North West Company would become widely known.

Slowly public opinion began to shift a little in Selkirk's favour. William Wilberforce wished to see "some opportunity of doing justice to your Lordship," on the ground that his venture "had been undertaken with a view to the improvement and benefit of your fellow creatures...I never had any misgivings on that head."[35] While there were grounds for optimism, Selkirk's future looked bleak. His health was failing rapidly. Having developed a serious chest complaint, he went with his family to live in Pau, in the south of France, in the hope that a warmer climate would bring improvements to his health. During the winter of 1819-20, the government increasingly put him under pressure to give his blessing to a merger between the two companies, but he resisted. The Colonial Office, the North West Company and many of Selkirk's friends were agreed that the time had come to put an end to the ancient dispute. The North West Company offered to buy his Hudson's Bay Company shares, a tempting proposition given his mounting debts. But Selkirk would not sell:

> Your observations as to the general state of my pecuniary affairs are undeniably just, but I fear the time for establishing a sinking fund is not yet come.... It is to be hoped that this state of things must soon be over and when that is the case I will retire to St. Mary's Isle and live on sixpence a day till I am out of debt."[36]

His good name was on the line. He would not hand power over to his enemies and leave his settlers vulnerable to the harm that they might do.

"Pecuniary advantage" was not his sole criterion. He would not give up on the settlement:

> I consider my character at stake upon the success of the undertaking and upon proving by the result that it was neither a wild and visionary scheme nor a trick and a cloak to cover sordid plans of agreement upon the property of others, charges which would be left in too ambiguous a state if I were to abandon the settlement at its present stage and, above all if I were to sell it to its enemies.[37]

Selkirk did not live to see the merger of the two companies on March 26, 1821. The Hudson's Bay Company was the victor. The North West Company's much longer inland routes made their transport costs more than double that of the Hudson's Bay Company.[38] They could not compete and in the end they were swallowed up by the more successful company. The older company, in which Selkirk had a controlling interest, prospered and the Red River settlement was no longer in danger. A victory of sorts for Selkirk. But not one that he could savour. A year before the merger he was at death's door. As Spring approached, his wife Jean reported that "mercifully there is hardly any suffering except from weakness, perfect tranquillity of mind and inexhaustible patience.... Everything like disturbance of mind had passed away, no bitter feeling seemed to remain."[39] He died at Pau, on the 8th day of April 1820 and he was buried at the nearest Protestant cemetery at Orthez, about twenty-five miles away. His obituary in the *Montreal Gazette,* with its somewhat caustic tone, reflected the feelings of those on the losing side of the fur trade dispute:

> On the 8th April, The Right Honourable Thomas Douglas, Earl of Selkirk, died on the Continent. It may be said of this Nobleman that the endowments of his mind, as well as his other qualification, made him be as much respected, as the exalted rank he inherited from his ancestors, a circumstance which but rarely happens.
>
> Perhaps some people will deduct something from his worth on account of his rage for colonization.
>
> *Sed de mortuis nil nisi bonum.*"[40]

The obituary in the Edinburgh-based *Scotsman* was far more favourable:

Lord Selkirk's tombstone. He died on April 8, 1820 in Pau in the south of France and was buried in the Protestant section of the nearby cemetery at Orthez. *Photograph by Geoff Campey.*

Few men were possessed of higher powers of mind, or capable of applying them with more indefatigable perseverance. His *Treatise on Emigration* has long been considered as a standard work and as having exhausted one of the most difficult subjects in the science of political economy. His Lordship is also advantageously known to the public as the author of some other literary productions, all of them remarkable for the enlargement and liberality of their views, the luminous perspicuity of their statements and that severe and patient spirit of induction which delights in the pursuit and is generally successful in the discovery of truth — To his friends the death of this beloved and eminent person is a loss which nothing can repair. His gentle and condescending manners wound themselves round the hearts of those admitted to his society and conciliated an attachment which every fresh interview seemed to confirm.[41]

The Red River settlers were understandably saddened by the news of Selkirk's death and feared that the colony "would be forsaken and neglected."[42] But they need not have been. The merger of the two great fur trade companies brought peace and stability to the region and Selkirk's family would continue to promote the settlers' interests. The settlement prospered, although not in the way that Selkirk might have foreseen. Redundancies followed the merger and brought fur trade workers to Red River as settlers. A great many were Scots who originated from the Orkney Islands, a region which had long supplied the Hudson's Bay Company with much of its overseas workforce. Taking Native wives, they and their children became a significant portion of the local population. They soon attracted the evangelical efforts of the Church Missionary Society. An Anglican organization, set up to promote the Christian faith in remote corners of the world, it promoted the ideals of a self-sufficient and agriculturally-based society. Thus, as Selkirk departed this world, his colony acquired different types of settlers and different people to guide it.

7. THE SCOTTISH SETTLERS
OF RED RIVER

A settlement once established on Red River, many flocked to it. Thus it was that ten years after the death of Governor Semple there were of Highlanders, de Meurons, Swiss, French voyageurs, Métis and Orkney half-breeds, not less than fifteen hundred settlers. It was certainly a motley throng. Mr. West, the first missionary tells us that he distributed copies of the Bible in English, Gaelic, German, Danish, Italian and French and they were all gratefully received in this polyglot community.[1]

B Y 1826 RED RIVER'S "MOTLEY THRONG" included people from many corners of the world. The fur trade had attracted men from Scotland, England, Ireland, Switzerland, Italy, Germany and Scandinavia. Canadians had also come to live in the region alongside the Native population, who were mainly the Cree and Saulteaux peoples. But, initially, the Red River Colony was almost entirely Scottish. Selkirk's aim in founding it had been to create a settlement which could derive its livelihood from farming, sell its produce to the Hudson's Bay Company and offer retired company workers somewhere to live. His recruitment efforts, from 1811 to 1815, brought large numbers of Scots to Frog Plain, just to the north of the Forks of the Red and Assiniboine rivers. River plots of between 50 and 100 acres were laid out for them "as far as possible to combine wood and plain in every lot."[2] Houses, a fort and a Colony store were built.[3] After many setbacks they eventually founded Kildonan, named after their mainly Sutherland roots; and they, with their descendants, would later colonize the neighbouring parish of St. John's.

Then Swiss colonists came in 1817. They were followed, a year later, by a small number of French Canadians who settled at what would later become St. Boniface.[4] The Swiss arrivals were ex-soldiers from the former de Meuron and de Watteville regiments, brought to the region by Selkirk after his occupation of Fort William in 1816. Settling near Point Douglas, they were joined four years later by a further 170 Swiss immigrants.[5]

The Swiss settlers, who were said to have consisted "principally of watch-makers and mechanics" had little success as farmers.[6] And, after the great flood of 1826, most left the Colony. However, the Scots and Canadians remained. There were no further attempts to recruit settlers from Scotland after 1815. But, as Selkirk had intended, retired fur trade workers came to live in the Colony and in doing so steadily increased its population. Initially most of those who settled were men who originated from the Orkney Islands in Scotland. When the two great fur trade companies merged under the name of the Hudson's Bay Company, a year after Selkirk's death in 1821, the situation changed dramatically. Around 1,300 fur-trade workers were made redundant and instead of returning home most took up residence in the new Colony. They were the former trappers, traders, clerks, labourers and voyageurs who were now superfluous labour.[7] As a consequence there was a rapid increase in Orcadian numbers and, for the first time, large numbers of French Canadians and Métis labourers also came to live in the settlement.[8] The Métis workers were principally the offspring of Orcadian and Canadian men who had taken First Nation women as wives. While the Orcadians had been mainly associated with the Hudson's Bay Company and the Canadians with the North West Company, the Métis had worked for both.[9]

Métis families had actually made enquiries about taking up residence in the new Colony even before the first Scottish settlers had arrived, a development which Selkirk welcomed:

> I shall be very much disposed to give encouragement to the people you mention as being inclined to join the settlement. The servants of both companies, who have families by Indian women, may be received with the exception of notoriously bad characters. You may assign lands to the extent of 90 or 100 acres per family.[10]

He directed Miles MacDonell to keep the English-speaking and French Métis families "a little distance apart so as to avoid the occasion of quarrels and disturbance."[11] Accordingly, the Orcadian families, who formed the principal part of the English-speaking Métis, were located to the north of Frog Plain, in what would later be known as Grand Rapids (or St. Andrews parish) while the Canadian families, who formed the French-speaking Métis, lived at the southern end of the colony (Figure 7).[12] Thus did a mixed-blood or Métis population develop at Red River, segregated according to whether they were English-speaking or French-speaking.

While Orcadian links with the Red River colony date back to the period of its foundation in 1812, their association with the Hudson's Bay Company stretches back even further.[13] They were recruited on a regular basis by the company from 1722 and, by the end of the eighteenth century, they represented nearly eighty per cent of its workforce. In 1812 they formed two-thirds of it.[14] Selkirk became involved in their recruitment from 1811. The conditions associated with his Assiniboia land grant from the Hudson's' Bay Company required him to take responsibility for recruiting company workers. He had to find about 200 men annually. To bolster the population of his new Colony, Selkirk hoped to recruit men who would wish to retire to Red River as permanent settlers, once their employment contracts were completed. Initially his search extended to all parts of the Highlands:

> A few stout and active young men for the service of the Hudson's Bay Company at their factories and settlements in America…wages depend on qualifications…very good hands may expect from £12–£15 per year…besides a sufficient allowance of oatmeal and other food equally good or wholesome…engaged initially for 3 years, at end of which he shall be brought home to Scotland free of expense unless he chooses to remain at the settlements of the company, where 30 acres of good land will be granted in perpetual feu to every man who has conducted himself to the satisfaction of his employer…families can be brought over at moderate freight.[15]

However, Selkirk quickly came to hold the long-accepted view that the men needed "are of a description that can be found only in Orkney."[16] Orcadian men, "though less alert and animated than the natives of some other parts of the Kingdom, make up that defect by other qualifications of at least equal importance and in particular are remarkably careful, steady and sober."[17] They were also known to be particularly good at adapting to harsh climatic conditions while Stromness, being the last port of call before leaving Britain, was an ideal place to load provisions on company ships.

So, Orcadians were well and truly established as the company's principal overseas workforce by the late eighteenth century (Figure 8). And some Orcadians were among the initial workers who had been recruited in 1811, to prepare the Red River site for colonization (Appendix C). But most would come to the Colony as retired workers. They generally had five year contracts but many worked for longer periods. Joshua Halcro, having joined the company in 1801, worked on the English River, east of Lake Winnipeg, for 21 years. Known to be "respectable, well-informed

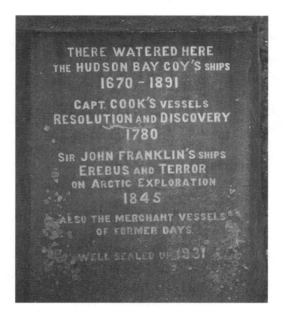

THERE WATERED HERE
THE HUDSON BAY COY'S SHIPS
1670 – 1891
CAPT. COOK'S VESSELS
RESOLUTION AND DISCOVERY
1780
SIR JOHN FRANKLIN'S SHIPS
EREBUS AND TERROR
ON ARCTIC EXPLORATION
1845
ALSO THE MERCHANT VESSELS
OF FORMER DAYS.
WELL SEALED UP 1931

The well at Stromness, in the Orkney Islands, which supplied Hudson's Bay Company ships with water. *Photograph by Geoff Campey.*

and an excellent clerk and trader," his poor health, which led to the decline in "his value as a trader," eventually caused him to return home. Andrew Wilson, from Orphir, who joined the company in 1806 when aged 19, returned home again in 1818 and then resumed his service with the company in 1820. Known for his boating skills, he was particularly "useful in going to Indian tents to fetch furs and provisions." And Thomas Isbister, who began work in 1812 as a labourer, "deficient in education," proved to be "a tolerable trader" and ended up as a company postmaster by 1830.[18]

Such work brought the prospect of good money. James Sutherland, from South Ronaldshay, who had joined the Hudson's Bay Company as a clerk at York Factory in 1797, advised his brother not to "come out as a labourer as you will have the chance of being a slave all your life and earn little or nothing."[19] Joshua Halcro, who originally looked set to join the North West Company, was told that if he behaved "well he has the chance of soon afterwards making a fortune; many who went with greater disadvantages have of late years returned with £20,000 to £30,000."[20] Although this was a wildly extravagant claim, ordinary labourers at this time could hope to accrue savings of around £60 after eight years service. Although

THE HAVEN
AGENTS OF THE
HUDSON'S BAY COMPANY
OPERATED FROM THIS
HOUSE. AND SIGNED MANY
ORCADIANS INTO
COMPANY SERVICE

Plaque, in Stromness, commemorating the building, close to the harbour, at which "Orkneymen" were recruited for the Hudson's Bay Company. *Photograph by Geoff Campey.*

not a fortune, it was enough money to buy a farm back in Orkney. And to the consternation of clergymen, these men, when they returned, could outbid local people in the competition for land. Writing in the 1790s, the Minister for the parish of Firth and Stenness felt such men made poor farmers and simply ended up in "mean circumstances." According to the Minister for Orphir, local men were hiring "themselves out for slaves in a savage land, where, in the language of the Scripture, they are literally employed as hewers of wood and drawers of water."[21]

The minister for Sandwick and Stromness parish blamed the departure of so many young men from Orkney on "a restlessness of disposition [and] the desire of change" and a willingness to accept low wages:

> These vessels usually arrive at the harbour of Stromness about the 5th of June, where they stop for two to three weeks to take aboard men for their settlements. They engage usually from 60 to 100 men…every year. They have about 400 or 500 men in these settlements, of whom it is presumed three-fourths are Orknese, as they find them more sober and tractable than the Irish and they engage for lower wages than either the English or the Irish.[22]

"Small as the wages" were, they were better "than the farmers here can afford to give."[23] Local clergymen may have poured scorn on them, but the young Orkney men clearly saw the economic attractions of working for the Hudson's Bay Company and they went out in large numbers over many decades.[24] Often three or four brothers would work for the company. James, the eldest son of the Tait family who joined the company in 1778, was joined in the following six years by John, William and one other younger brother.[25] James, John and William later settled at Red River. Thus whole families were being attracted to the way of life which the fur trade and the region had to offer.

Like the Tait brothers, many Orcadians never returned home and instead retired to the new Colony. By 1816 there were so many Orcadians in the area that the French-speaking Métis saw fit to call Red River's inhabitants "les Orcanais," although most were, in fact, Highlanders from Sutherland.[26] Even more Orcadians arrived in 1818. "Orkneymen, with their wives, white and brown," together with their children chose lots "on the Assiniboine River, some leagues up at the Plaine du Cheval Blanc," where they "laid the foundations of Orkney Town," in what would later become St. James parish. In addition to these recent arrivals, the Colony, at the time, had just 153 Scots, 45 de Meurons and 26

In memory of John Tait from South Ronaldshay, in the Orkney Islands, who died in 1879. Plaque in St. Andrew's Anglican Church. *Photograph by Geoff Campey.*

Canadians.[27] It was no longer under attack, but its population remained small. Food was scarce and agricultural production increased only very slowly. Selkirk's concept of a self-sufficient, agricultural society was still a distant pipe-dream. The settlers were adapting to their difficult circumstances by becoming accomplished hunters. "They could kill buffalo, walk on snowshoes, had trains of dogs trimmed with ribbons, bells and feathers in true Indian style; and in other respects were making rapid steps in the arts of savage life."[28] It was just as well since they were about to face a plague of locusts.

The locusts came in 1818 and again the following year, leaving the Colony without seed grain. Rumours abounded that the Kildonan settlers had become so dispirited that they were "praying to be removed from their exile and relieved from the danger of perishing by famine."[29] Once more the settlers were forced to seek a winter refuge at Pembina.[30] Acting on Lord Selkirk's realization that "our people might draw their supplies of many articles, by way of the Mississippi and River St. Peters (Minnesota), with greater facility than from Canada or from Europe," some of the settlers went off, in the dead of winter, on snowshoes, to the nearest American settlement at Prairie du Chien (now Wisconsin).[31] Loading 250 bushels of wheat, 100 bushels of oats and 30 bushels of peas onto boats, they transported their supplies back home by going up the Mississippi and Minnesota rivers and down the Bois de Sioux to the Red River. The 1819 expedition had cost Lord Selkirk a total of £1,040, but it had been successful. The seed reached Kildonan in June and, after being planted immediately, grew quickly enough to provide sufficient seed for the following year. Around 500 colonists lived at Red River by this time, of whom about 200 were the Kildonan settlers and their descendants.[32]

Selkirk had arranged for a Colony Store to be built in 1812 and regularly supplied shipments from Britain. He had "sent out a supply of goods and clothing after the departure of the first colonists, as well as a general assortment of the implements of husbandry, arms and ammunition for defence, and a supply of oatmeal to fall back upon in the last extremity...and during the dispersion of the settlers towards Pembina, the supplies, when practicable, followed them to that quarter."[33]

More Canadians came in 1820 from Montreal and Green Bay, "in the neighbourhood of Sault Ste. Marie."[34] And although the locusts returned that year, their worst ravages were over. But more gloom descended on the Colony when news of Selkirk's death reached the settlers. Their worries were mollified by Governor Simpson assurances that Selkirk's family and relatives would continue his work at Red River.[35] And they did so with great vigour. Their first expressed aim was to recruit 600 additional colonists for Red River, although this was never achieved.[36] Andrew Colvile, his wife's brother, and John Halkett, husband of Katherine, his sister, had been two of Selkirk's staunchest allies. Both were Hudson's' Bay Company grandees. Colvile, a senior partner in a firm of sugar brokers, had been a leading light in the merger negotiation with the North West Company, while Halkett had helped Selkirk in his earlier battles with the Colonial Office.[37] Halkett was quite clear that Selkirk's dream would live on:

> My opinion is, we must do everything in our power to carry on the settlement by a fair and reasonable trial for if we do not Lord Selkirk's plans will be at once knocked on the head and the whole expense which he has been at thrown away, which in fact, may eventually be regained by his family.[38]

Acting as Selkirk's representatives in Red River, Colvile and Halkett kept a close eye on land grants, the circumstances of the settlers and their progress in farming and cultivating land.[39] There were reports that the settlement had become unruly and complaints over the way the Colony was being governed.[40] Apparently promises made by Selkirk at Montreal to supply some Canadian settlers with cattle and "the articles necessary to cultivate their lands" were not being honoured. Lawlessness was rife and it was claimed that a military force was needed to protect the colonists.[41] These concerns were verified and acted upon. And their watching brief even included visits, from time to time, to the Red River settlement.[42]

The settlers' growing discontent was understandable. The merger of the two companies, in 1821, had caused a mushrooming of the Métis population to several hundred.[43] And there were conflicting lifestyles to reconcile. The Métis had hunting and fur trapping traditions, while the Kildonan settlers were trying to become full-time farmers.[44] There were also religious differences. The French Métis community was Roman Catholic and the English-speaking Métis families were on their way to becoming Anglicans. Father Joseph-Norbert Provencher had been in the Colony since 1818 while the Reverend John West, an Anglican from the Church Missionary Society, came two years later.[45] The initial steps in establishing a Catholic Mission had been taken by Selkirk, who had earmarked a fund for its support in 1815.[46] But nothing had been done for the Gaelic-speaking, Presbyterians of Kildonan. Numbering "upwards of fifty heads of family," they desperately wanted "a minister of their own tenets" who could preach in "their own language."[47]

Selkirk had promised, in 1817, that a Presbyterian clergymen would be sent; but it would take nearly 35 years for this to happen. He apparently "did not intend to go to a greater expense than £50 p.a. with board and lodgings for such a clergyman."[48] For years the Kildonan settlers would complain about "having no minister of their own" and having to attend an Anglican Church, where "they never became reconciled to the Prayer Book and would take no part in the response."[49] It was a promise that Selkirk probably wished he had never made. The Church of Scotland's North American missionary work would not begin until 1825.

The only body that he could turn to was the Anglican Church Missionary Society, whose missions had been promoting the Christian faith in remote corners of the world since 1799. One of his last deeds was to ask them to send a clergyman to act as the Protestant chaplain to the Colony. Reverend John West was appointed chaplain just seventeen days after Selkirk's death in April 1820. Travelling to Hudson Bay with John Pritchard, Selkirk's London agent, he arrived at York Factory on August 13, 1820. And Andrew Colvile had done his best to smooth the way for him. He pointedly told the Roman Catholic Governor, Alexander MacDonell, to "encourage all Protestants, Presbyterians as well as others, to attend divine service as performed by Mr. West. He will also open schools."[50]

George Simpson was pleased with the new arrivals of 1823, believing they would "relieve our establishment greatly," but it would be "necessary to assist many of them through the winter." Amongst those who came were "several who have saved considerable sums and will become useful and respectable colonists."[51] The new arrivals included Orcadians

Peter Rindisbacher's painting of the Anglican clergyman's house, Red River, Summer, 1822. *Courtesy National Archives of Canada, C-001933.*

like William Flett. Having joined the company in 1784, he retired in 1823, when "he was getting infirm." His brother George, who began work in 1796, also retired that same year and joined him. He had been "a faithful interested old servant, deficient in education, but a good trader." The Morayshire-born Alexander Ross arrived two years later with his Native wife, Sally, and four children. Having worked as a trader with the North West Company from 1813, he had led expeditions for the Hudson's Bay Company's Northern Department after the merger. He would later play a particularly active part in the social and religious life of Red River.[52]

James Sutherland, another Orcadian, from Ronaldshay, worked first as a trader at Cumberland House, on the Saskatchewan River and later as Chief Factor in charge of the Swan district.[53] He retired, in 1827, to live in the Rapids (St. Andrew's) with his Native wife, Jane Flett. A year later he told his brother in Orkney:

> I do not see what I have to go in search of in another Country – here I have everything that man requires for the good of both soul and body. Religion in its purity, the best of Climates, a soil that produces all the productions of the earth in perfection with very little labour, the society is not extensive but agreeable.[54]

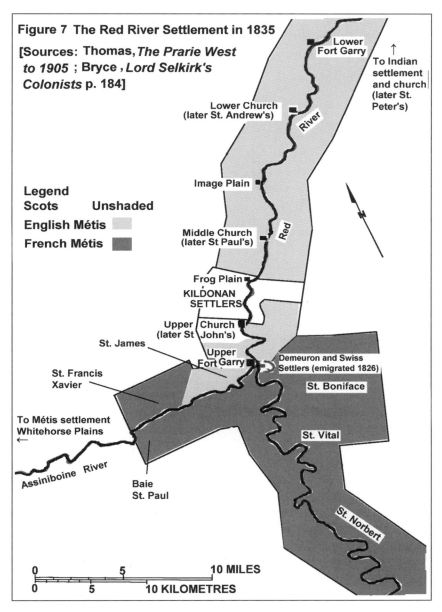

Figure 7 The Red River Settlement in 1835

[Sources: Thomas, *The Prarie West to 1905* ; Bryce , *Lord Selkirk's Colonists* p. 184]

Like Alexander Ross, James Sutherland would become a prominent settler and the Rapid's most successful farmer. In just four years he could boast about his "farm, well stocked with cattle, horses, pigs" and his ownership of "800 acres, of the best land"[55]

129

The French Métis population rose even further in 1824, when a large number of families moved to the Colony from Pembina, an area to the south of Red River. They settled along the Assiniboine River, later forming the parishes of St. Charles, St. Francois Xavier and Baie St. Paul, and along the Red River at what would later become the parishes of St. Boniface, St. Vital and St. Norbert (Figure 7).[56] Then, in 1829, a further thirty-six Orcadian families, four English and twenty Métis families came to Red River from James Bay, taking the Colony's population up to nearly 1,500.[57] Governor Simpson found them "very formidable in point of numbers." Some lived "entirely by the chase" and could not "immediately be brought to agricultural pursuits." But, although most relied on buffalo hunts, fishing and seasonal work with the Hudson's Bay Company to support themselves, most also had small farms.[58] By 1835 both the French and English-speaking Métis communities were cultivating, on average, around five to six acres annually, which was roughly half the amount cultivated by the Kildonan settlers.[59]

Then, a change in the Hudson's Bay Company recruitment policy suddenly brought men from Lewis, in the Outer Hebrides, to the region. Having faced increasing difficulties in finding suitable Orcadian men for the company's Northern Department, Governor Simpson recommended that men from Lewis should be employed as labourers. In 1831, twelve men were collected at Stromness in Orkney but, in 1832, the company ships actually came to Stornoway. Alexander Stewart, Factor of the Seaforth estate, could hardly contain his excitement:

The Hudson's Bay squadron have been in the harbour [at Stornoway] for the last four days – they have taken on board forty young men and sailed last evening.... I have taken upon myself as a present, from you, to have sent on board the ships a small supply of vegetables from the Lodge garden...they are to touch here next year and will probably continue to do so; they have not touched here before now since the year 1810.[60]

The arrival of men from Lewis soon became a regular event, making it the second most important labour source after the Orkney Islands.[61] And three men from Uig, in Lewis, had been some of the first to arrive at the Colony in 1812 (Appendices B & C). But, unlike the Orcadians, very few Lewis men remained at Red River. They never sought a lifelong career in the fur trade nor access to the farming opportunities to be had in the Colony.

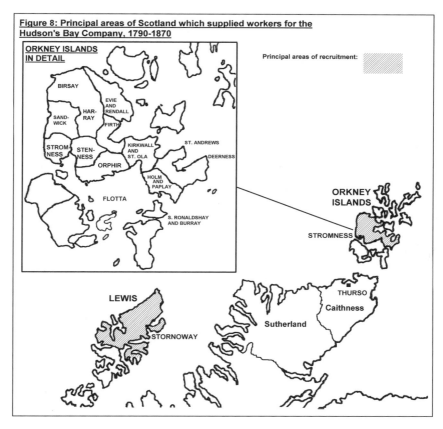

Figure 8: Principal areas of Scotland which supplied workers for the Hudson's Bay Company, 1790-1870

By 1835 Red River was principally a Métis society of some 3,000 people who derived their livelihood from the combined pursuits of fishing, hunting and farming.[62] The Kildonan settlers, were its principal farmers, but in numeric terms they were a diminishing element. Of 533 adult males, only sixty were classed as Scottish and seventy as Orcadians (Table 8).[63] They were a tiny minority. People like Thomas Anderson, Margaret Garrioch, Mary Tait and George Spence, who might be mistaken for Orcadians, had become assimilated into the Métis community.[64] More than anything the Colony was a very cosmopolitan place, having attracted retired fur traders from many countries – men like Ferdinando Sebeller from Italy, Andre Jankasky from Poland, Joseph Gugoretz from Switzerland, Peter Ezasmus from Denmark and Henry HicKenberger from Guernsey.[65] But its principal European arrivals continued to come from the Orkney Islands:

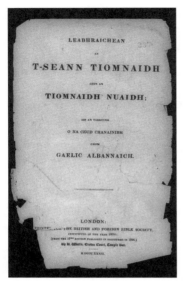

LEABHRAICHEAN
AN
T-SEANN TIOMNAIDH
AGUS AN
TIOMNAIDH NUAIDH;
AIR AN TARRUING
O NA CEUD CHANAINIBH
CHUM
GAELIC ALBANNAICH.

LONDON:
PRINTED ... BY BRITISH AND FOREIGN BIBLE SOCIETY,
(INSTITUTED IN THE YEAR 1804;)
(FROM THE 1ST EDITION PUBLISHED IN EDINBURGH IN 1826.)
By R. Watts, Crown Court, Temple Bar.
M.DCCC.XXXIX.

Front page of Gaelic Bible. It belonged to Alexander Sutherland (1784–1867) who originated from Kildonan in Sutherland. *Courtesy National Archives of Canada, C-149651.*

In whatever sphere of life they [Orkneymen] are placed, either high or low, in prosperity or adversity, their well-known habits of industry and frugality follow them…and as they had come out, not as settlers, but as servants of the Hudson's Bay Company, the greater part of them had saved more or less money, with which, when their term expired, they at once became comfortably settled…. They are generally speaking, a degree behind the Scotch settlers in point of agricultural skill, though not in point of economy.[66]

While the transformation of retired fur trade worker to Métis settler continued to augment both the French and English-speaking Métis communities, the Kildonan settlers attracted few newcomers. Selkirk had assumed that they would become "the means of attracting a great body of their friends and others from the same county." After all they had ready access to Stromness in the Orkney Islands, the port where Hudson's Bay Company ships called at regular intervals. He even hoped that the company might use its ships to take timber to Stromness and return with emigrants.[67] But timber ships never called and very few emigrants from the north of Scotland sought passages to Hudson Bay on company ships.

Alexander Sutherland's family was quite typical. He and Catherine McPherson married soon after his arrival in 1815 and moved to a river lot just outside of Kildonan, purchased from Selkirk. Both had come from "Old Kildonan."[68] The news from home was of the great numbers from both of their families who had moved to Upper Canada. Alexander's brother-in-law, William McPherson, reported that by 1823 "all the family went to Upper Canada three years this month, except Hector and me." Upper Canada's accessibility, climate and opportunities were far better than anything Red River had to offer. Two of Alexander's sisters had toyed with the idea of going to Red River in 1831 "but the Agent at Thurso would not take them without paying £10.10s. for their passage, which they did not have."[69]

TABLE 8: SCOTS AND ORCADIANS IN RED RIVER, FROM
THE 1834–35 CENSUS RETURNS*

Name	Orcadian/Scottish	Age
Anderson, Jas	O (Orcadian)	60
Arcus, George	O	n/k
Bannerman, Donald	S (Scottish)	30
Bannerman, Wm.	S	71
Bannerman, Alex.	S	28
Bram, Henry	O	36
Bremner, Jos.	S	36
Briston, Magnes	O	66
Brown, Peter	O	24
Campbell, Rob't.	S	44
Clauston, Rob't.	O	42
Corrigal, Jas.	O	n/k
Corrigall, Peter	O	n/k
Cameron, Hugh	S	41
Dunnet, Wm.	O	51
Esson, David	O	35
Firth, Thomas	O	n/k
Flett, George	O	56
Flett, John	O	51
Flett, William	O	49
Folster, John	O	65
Folster, Jas.	O	51
Forbisher, John	O	n/k
Fraser, Jas.	S	46
Gaddie, Jas.	O	n/k
Garrioch, Wm.	O	50
Gibson, Hugh	O	48
Gibson, Wm.	O	47
Gibson, Heugh	O	51
Gunn, John	S	45
Gunn, Donald	S	38
Halcro, Thomas	O	53
Henderson, Samuel	O	46
Henderson, Peter	O	40
Hourrie, John	O	56
Inkster, James	O	62
Inkster, James	O (Orcadian)	30
Inkster, James	O	n/k
Inkster, John	O	n/k
Irvine, George	O	28
Johnson, David	O	63
Johnston, George	O	38
Knight, Jas.	O	51

Name	Orcadian/Scottish	Age
Kennedy, Alexr.	O	n/k
Livingstone, Neil	S (Scottish)	74
Livingstone, James	S	42
Livingstone, John	S	27
Livingstone, Donald	S	44
Livingstone, Hugh	S	34
Logan, Robert	S	56
Luth, William	O	51
Linklater, Andrew	O	33
MacDonald, Donald	O	n/k
McDonald, Neil	S	35
McDonald, Kenneth	S	35
McDonald, Donald	S	39
McDonald, John	S	43
McLean, John	S	41
McLean, Alexander	S	43
McIntyre, John	S	44
McKay, George	S	n/k
McKay, Wm.	S	61
McKay, Robert	S	60
McBeath, Alex'r.	S	81
McBeath, John	S	44
McBeath, George	S	35
McBeath, Roderick	S	31
McBeath, Robert	S	26
McLeod, John	S	35
McKay, Charles	S	n/k
Matheson, Angus	S	22
Matheson, Angus	S	31
Matheson, Alex'r	S	53
Matheson, Alex'r.	S	63
Matheson, Angus	S	22
Matheson, James	S	32
Matheson, John	S	37
Micklejohn, William	S (Scottish)	45
Moar, John	O (Orcadian)	55
Mowat, Adam	O	63
Mowat, Edward	O	49
Mowat, Edward	O	50
Morwick, James	O	57
Morwick, John	O	49
Murray, James	S	37
Murray, Donald	S	35
Mitchell. John	S	39
Munroe, George	S	n/k
Norn, William	O	32
Oman, James	O	37

Name	Orcadian/Scottish	Age
Park, John	O	66
Polson, Alex'r.	S	58
Rose, Alex'r.	S	61
Rawland, Robert	O	51
Robertson, George	O	61
Ross, Alex'r	S	50
Ross, George	O	37
Scarth, John	O	n/k
Setter, Andrew	O	54
Sinclair, Wm.	O	46
Sinclair, Wm.	O	49
Sinclair, Donald	S	39
Slater, Jas.	O	58
Slater, John	O	34
Spence, Magnus	O	71
Spence, George	O	65
Spence, James	O	55
Spence, Joseph	O	69
Spence, Archibald	O	34
Sutherland, Alex'r. Jnr.	S	46
Sutherland, Donald	S	29
Sutherland, Ebeneezer	S	31
Sutherland, James Snr.	O	58
Sutherland, John Sr.	S	61
Sutherland, John Jr.	S	27
Sutherland, John	S	41
Sutherland, John	S	35
Sutherland, Wm.	S (Scottish)	76
Sutherland, Alex'r.	S	54
Sutherland, James	S	58
Sutherland, George	S	n/k
Tait, Jas.	O (Orcadian)	48
Tait, Wm	O	40
Tait, John	O	29
Taylor, Wm.	O	46
Taylor, James	O	41
Whiteway, James	O	53
Work, Alex'r.	O	48
Wishart, Thomas	S	n/k

* Source: NAC (C-2170)

There were many factors to deter people. The Colony had suffered violent attacks and had endured many natural disasters. There were huge distances to travel and a harsh climate. The prospect of life in a highly regulated regime, administered by the Hudson's Bay Company, was hardly going to suit most independently minded colonizers. And yet, Selkirk's vision of agricultural colonization became a reality. It seems ironic, that it was the fur trade which gave his Colony new life. It brought large numbers of Métis settlers to the Colony, giving it a viable population base. And while the many Orcadians became assimilated as Métis settlers and were separated geographically as well as culturally from the Kildonan settlers, they attracted the Anglican missionaries who would encourage the ideals of a settled, agricultural society.

The missionaries were to have a profound effect. They extolled the virtues of Christian beliefs, education and a society which derived its living from tilling the soil. They exhorted Métis and Native communities to forsake hunting and take up farming. In other words, their remit extended far beyond the task of spreading the gospel. This was the heyday of Empire, when Anglican missionaries spoke out in praise of all things British. Agriculture created settled communities, where people shared in both the work and the produce. Education and religion could build on this new form of co-operation and help create a more "civilized society." This was the doctrine they preached and sought to implement. Reverend West, and the missionaries who followed him, thus became promoters of British values.[70] Kildonan settlers now had in their midst, highly influential clergymen who shared their desire to realize Selkirk's vision of a viable, agriculturally-based society. The small log building put up by Reverend West in 1823, just to the north of the forks of the Red and Assiniboine rivers would be the Colony's first church and school.[71] Subsequently, four churches would occupy the site, with the last, built in 1926, becoming the present St. John's Cathedral.

Reverend William Cockran, who arrived in 1825, was one of the most popular of the missionaries. Concentrating his efforts, initially, on the English-speaking Métis, who lived at the Rapids, he founded a log church (later St. Andrew's) and school in 1831, which was replaced by the present stone church, completed in 1849. However, his other important achievement was in helping some of the Cree and Saulteaux peoples, who resided at the northern end of Red River, to take up farming. He would establish a new church and a new settlement:

Mr. Cockran's services at Lower Church or St. Andrew's were usually attended by a goodly sprinkling of Indians; but as the services were in English, and for that reason not very profitable to them, he decided to extend his efforts downstream, and form an Indian settlement there

St. Andrew's Anglican Church, the oldest stone church in western
Canada. Built from 1844–49, it replaced an earlier church,
founded in 1831 by Reverend William Cockran. *Photograph by
Geoff Campey.*

so that they could enjoy near home, services which could be held in
their own tongue.[72]

Cockran was lucky in having Chief Peguis' support in this venture.
By 1833, Peguis had convinced a small number of Native families to settle at Sugar Point, near present-day Selkirk. Houses were built and a
wooden church (later St. Peter's) was constructed in 1836. And while
Cockran "was initiating his protégés into the mysteries of agriculture, he
lived in his own tepee or lodge, which was made of dressed hides of buffalo or moose."[73] Around 35 acres of mission farmland were cultivated
by 1835, representing an average of one acre per person. Cultivated
acreages and livestock numbers would increase dramatically in later
years.[74] Appropriately, a memorial, at St. Peter's Church, commends Chief
Peguis for "his good offices to the early settlers" and for being "one of
the first converts to Christianity of his race."

In his brief time at Red River, John West had managed to irritate the
Presbyterian settlers by pressuring them to accept traditional Anglican
services. Relations between the two groups remained at a low ebb under
his successor, David Jones. The problem was that enormous frustration
and bitterness had been building up for years. Presbyterian Scots had contributed to the Church Missionary Society's fund-raising efforts and
supported their work, but they felt cheated by the lack of progress made

on their behalf.[75] Alexander Ross, leader of the campaign to get a Presbyterian clergyman, sent a petition to Governor Simpson in 1844.[76] It was on behalf of the "2000 persons, who may now be considered without a pastor," who complained of a broken promise:

> They had been given a solemn promise from the late earl of Selkirk that a clergyman of their own church would either accompany them…or shortly after join them…but the state of his health which rendered it necessary for him to travel to the Continent of Europe, where he unfortunately died, put an end to the hope which, then up to that period we cherished, and which has not since been realized.[77]

In the end, Ross's numerous petitions to the Hudson's Bay Company yielded results. Eden Colvile, the associate Governor of Rupert's Land offered "the sum of £150…and the grant of a reserve lot in Frog Plain in which they may erect a Church."[78] And, John Black, a Presbyterian minister finally arrived in 1851:

> Three hundred of the Selkirk colonists immediately gathered around Mr. Black and though interrupted for a year by the great flood…they erected in the following year, the stone Church of Kildonan…which still remains.[79]

The Reverend Black had not been sent from Scotland as might have been expected. Having emigrated to New York as a young boy and later

The Kildonan Church built at Frog Plain and completed in 1853.
Photograph by Geoff Campey.

A Kildonan house, built c.1830, now at Lower Fort Garry. It was originally the home of James Fraser, a Hudson's Bay Company employee and his wife Ann Bannerman. *Photograph by Geoff Campey.*

moving to Toronto, where he attended the Presbyterian Church's Free Church College (now Knox College), he became immersed in the work of the students' missionary society. Later while working in Montreal as a Presbyterian minister, he received a request from representatives of the Selkirk settlers to serve in Red River. "Nobody else would go," he told his brother, "and so I am called to go." He was an outstanding success, remaining at Kildonan for the rest of his life, and was instrumental in establishing Manitoba College.[80]

More European women had been arriving since the 1840s, changing the social balance of the Colony.[81] Fashion mattered now. Ladies like Miss Bannerman would come into Church "wearing a hoop-skirt" and "with a graceful swish of it to one side" would come "through the door into the Bannerman pew."[82] Attitudes to race and class were becoming polarized. White wives were seen as being more desirable than Métis or Native wives, and men were abandoning their Métis and Native "wives" to marry them.[83] Going against the trend, the Reverend John Black had caused quite a stir when he married Henrietta Ross, the Métis daughter of Alexander Ross. New elites were forming in a new social order, which left people of mixed ancestry increasingly marginalized. James Sutherland remained faithful to Jane, his Native wife, but he clearly felt that he had to keep up with the changes:

We now have here some rich old fellows, that [have] acquired large fortunes in the service, have got married to European females and cut a dash and have introduced a system of extravagance in the place that is followed by all who can afford it and I, to keep up a little respectability, have followed it in some way, my housekeeping expenses is double of what they were when I first came to Red River.[84]

And he was worried about his son's prospects. Although "a good scholar," he faced a future where he would be denied social advancement and employment opportunities. "Half-breeds, as they are called, have no chance, nor are they respected, whatever their abilities may be, by a parcel of upstart Scotchmen who now hold the power and control."[85] It was the same for Alexander Ross's, son James. Even, after being educated at the University of Toronto and winning prizes for his scholastic abilities, his mixed-blood origins would later prevent him from playing a part in the Colony's governing bodies.[86] Yet, while these changes brought about added tensions, the different communities appeared, for the most part, to be living comfortably with one another.

Narcisse Marion's house in St. Boniface had been the first place that Reverend John Black visited when he arrived at the colony. Narcisse, a French-speaking Roman Catholic, was renowned for his party-giving and "his house was a centre of hospitality on the St. Boniface side.... Many of the Kildonan people and the other people across the river used to come to our parties and we went to theirs." And St. John's School was attended both by the Kildonan settlers as well by "several boys and girls...belonging to the well-to-do Roman Catholic French-speaking families."[87] Alexander Sutherland's granddaughter, Catherine, could remember that "the French people used to come to the house constantly to consult my father about their affairs and in that way he came to be a link between them and the Kildonan people." As a result of this regular contact, she and her whole family "came to speak French as well as English and as we saw a great deal of the Indians, we also had a working knowledge of Cree."[88] Socializing was also free and easy. There were "the fine parties in winter" when young people would be gathered up by sleigh and taken to a house "where they knew we were coming.... The suppers at those dances were more like banquets. For music we used to have to depend on the fiddle."[89]

By 1856, Red River's population had risen to 6,522. There were 8,371 acres of land in cultivation, sixteen windmills, nine water mills and property valued at £111,000.[90] And a new economic order was evolving. After many years of opposition, the Métis had finally broken the Hudson's Bay Company fur monopoly and were becoming free traders.[91] As the fur trade economy developed, they found new occupations in the Great Lakes region, principally in the buffalo robe trade. More and more Métis were abandoning their farms and leaving the region.[92] At the same time those who remained were finding their interests increasingly jeopardized by the expected influx of settlers from Ontario. The character of the place had changed beyond all recognition and when the transition from Colony to Province came, it was marked by violence and racial strife.

In 1863, just seven years before Rupert's Land became confederated as Manitoba, the sixth Earl of Selkirk severed his family's connections with Red River:

> The Committee adjourned today at half past three. I at once got into a cab and came here to sign papers with a view to the end of our connection with the old Hudson's Bay Company. I cannot help regretting that this is the last time I shall sit here in my old place in the old Board Room, however as an old story must have an end, the Company has come to its end well and creditably and with no disadvantage to its shareholders.[93]

He received £100,000 from the sale of his shares which he planned to put into Government securities. Assiniboia, itself, had already been returned to the Company and even earlier, the Selkirk estate had been forced to relinquish its claim to that part of Assiniboia which lay south of the forty-ninth parallel.[94] The Hudson's Bay Company resigned its charter into the hands of the Crown and the British government then sold Rupert's Land to Canada for £300,000.

Selkirk's so-called "rage for colonization" had brought many Scots to Northwest Canada at a crucial point in its history. A reluctant British government stood by as Selkirk launched his Colony, not believing the region to have any value. He alone had recognized its agricultural potential. The venture had cost the lives of at least twenty-one of his colonists, shortened his own life and consumed much of his fortune. But by establishing this British anchor, in a region deemed fit only for the fur trade, Selkirk and his settlers ensured that Canada's vast western territories remained intact until they could be incorporated into the Canadian Confederation. It was a momentous achievement.

Selkirk always regarded himself as directing the exodus from Scotland rather than promoting it. He chose both his recruits and where they went very carefully. Belfast, in Prince Edward Island was the one region of British America where he could acquire large quantities of land on which to settle several hundred colonizers. On the other hand, Baldoon and Red

River were chosen for their strategic locations, not because they could accommodate large numbers of settlers. Belfast's colonizers came primarily from Skye, Wester Ross and South Uist, Baldoon's settlers from Argyll and Red River's colonizers from Sutherland and the Orkney Islands. In each case, Selkirk's recruitment campaigns had been well targeted. Together, these colonizers would contribute greatly to Canada's rich Scottish heritage and influence the development of Canadian society.

8. LATER DEVELOPMENTS AT BELFAST, BALDOON & RED RIVER

It is with regret I have heard persons of distinguished judgement and information give way to the opinion, that all our colonies on the continent of America, and particularly the Canadas, must inevitably fall, at no distant period of time, under the dominion of the United States. That continued mismanagement may bring this about, cannot be denied; but, I think it equally clear, that, by steadily pursuing a proper system, such an event may be rendered not only improbable, but also impossible.

The danger to be apprehended, is not merely from an invading military force, but much more from the disposition of the colonists themselves, the republican principles of some, and the lukewarm affection of others.[1]

WHEN SELKIRK WROTE HIS *Observations on the Present State of the Highlands*, published in 1805, he provided the first ever blueprint for colonization. It gave a coherent strategy for relocating Scots to British America and set out actual procedures for creating pioneer settlements. No one else at that time came close to understanding the issues involved. The British government's policies for promoting colonization were based on devolving responsibility for settlement creation to proprietors. They were expected to relocate emigrants on the land granted to them, but few did. Only land speculators prospered under the government's approach while settlers had obstacles placed in their way. They had only limited access to land and had to cope with a bureaucratic muddle which placed their needs last. Small settlements, scattered over huge distances, were the result.[2]

Selkirk had discovered this pattern of small, pioneer settlements in some areas of the United States. In his visit to the Highlands in 1792, he had met people whose relatives and friends had emigrated to New York and Georgia. He noticed that they had settled in distinct groups. There was a separate settlement for each Highland district involved in the exodus.

And as news of each group's success filtered home, each continued to attract "the peculiar attention" of the Highland district from which they came. Thus, "no one of these settlements gained a universal ascendancy." While Selkirk certainly had no desire to help in the colonization of the United States, there was a valuable lesson to be learned. Left to themselves, emigrants created a number of small settlements rather than one or two major centres of population. And Selkirk was concerned that if this trend continued in the British American colonies, they would suffer interference from their neighbour to the south. American "intruders" were beginning to dominate in some areas and soon they would be "infecting the mass of the people throughout the provinces."[3]

While there was always the risk of an attack from the United States, Selkirk believed that the more immediate danger came from what he termed "American influences." He believed that American culture was so pervasive that it threatened to take over whole communities. Settlers, who were distributed in small clusters, over large areas, were particularly vulnerable. He advocated the bringing together of emigrants to one or two locations. This would produce well-populated and culturally distinctive settlements. Highland emigrants were his first choice. Their Gaelic language and strong Highland traditions would set them apart. Once relocated they would defend their way of life and be confident enough to withstand external pressures. Thus, Selkirk sought to direct the Highland exodus to specific locations in British America. His principal aim was to strengthen British America's security, although he also had humanitarian motives at heart.

Persistent poverty in the Highlands and the displacement caused by the introduction of new farming methods were factors in the growing zeal being shown for emigration. Selkirk had been moved by the extreme poverty that he had witnessed during his visit. While most of his contemporaries fretted about the harm being done to Scotland, by the loss of Highlanders to the colonies, Selkirk sought to help those who wished to emigrate. He realized that, while many Highlanders were looking for an orderly escape from their poverty, they also wanted to maintain their way of life. Factory jobs in the manufacturing Lowlands would require them to surrender their cultural roots, but emigration provided the means to transplant Highland customs and traditions into New World communities. It was this prospect, more than anything else, which made emigration such an unstoppable force in the Highlands. Scottish landlords flatly refused to accept Selkirk's assertion that emigration was an inevitable outcome of very harsh economic conditions. They believed that, with a sufficient amount of persuasion, their tenants would see the error of their ways. They accused Selkirk of stimulating the exodus by offering inducements. His well-financed colonization schemes have to be seen as great facilitators of the emigration process, but they were not inducements. As Selkirk realized, people did not take the decision to emigrate lightly. "To emigrate implies a degree of violence to many of the strongest feelings of human nature – a separation from a number of connections dear to the heart," which few people "can resolve upon without absolute necessity."[4] Selkirk sought only to intervene in the choice of location, not the decision to emigrate.

For him, emigration was a socially desirable mechanism. It had the potential to bring material benefits to Highlanders and a much-needed population to the British American colonies. Many years later, public opinion would come to recognize the wisdom of Selkirk's arguments, but in 1803, when he sought to launch his first venture, emigration was resisted with great fury and determination. Even so, Selkirk's contribution to the debate ought to have pleased Whitehall since the government shared his view that British America's security needed to be strengthened.

It had long been government policy to build up civilian populations in areas which were thought to be vulnerable to American attacks. This had been done by relocating discharged soldiers and officers to key boundary areas in Upper and Lower Canada and in the Maritimes. Selkirk was planning to use Highlanders to achieve the same end. And he was offering to finance their relocation himself. His proposal to bring large numbers of Highlanders to Sault Ste. Marie would have placed them at a highly strategic site on the American border. Yet, his request for land was rejected. Given the strength of anti-emigration feeling, the government could not be seen to be supporting him directly by granting him land.

However, the government sensibly found discreet ways of directing Selkirk's colonization efforts. Prince Edward Island desperately needed more settlers and much of its land could be purchased from private individuals. So he was steered in that direction, with the result that hundreds of Highlanders emigrated to Belfast. He then acquired a small quantity of land, in an important location, next to the American border and established Baldoon in Upper Canada. He had wanted to found a much bigger colony but had failed to get sufficient land from the government. He essentially lost out to Upper Canada's chief colonizer, Colonel Thomas Talbot.[5] Unlike Selkirk, Talbot was based entirely in Upper Canada. He never tried to recruit settlers, but merely accepted, or rejected, those who came to him. He played no part in the Scottish emigration controversy and could

145

thus be granted land without antagonizing Scottish landlords. Selkirk's only real success in obtaining both a large quantity of land and a strategic location was at Red River. There he had dealt with the Hudson's Bay Company rather than the government.

The Prince Edward Island expedition of 1803 was an immediate success; so much so, that Selkirk devoted a whole chapter, in his book, *Observations on the Present State of the Highlands,* to the colonization principles he had adopted.[6] His illustrations, using actual examples of settler experiences on the Island, had a powerful effect on the emigration debate. Public opinion began to move in Selkirk's direction as people comprehended how emigrants had been able to grasp farming opportunities in Prince Edward Island. And he built on these initial successes. For seven years after the initial founding of his P.E.I. settlements, Selkirk continued to employ agents to organize ship departures for Highlanders who wished to relocate to the Island.

In 1810, his former agent, Dr. Angus MacAulay, claimed that the ships, which were arriving from Scotland, carried "poor ignorant wretches," who were being "deluded by false and exaggerated accounts of the Island." This was a blatant attack on Selkirk, but it failed. It was known that MacAulay felt extremely bitter over Selkirk's choice of James Williams, over himself, as his principal agent in Prince Edward Island. As well, he could offer no proof for his allegations. John MacDonald of Glenaladale thought MacAulay "mischievous on every occasion" and "considered him as a madman." Belfast was "as respectable a settlement as any in the Colony, if not more so" wrote Glenaladale. "I hear that they have cleared a great deal from the woods and that they are far more sober than the others."[7]

Ten years later William Johnston, who later succeeded James Williams as agent, gave Selkirk another heartening account of life at Belfast. "These poor people whom your Lordship brought hither have universally bettered their condition" and "are contented and happy."[8] And two years after this, another Walter Johnstone commented on Belfast's residents. A staunch Presbyterian, he had arrived on a Sunday:

> Many of them could read none, and scarcely any of them had a single copy of the Scriptures in their possession. They were in the habit of meeting on this day in crowds, and in open places in the woods, and then all kinds of amusements went on. Feats of bodily strength, or vigour were performed, such as running, wrestling, leaping and throwing stones. The older people looked on at the feats of the young and filled up vacant moments with worldly and corrupt conversation.[9]

Photograph of Uig Bay in Skye taken c. 1909. Large numbers of emigrants came from Uig in 1829 to found Uigg (Lot 50) in Prince Edward Island. *Courtesy of Aberdeen University, George Washington Wilson Photographic Archive, E3603.*

Not to Walter Johnstone's liking, but this is exactly what Selkirk had intended would happen. A vigorous and lively group of Highlanders were upholding their traditions. And when eighty-four families from Skye arrived in 1829 to settle next to Belfast, at lot 50, the region's distinctively Scottish way of life received an added boost.

The newly arrived families appropriately dubbed their new home Uigg, in honour of Uig, their former home in northeast Skye. The influx, which had been triggered by a severe downturn in kelp production and a general industrial depression, was followed by even more arrivals from Skye, Rasaay and North Uist throughout the 1830s and 1840s (Figure 9).[10] As was the case before, these were groups of extended families from Lord MacDonald's estates.[11] They immediately assembled themselves together in cohesive communities, settling at previously-established Skye footholds in Belfast (lots 57 and 58) Flat River (lot 60) and Wood Islands (lot 62) and opening up new ones at Murray Harbour (lot 64), Dundas (lot 55) and Breadalbane (lot 67).[12]

While the Island attracted many families from Skye, it also lost some if its original Wester Ross families to Cape Breton. Angus MacAulay had led the initial attempt, in 1807, to relocate "a considerable number of Protestant families" but this had failed. Success came in 1811 when a number of MacRae and Campbell families, from Applecross, who had emigrated to the Island in 1803, established a major settlement at Middle River, to the north of Bras d'Or Lake.[13] Thus, a by-product of Selkirk's 1803 venture had been the founding of one of Cape Breton's first Scottish Presbyterian communities.[14]

However, most of the original families remained on the Island. They continued to attract further emigrants from Scotland, for a short while; but numbers declined to a trickle, from the 1830s, as Upper Canada's greater accessibility and better prospects made it the preferred option for most people. But Skye was different. Skye emigrants rejected Upper Canada and remained loyal to the Island. This is what Selkirk had hoped would happen. Large, culturally-distinctive Scottish settlements, begun in 1803, were able to draw fresh recruits from Skye over a period of some forty years. They attracted Skye people precisely because they had preserved their cultural identity. It was a virtuous cycle which would ensure the dominance of Highland culture in Belfast and nearby townships.

Highland culture would prevail at Baldoon, as well, although to a much more limited extent. If Selkirk's contemporaries and many later commentators are to be believed, Baldoon was an unmitigated disaster.[15] But this was not so. Selkirk's Home Farm certainly proved a dismal failure. After experiencing heavy losses he had to sell up, to recover what he could; but his colonists surpassed themselves. They persevered against all the odds, remaining immensely loyal both to Baldoon and to their Scottish roots. From 1822 they began moving the nucleus of their settlement, a

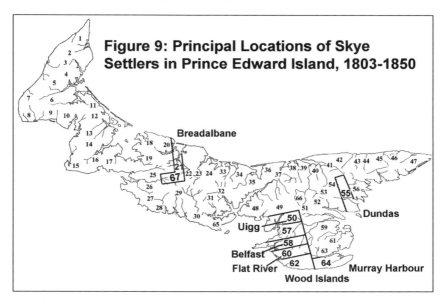

Figure 9: Principal Locations of Skye Settlers in Prince Edward Island, 1803-1850

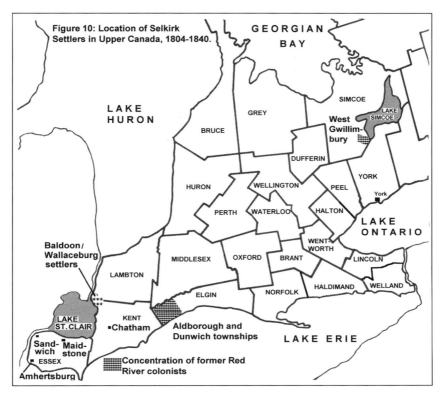

Figure 10: Location of Selkirk Settlers in Upper Canada, 1804-1840.

short distance to the north, to a better site in Chatham Gore. Naming their new settlement, in 1830, after no less a man than Sir William Wallace, the founder of Scottish nationalism, the Baldoon settlers created the important commercial centre of Wallaceburg. In all the circumstances this was an amazing and heroic achievement.

Of course, looked at in terms of just size, Baldoon was a small and fairly insignificant Highland community. But when location is taken into account its importance increases. Situated close to the American border, the Baldoon settlers were Selkirk's civilian army. Baldoon was invaded and pillaged twice by American soldiers in 1812, and again in 1814; each time his settlers were there to pick up the pieces and rebuild their communities. They were defenders of territory and upholders of Highland customs and traditions, just as Selkirk had intended. And with their mainly Argyll origins, they helped to re-enforce Argyll's dominance amongst Scots in Kent County.[16] It may be that they also played some part in the founding, in 1830, of another "Scotch Settlement," in Maidstone township, in

Memorial plaque commemorating the founding, in 1819, of the "Scotch Settlement" at West Gwillimbury (now Bradford) in Simcoe County Ontario. *Photograph by Geoff Campey.*

Essex County, at the southern end of Lake St. Clair (Figure 10).[17] It, too, was close to the American border. But Selkirk's influence in Upper Canada went beyond what was achieved with his Baldoon venture.

Upper Canada had attracted some of his Red River colonists. The turmoil, which came to a head in 1815, and the North West Company's offer of land and free passages to Upper Canada had persuaded one hundred and thirty-four people to leave Red River. Travelling by canoe with a North West Company escort, they first went to Fort William. Then having transferred to a fleet of small boats, they crossed Lake Superior and entered Lake Huron. There they split into two groups. The first group went down Lake Huron to Lake St. Clair and on to Lake Erie, to settle at Aldborough and Dunwich townships, in Elgin County, on land which belonged to Thomas Talbot.[18] The second group crossed into Georgian Bay, landed at Penetanguishene and waited for land to become available.

From an initial grant of 5,000 acres, Talbot managed to gain control over hundreds of thousands of acres. He had acquired what Selkirk so passionately desired and failed to get. He commanded colonization operations, on a grand scale, in border country. His land was on the north shore of Lake Erie along the American border. However, Selkirk could

Site of the "Auld Kirk" at West Gwillimbury. A timber-framed church, constructed in 1827, replaced a log cabin built in 1823. *Photograph by Geoff Campey.*

take some satisfaction. The government's instructions to Talbot stipulated the creation of a compact colony. The strategy he had recommended to government was being adopted, although Talbot gave it his own interpretation.[19]

While Talbot was considered to be a good manager, he hoarded land, much as a speculator would. He ignored the conditions of his grant and systematically withheld huge tracts of land from settlement or even improvement. Thus large areas were left vacant, creating dispersed settlements. And yet Talbot was Upper Canada's most successful colonizer. He spent considerable sums of his own money on road building, set strict targets for his settlers and, in the end, produced a string of flourishing settlements.[20] In fact, it was Talbot's road, linking Sandwich with Aldborough and Dunwich townships which had enabled Selkirk's Red River colonists to actually get to his land. They were joined three years later by a large influx of Argyll colonists, who settled in Aldborough, about 30 miles to the west of present-day St. Thomas.[21]

Meanwhile, the second Red River group reached to Simcoe County in 1815. Having arrived at Penetanguishene, they travelled by road to Kempenfelt Bay, then crossed Lake Simcoe to the mouth of the Holland River, arriving at frontier settlements on Yonge Street. They acquired their land at West Gwillimbury some four years later. Travelling up the Holland River, they landed at the 3rd Concession and founded the "Scotch Settlement." Included amongst its first settlers were: Donald Sutherland,

151

James Wallace, John Armstrong, Hanan and William Sutherland, James and Roderick MacKay.[22] Located on the west side of the River, at the southern end of the township, it acquired its first Presbyterian church on lot 8, in the 6th Concession, in 1823. A log cabin, it was replaced by a small timber-framed church four years later. While the settlement prospered initially, it later became a deserted site with an "Auld Kirk."[23]

Thus, the former Red River colonists succeeded in re-enforcing major Scottish settlements at Aldborough and Dunwich and in establishing a small, but short-lived, population centre of their own at West Gwillimbury. Aldborough and Dunwich became predominantly Argyll centres of population, while West Gwillimbury probably lost its later inhabitants to the large Scottish enclaves which developed at Nottawasaga, further to the north in Simcoe County, and in Grey County.[24]

People like Catherine MacPherson, who remained in Red River throughout the troubles, would have lost some of their relatives and friends to Elgin and Simcoe counties. Her husband, Alexander Sutherland, who arrived after the removals of 1815, also ended up being separated from much of his family. His branch of the Sutherland family emigrated from Kildonan, in Sutherland to Upper Canada during the 1820s. Catherine and Alexander's mutual friends included, George Bannerman, great-grandfather of John Deifenbaker, who by 1844 was installed at West Gwillimbury, and George McBeath who had become one of Thomas Talbot's agents, and who was said to "help him greatly."[25] None of their relatives and friends joined them at Red River.[26] This was typical of the others as well. And yet, the Red River colony produced as strong a bastion of Highland culture and tradition as was ever to be found in British America.

Selkirk's policy, of granting the various communities in Red River their own separate lands, ensured that each community would expand within its particular boundaries. W.L. Morton tells us of the "solidly occupied" Red River lots of 1871 where "the farmsteads of the half-breeds and the Orkney and Kildonan Scottish settlers presented an almost unbroken line along the west bank" of the Red River.[27] This is exactly how Red River would have appeared in 1835 (Figure 7); and, but for the loss of the de Meuron and Swiss settlers, how it would have been described in the 1820s. Consequently, over the years, Métis and Kildonan families had been able to preserve quite separate communities in their own designated parishes. But these harmonious arrangement became increasingly unstable as pressure mounted, in the late 1850s, to hasten the end of Hudson's Bay Company rule in the region and to transfer Red River to Canada.

John Gunn wrote to his brother, James Ross in Toronto, that Red River was "in a regular ferment about getting joined to Canada.... We are determined never to relax our efforts until their [the Hudson's Bay Company] despotic power is laid in the dust, and we are protected by the noble fabric of the British constitution which has been reared by wisdom and cemented by the blood of our forefathers." Gunn was certain that a petition, requesting "the protection of the Canadian government's laws and institutions," would be "a numerously signed one."[28] It was. The petition won wholehearted support from Red River's Scots and English-speaking Métis. Organized by Captain William Kennedy, a Métis, of Orcadian and Cree descent, it was presented to the Parliamentary Select Committee on the Hudson's Bay Company which sat in 1857.[29] The government was persuaded to act.

Plans to transfer the Northwest to Canada began in earnest in 1869, arousing strong feelings from the French Métis, who were understandably outraged at not being consulted in the matter. Concerned that their status, land rights and way of life would be threatened by Canada's takeover of their region, they mounted a campaign of resistance, which was led by Louis Riel.[30] With their support concentrated almost entirely amongst French-speaking Métis, the Resistance of 1869-70 ultimately failed. A military expedition sent in 1870 to Red River, by the Canadian government, secured Canada's authority over the new province, but the resentment and bitter feelings lived on.[31]

Selkirk's Red River colonists focused the attention of both the British and Canadian governments at a particularly crucial time. Their protestations, that they were British and wanted to be treated "like all Her Majesty's subjects in any other British colony," put down an important marker. In 1869, just a year before Manitoba joined the Dominion, the Hudson's Bay Company Governor had been predicting that Rupert's Land's annexation to the United States was unavoidable. The Americans had been hankering after the region's fertile lands for some thirty years. But for the existence of the Red River colony, this vast territory would almost certainly have been lost to the United States. Once again, Selkirk had been proved right. He had foreseen these possibilities decades before anyone else. His colonists had presided over the region and kept it intact until Britain and Canada woke up to its potential and sought to include it in the Confederation of Canada.[32]

Although people from Kildonan and St. Andrew's had campaigned as one on the annexation issue, they did not benefit equally from the outcome. The Métis of St. Andrew's, who were predominately of Orcadian ancestry, had expected to do well out of the new arrangements. They broadly welcomed the expected influx into the region of large numbers of Protestant, English-speaking settlers from Ontario. They hoped to play a major part in Manitoba's development; but their influence waned as political power moved into the hands of the new arrivals from Ontario.[33] The bigotry and intolerance shown to so-called "half-breed's" blocked their integration into Red River society and many left the area. In this way, the Kildonan Scots of Red River lost many of their Orcadian mixed-blood neighbours and in their place came large numbers of migrants from Ontario, many of whom were Scots. And as Red River became Winnipeg, and colonization progressed beyond its boundaries, the influx from Ontario and Britain gathered pace.

New settlements began to appear in the early 1880s, even before the railway networks were fully completed. Initially, they formed along the old Saskatchewan Trail. A wagon trail, which went west from Upper Fort Garry, at the forks of the Red and Assiniboine rivers, it extended some 500 miles to Fort Carleton. A branch of the Trail went southwest from Beaver Hill to South Qu'Appelle (Figure 11).[34] And Scottish immigrants were to be found in small settlements along or near this trail. With their early domination of the fur trade, and their extensive investment in the railways and land companies, it is not surprising that Scots would be so well-represented.[35] But, curiously, most Scots who came to settle, at this time, originated from the Orkney and Outer Hebridean Islands. These were regions which had associations with the North American fur trade, and more specifically with the Hudson's Bay Company.

Orcadian and Lewis men had been employed regularly by the company on short-term contracts. Returning home to the Orkney Islands, when they completed their contracts, men like John Thomson of Eday and Alexander Watt from Stromness, who worked for the Hudson's Bay Company in the early 1870s, could bring back first-hand accounts of their experiences.[36] Donald MacLeod, from Berneray in Harris, had worked in the region during the 1850s, and after returning home acquired the new name of *Talmhainn Fhuair* – Donald of the Cold Country. There were probably several men like Donald Macleod in the Outer Hebrides who could describe the agricultural and job prospects of the Canadian North West from personal observation. This was an inside track which they alone possessed. Going west in Red River carts along the old Sasketchewan Trail, settlers from the Orkney Islands, Harris, Lewis, Benbecula and North and South Uist were amongst the first emigrant Scots to come to the region after Confederation.[37]

154

Once again, the fur trade, which had initially hampered agricultural progress in the North West, drew Scots to the region. Impoverished crofters came in search of better prospects just as they had done decades earlier, only now they came as settlers, with their families, not as fur trade workers. And in doing this, they had to make the gigantic leap from small crofter to prairie homesteader, without the requisite farming skills. In 1882, a group from Eday in the Orkney Islands founded Orcadia, north of what is now Yorkton in 1882, having purchased their land from the York Farmers' Colonization Company. And many more Orkney families came in the years which followed.[38] A year later Binscarth was founded. Named after William Bain Scarth, a descendant of the Binscarths of the Orkney Islands, who was a director of the Ontario and Manitoba Land Company, it initially attracted 70 Scottish families from Ontario.[39]

Tombstone, West Gwillimbury cemetery – "To the memory of Isabella, wife of George MacKay, who died Feb. 18, 1851 aged 95 years, native of County Sutherland, Scotland." *Photograph by Geoff Campey.*

A year later around three hundred and fifty crofters, from Benbecula and South Uist, in the Outer Hebrides, founded St. Andrew's and Benbecula near Moosomin and Wapella, having been assisted financially by Lady Cathcart, their landlord. Some five years later about seventy-nine families from Lewis, Harris and North Uist established homesteads at Killarney and Saltcoats under a colonization scheme, which was financed by the British government. All were successful apart from the Saltcoats settlement which failed largely because of administrative failures, its poor location and adverse climatic conditions.[40]

The Lowlanders who came to Moffat, near Wolseley, were part of the later influx which came with the completion of the railroads. Moffat had been founded by English and Irish settlers from Ontario and Quebec and these later arrivals from Scotland eventually became the predominant settlers.[41] This pattern would continue and escalate. Spurred on by the region's agricultural potential and the onset of a great agricultural depression at home, the flow of British immigration reached flood proportions from the early twentieth century.

Reconstructed Red River Cart at Lower Fort Garry. Constructed entirely of wood and leather, the carts were pulled by oxen or horses. *Photograph by Geoff Campey.*

When Selkirk began his colonization ventures a century earlier, success was far from guaranteed. Belfast's progress won grudging acceptance, but he and his settlers were judged to have floundered at Baldoon and Red River. Few people understood that Selkirk was a driven man. Strong humanitarian and patriotic emotions caused him to devote his life and fortune to the relocation of impoverished Highlanders. The vested interest groups of his day hoped he would fail and discredited him and all he stood for. He died without realizing just how colossal his impact would be. And important as he was to Belfast, Baldoon and Red River, Selkirk's influence on Canada extended even further.

9. SELKIRK & HIS SETTLERS

He was a philanthropist. Some of his contemporaries said that he was a hundred years ahead of his time not knowing that they were one hundred years behind theirs.[1]

WITH REMARKABLE BREVITY, REVEREND A.C. Garrioch outlines Selkirk's dilemma. To modern eyes, Selkirk's desire to alleviate suffering in the Highlands seems highly commendable. But in an era when the masses were meant to serve the needs of the few, such thinking was controversial and threatening. In the early nineteenth century, Highland society was still steeped in feudal traditions and attitudes. Landlords' private interests determined how they treated their tenants. They had adopted more productive farming methods and, in doing so, caused considerable upheaval and devastation to their tenantry. Life in the Highlands was precarious at the best of times; these developments made a bad situation worse and greatly heightened the temptation to emigrate. Selkirk offered people an escape route to British America. But this was a time when landlords felt that they should dictate what happened to their tenantry.

Fearing the depletion of their estates, landlords opposed his colonization schemes, even when their tenants were surplus to requirements. The owners of great estates were simply "unwilling to relinquish the ancient splendour of a numerous train of dependants."[2] They put obstacles in Selkirk's way and accused him of being a self-seeking, land speculator. But he was driven entirely by humanitarian motives. He had grasped the new concepts of social justice and liberty which flowed from the Scottish Enlightenment and offered emigration as a practical remedy for the poor and dispossessed. Although some of his thinking may have found support within the Edinburgh intelligentsia, his views on emigration were fiercely opposed by Scotland's ruling classes. Seeing the world differently, he lived ahead of his time. He would introduce his radical schemes, challenge vested interests and ultimately be proven right.

Although Selkirk was himself a wealthy aristocrat, he transcended and challenged the world of the rich and powerful. By becoming an advocate for emigration, he sided with the people over the landlords. His Edinburgh professor, Dugald Stewart, warned him of the dangers he faced in doing battle with well-connected and prestigious men. He would become "obnoxious to government," risk being ridiculed and vilified by his peers and, if he were to fail, he would suffer "the reproach of being the author of all the disappointments and miseries" which lay ahead.[3]

Selkirk pressed on. His critics thought him obstinate and foolhardy, but his settlers and friends admired his persistence and courage. He was a forceful, yet shy man. When he made his maiden speech in the House of Lords he spoke in such a low voice that he could hardly be heard. Yet this was the same charismatic man who raised the spirits of his settlers through the force of his character and commanding presence. It was his liberal views that freed him from religious prejudice and constraints. His first colonization proposal had been designed for Irish Catholics. He took Catholic settlers from South Uist to Prince Edward Island, tried to attract Catholic Glengarry Highlanders to his Baldoon settlement, appointed Miles MacDonell, a Roman Catholic, as Red River's first Governor and helped its local Métis community acquire a Catholic priest. In addition to being broad-minded, he was also compassionate. He hated the cruelty and brutality of the fur trade and, with William Wilberforce's help, campaigned for improved working practices and conditions.[4] But he also had the practical and hard-nosed skills of a good administrator and planner.

He was a kind-hearted man with a keen intellect and had boundless energy, masterly gifts in assembling ideas and people, and a steely determination to succeed. Arriving at Prince Edward Island in 1803 with 800 frightened and sceptical Highlanders, he broke through the confusion and conflict, and within a month had the new arrivals building houses and clearing land. Of course his other important asset was his great wealth. It enabled him to turn his intellectual theories into practice. And he spent quite staggering sums, so much so, that his wife wondered whether their son would live to see his inheritance:

> I acknowledge I cannot swallow the exchange of St. Mary's Isle for your kingdom on Red River. Could you please deprive Daer [their son] of his title; you have a right to prefer that exchange if you like but, as it is, while he lives, you are in duty bound to leave him independent at home…year after year passed and we are always deeper into the mire.[5]

At the time of his death, in 1820, his debts amounted to £160,000, his property in North America was considered unsaleable and the Hudson's Bay Company, whose shares he held, was nearly bankrupt.[6] Peter Fidler estimated that, by 1816, Red River had cost him £40,000.[7] Between 1815 and 1823 Selkirk or his family were said to have spent around £114,000 on his three settlements. That is nearly six million pounds in today's money.[8] But although these vast sums were spent, the family remained solvent and later benefited from the steep rise in the value of their Hudson's Bay Company shares.[9]

Dugald Stewart was right when he predicted that Selkirk would suffer for his convictions. But some battles were easier to win than others. His book, *Observations on the Present State of the Highlands,* changed attitudes fairly quickly, largely because he could demonstrate the feasibility of his colonization ideas from his experiences at Belfast. He won the intellectual argument convincingly and caused public opinion to shift in his favour. He would live to see his policies on emigration being adopted by the British government and pursued with great eagerness by the very landlords who had earlier thrown obstacles in his way.[10] But Baldoon and Red River marked a downturn in his fortunes. Early setbacks at Baldoon led to premature predictions of failure while his conflicts with the North West Company over Red River left his reputation in tatters. Even so, his gritty determination to defend his beliefs and his settlers never wavered.

Selkirk's actions were judged most harshly and unfairly at Red River. He was criticized for having taken settlers to a dangerous and "dreary wilderness." Dr. John Strachan claimed that his Red River venture was "one of the most gross impositions that was ever attempted on the British public."[11] His conduct in seeking to rescue his settlers from the misdeeds and treachery of the North West Company, through the use of a private army, greatly damaged his public persona. No longer the shy and kindly colonizer, he became the bold and aggressive enemy of the fur trade. By resisting arrest he became a common outlaw, on the run. And from the Colonial Office down, the entire British establishment turned against him.

He was blamed for the downfall of the North West Company and the job losses which followed the merger with the Hudson's Bay Company. His intervention had "meant the end of that picturesque group of fur-trade magnates who had made Montreal famous for its hospitality." And, after a little more than a century, no more than "a handful of those in whose veins runs the blood of the lords of the lakes and forests" were still to be found in Montreal.[12] Such romantic imagery of the dashing and daring men of the fur trade, and the dangers inherent in the trade itself, helped the North West Company to win public sympathy. Selkirk's venture threatened their very survival. In Chief Peguis' words it was like "a dagger at their heart, striking at the vitals of their commerce."[13]

Although Selkirk had hastened the company's downfall; he had not caused it. The fur trade was a transport and bartering business. The North West Company's much longer, inland routes made its transport costs more than double those of the Hudson's Bay Company. As the beaver was hunted almost to extinction, in the westward progression of the fur trade, the competitive gap widened. The company's efforts in opposing Selkirk would have added to its financial difficulties, but in the end, the company was bound to go under. Even so, Selkirk got the blame and, as George Bryce ruefully observed many years later:

> Instead of being the philanthropic promoter of settlement at Red River he was represented as the greedy, vindictive and unscrupulous invader of the rights of that meek and docile flock – the North West Company.[14]

Unfortunately, Selkirk's Red River battles diverted attention away from his other activities and achievements. He, more than anyone else in his day, recognized the importance of strategically-placed settlements to British America's long-term security. Government measures had dealt with the security of some vulnerable boundaries, but Selkirk's thinking went beyond this. He realized that insufficient regard was being given to the process of settlement. The colonies were perceived to have little value beyond their role in serving Britain's military and mercantile interests. Coherent policies were needed to promote compact settlements at advantageous sites. Failure to do so would leave them sparsely populated and vulnerable to American expansionism and influence.

His foresight, and willingness to take action himself, helped to stem American influences at a critical time in Canada's development. Yet, he got no credit for having raised the alarm. By bringing 800 Highlanders to Prince Edward Island, in 1803, he established an early and major Scottish nucleus in the eastern Maritimes. His many Skye emigrants would have quite happily gone to North Carolina had he not intervened.[15] They attracted many followers and contributed greatly to the growing influx to Prince Edward Island from the Highlands and Islands. And there were also spin-offs for Cape Breton and Nova Scotia. They too attracted great numbers from the same Highland areas where Selkirk's agents had been most active. Knowledge of New World opportunities and the

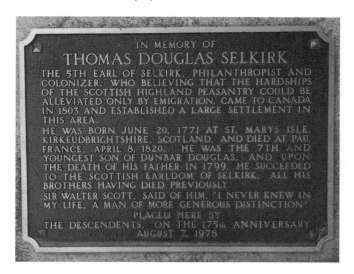

Memorial to Lord Selkirk at Orwell Bay, Prince Edward Island.
Photograph by Geoff Campey.

proven successes of those who had gone before all stimulated interest in emigration. The vital point for Canada was that instead of being drawn to the United States, these people were relocating themselves in the Eastern Maritimes. They brought their rich traditions of Scottish culture to Canada and in doing so helped to secure its distinctively Canadian future.

Selkirk developed his thinking a stage further at Baldoon. This was a site he chose for its strategic importance in relation to the American border along the north west side of Lake Erie. The government later incorporated his schemes and arguments in using civilian settlers to defend key border areas.[16] Upper Canada's sparse and scattered population had been put in jeopardy during the War of 1812. This prompted the government to take preventative action. Realizing the immense cost and impracticality of defending its long borders with military personnel, it encouraged emigrant Scots to take up land in designated areas within the Rideau Valley. There were even public subsidies to fund emigrant transport and land. Around 700 Scots went to the militarily-designated townships in Lanark County in 1815, and were followed by hundreds more in 1818, 1820 and 1821.[17] The government acknowledged that emigration had its uses. Selkirk had been right all along.

Selkirk's battles with the North West Company have excited much interest from historians. Far less attention has been paid to his colonization policies and the contribution of his settlers. There was no guarantee

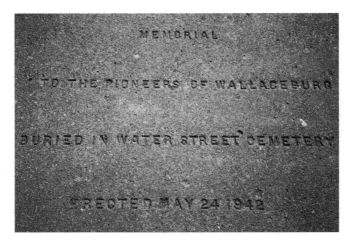

Plaque at the pioneer cemetery in Wallaceburg. *Courtesy of the Wallaceburg and District Museum.*

of success. Selkirk painstakingly researched and planned every detail of each enterprise he undertook. The layout of settler lots, the building of mills and roads, methods for transporting sheep, how food supplies would be stored, were all considered in meticulous detail. He was familiar with the methods which Charles Williamson used in forming his settlements at Genesee in New York State. His Diary reveals that he had been "anxious to apply Williamson's principle of setting down the lots round a central point for a village." Then, after seeing the lie of the land at Belfast, he modified this principle in line with settler preferences.[18] At Baldoon, he had recognized the crucial importance of recruiting families with teenage sons. Without them the settlement would never have survived the terrible malaria outbreak which claimed so many lives. And at Red River, his foresight in offering land to retired fur trade workers from the Orkney Islands, his allocation of separate territories to the different ethnic groups, and the encouragement given to Anglican missionaries by him and his family were key factors in its success.

Selkirk's settlers are wrongly perceived as having only peripheral importance. They were crucial players in their own right. As Selkirk realized when he arrived at Prince Edward Island, they were tough and skilful negotiators. He only won their co-operation after very hard bargaining. His settlers sought the best possible outcome for themselves. They did the same at Red River. This was why so many of them took up Duncan Cameron's offer to go to Upper Canada. They chose what they considered to be the better alternative in changed circumstances. And when problems arose, they showed their ability to adapt to the uncertainties and rigours of pioneer life. When faced with swampy conditions at Baldoon, the settlers moved, of their own accord, to more favourable locations of their own choosing. Having won the friendship and support of the Native Peoples, the Red River settlers could cope with food shortages. They learned how to kill buffalo and survive winters by eating pemmican; and when locusts came, they trudged hundreds of miles into the United States to get fresh supplies of seed grain. These people had to be resilient and independently-minded. Their settlements would not have succeeded otherwise.

It would seem that Selkirk showed poor judgement in his choice of agents and managers. Alexander McDonell stands out as having been particularly unreliable. His allegations that Baldoon was packed full of drunken brutes have to be taken with a large pinch of salt. James Williams had a stormy relationship with many of the Belfast settlers, while Miles MacDonell hated Orcadians. They were "lazy, spiritless and ill disposed" men who "were wedded to old habits and strongly prejudicial against any change however beneficial."[19] As for the Irish, "they were worthless blackguards in need of the lash."[20] And his Roman Catholic faith could hardly have endeared him to the Kildonan Scots. These men were far from perfect choices, but Selkirk's options were extremely limited. They managed his financial affairs and interests, but were not necessarily in control of everything that his settlers did. As the settlers became more experienced, the managers' instructions were probably widely ignored.

They came as free spirits who were not subservient to anyone. Just four days after their arrival in Prince Edward Island, the *Polly*'s passengers had already built wigwams "along a mile of shore," thatched "in general with spruce boughs," some of them "very close and fit to turn a good rain." By the middle of the month, "log-houses in different lots were up" and by the end of the month their various settlements were already taking shape.[21] John MacDougald, one of the Baldoon settlers, wrote to his brother, in the height of a malaria outbreak which had claimed many lives, to tell him "that there was not a place under the sun better than this place."[22] They coped with extreme adversity and never lost sight of the opportunities which lay ahead.

And after the North West Company's attack on the Red River settlement in the summer of 1815, John MacLeod, one of three Hudson's Bay Company workers to stay behind, took matters into his own hands:

The "Scots Monument," located at the Fort Douglas site in Winnipeg, commemorating the emigrant Scots who came to Red River. *Photograph by Geoff Campey.*

The next day, after our people's departure from here, there came from 40 to 50 men led by some of the North West Company's clerks and set fire to all of your lordship's houses…they pillaged and robbed…took all the Colony horses. With the three men left I have got the savings of 100 kegs…have weeded and howed…am now busy making hay. I am now building a house of 40 feet long, and 20 feet wide and 16 feet high. This may be disapproved of, but, to defer it until the arrival of the boats would be too late for the people that may come up in the fall.[23]

These qualities of resilience and self-reliance were the hallmark of Selkirk's recruits. And we should also pay tribute to the pioneer women. Mrs. McLean gave birth on board the *Robert Taylor,* as the ship approached York Factory in 1812, in the midst of a raging storm.[24] Catherine MacPherson, who arrived at Churchill on the *Prince of Wales,* in 1813, nursed the victims of the typhus outbreak on board ship. And in the long "march to York Factory, the courage of Kate MacPherson had strengthened the wavers in the line."[25] The women too were an object lesson in steadfastness and courage and contributed greatly to the success of the Selkirk settlements.

Figure 11: Early Scottish Settlements along the Saskatchewan Trail.

Selkirk's philanthropic image took many years to recover. There were lingering sympathies for the North West Company and concerns for the suffering endured by the early settlers. Understandably, a great sadness was felt in Scotland over the loss of so many Highlander emigrants to British America. While he had won the intellectual arguments and could demonstrate the benefits of emigration, there were emotional undercurrents which were impervious to reason. Emigration had hurtful associations. As the Highland Clearances gathered pace from the 1830s, feelings of outrage intensified. Fiery critics like Hugh Miller exposed the forced removals and suffering in his various publications.[26] However, Miller was harking back to a previous "golden age" which never actually existed. Selkirk's positive stance on emigration accepted the realities of the present and looked to the future. But the moral indignation felt in Scotland over the Clearances largely engulfed his work and achievements.

As such, vindication was unlikely to come from Scotland. In the end, it came from Manitoba. In 1880, the Reverend George Bryce, a Presbyterian clergyman and Manitoba scholar began poring through countless papers and, after weighing up the arguments and evidence, offered his conclusions to the world two years later:

It is true he suffered a wearisome persecution. It is true he may have had heart burnings at the baseless charges hurled at him before the

165

Selkirk died at Pau in 1820 and was
buried at Orthez, a few miles distant.
Photograph by Geoff Campey.

British public, whose opinion he valued as a high-minded and sensitive man; but that he broke down single-handed a system of organized terrorism in the heart of North America; that he established a thriving colony; the good he did; the vision he cherished; and the untainted and resolute soul he bore; these are his reward.[27]

I paid my respects to George Bryce when I visited his grave in the cemetery at Kildonan Church. It struck me that he was among friends. He rediscovered the compassionate man of principle, who had achieved so much for his settlers and for Canada. As a young man, Bryce had spoken to people who could recollect the original settlers and I wondered whether these insights had inspired his determination to root out the truth.

Whatever the outside world may have thought of him at the time, Selkirk's settlers always remained loyal to him. Rows and rows of graves lie close to his monument at Belfast, while at Wallaceburg a cherished plaque still keeps his memory alive. The Scots Monument in Winnipeg, now stands at the place where Selkirk first landed in 1817. Framed by a circular wall in which are encased stones from different Scottish parishes, it is dedicated to Selkirk and "honours all Scots and their descendants who settles the provinces, territories and districts of Canada."[28] He and they could have no finer tribute.

August 2003 marks the bicentenary of the founding of Belfast. As we look back now, we can see that, beyond the goodness, greatness and importance of the Silver Chief, lie those many Highlanders who made his plans and ideas a reality in Canada. They succeeded against overwhelming odds and we should honour their determination, skills and achievements. Together with Selkirk, they undertook tasks of enormous magnitude and altered the course of Canadian history.

APPENDIX A

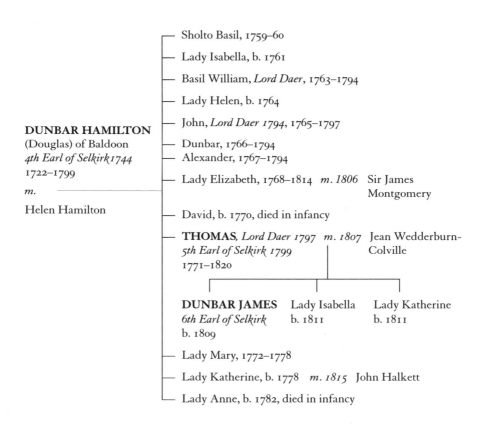

DUNBAR HAMILTON
(Douglas) of Baldoon
4th Earl of Selkirk 1744
1722–1799

m.

Helen Hamilton

Sholto Basil, 1759–60

Lady Isabella, b. 1761

Basil William, *Lord Daer*, 1763–1794

Lady Helen, b. 1764

John, *Lord Daer 1794*, 1765–1797

Dunbar, 1766–1794
Alexander, 1767–1794

Lady Elizabeth, 1768–1814 *m. 1806* Sir James
Montgomery

David, b. 1770, died in infancy

THOMAS, *Lord Daer 1797* *m. 1807* Jean Wedderburn-
5th Earl of Selkirk 1799 Colville
1771–1820

DUNBAR JAMES   Lady Isabella   Lady Katherine
6th Earl of Selkirk   b. 1811   b. 1811
b. 1809

Lady Mary, 1772–1778

Lady Katherine, b. 1778 *m. 1815* John Halkett

Lady Anne, b. 1782, died in infancy

Source: John Moran Gray, *Lord Selkirk of Red River* (Macmillan, 1963) 370–1.

APPENDIX B

Names	Age	Parish	County
John McIntyre	19	Paisley	Renfrew
William Anderson	28	Aberdalgie	Perth
Robert Montgomerie	19	Kilmaurs	Ayr
William Brown	20	Kilmaurs	Ayr
James Robertson	23	Kilmaurs	Ayr
James Urie	22	Cowal	Argyle
John Walker	21	Bunhill	Dumbarton
William Wallace	23	Riccarton	Ayr
Daniel Campbell	24	Row	Dumbarton
Andrew McFarlane	17	Luss	Dumbarton
Walter Colquhoun	25	Row	Dumbarton
Peter Barr	25	Houston	Renfrew
Colin Campbell	21	Isla	Argyll
Duncan McCaskill	24	Harris	Inverness-shire
Beth Bethune	19	Uig (Lewis)	Ross-shire
John McLennan	23	Uig (Lewis)	Ross-shire
Donald McKay	17	Uig (Lewis)	Ross-shire
John McKay	n/k	Ardrocullis	Sutherland
Jacob Folstrom	17		Sweden
Thomas McKim	18		Sligo
James Green	21		Sligo
Pat Corkoran	24	Killala	Mayo, Ireland
Anthony McDonnell	23	Killala	Mayo, Ireland
Michael Higgins	n/k	Killala	Mayo, Ireland
John O'Rourke	20	Killala	Mayo, Ireland
James Toomy	20		
James Dickson	23	Harra	Orkney
John Chambers	19	Walls	Orkney
Murdock Rosie	20	Bura	Orkney
George Merriman	22	Hara	Orkney
Peter Spence	20	Sandwick	Orkney
John Cooper	19	Sanda	Orkney

Names	Age	Parish	County
James Robertson*	18	Sandwick	Orkney
William Finlay		Stromness	Orkney
George Gibbon*	30	Sandwick	Orkney
Thomas Angus	33	Stromness	Orkney
A. Simpson*	24	Hara	Orkney
Nichol Harper	34	Birsay	Orkney
James Johnston	29	Birsay	Orkney

*—A line is run through the three names in the original.
Source: Original in NAC MG 19 E4 vol. 1, 145 – transcript in Martin, *Red River Settlement, Papers in the Canadian Archives*, 13

APPENDIX C

Name	Age	Where from
Colin Campbell	21	Argyll
John McKay*	22	Ross-shire
John McLennan	23	Ross-shire
Beth Bethune	19	Ross-shire
Donald McKay	17	Ross-shire
William Wallace	21	Ayr
John Cooper	26	Orkney
Nicholas Harper	34	Orkney
Magnus Isbister*	21	Orkney
George Gibbon	50	Orkney
Thomas McKim	38	Sligo (Ireland)
Patt Corcoran	24	Crosmalina (Ireland)
John Green	21	Sligo
Patt Quin*	21	Killala (Ireland)
Martin Jordan*	16	Killala
John O'Rourke	20	Killala
Anthony McDonnell	23	Killala
James Toomy	20	Sligo

* Except for Magnus Isbister, Patt Quin, John McKay (Ross-shire) and Martin Jordan, all of the other names appear in Appendix B.
All persons on this list had agreed to serve for a period of three years.
Source: Original NAC MG19 E4 vol.1, 151 – transcript in Martin, *Red River Settlement, Papers in the Canadian Archives*, 10

171

APPENDIX D

LIST OF PEOPLE RECRUITED, IN 1812, BY CHARLES MCLEAN IN MULL
FOR THE RED RIVER SETTLEMENT AND THE HUDSON'S BAY COMPANY*

Names	Residence of Head of Families	Status	Age	Parish
Angus McDonald	Balinahard	Settler	45	Kilfinichen, Mull
Mary McLugash			40	Kilfinichen, Mull
Donald McDonald		Labourer	18	Kilfinichen, Mull
Archibald McDonald			14	Kilfinichen, Mull
Alexander McDonald			8	Kilfinichen, Mull
Jean McDonald			16	Kilfinichen, Mull
Ann McDonald			14	Kilfinichen, Mull
Donald McLean	Kilnienen	Settler and Wright	30	Kilmore, Mull
Catherine Morison, his wife			22	Kilmore, Mull
John McLean	Kilbrianin	Settler	28	Kilmore, Mull
—McLean, his wife			24	Kilmore, Mull
2 children			2 & 4	
Charles Campbell	Calich	Settler	27	
Catherine Livingstone his wife			20	
Mary			2	
Alexander			infant	
Archibald McKinnon	Torinbeg	Settler	40	Kilfinichen, Mull
Marion McLean, his wife			36	Kilfinichen, Mull
John McKinnon			14	Kilfinichen, Mull
Hector McKinnon			12	Kilfinichen, Mull
Duncan McKinnon			10	Kilfinichen, Mull
Effie McKinnon			6	Kilfinichen, Mull
Neil Campbell	Torin Uichdrich	Settler	24	Kilfinichen, Mull
Flora McKinnin			45	Kilfinichen, Mull
John Campbell		Labourer	18	Kilfinichen, Mull

Names	Residence of Head of Families	Status	Age	Parish
Malcolm Campbell		Labourer	16	Kilfinichen, Mull
John Campbell			14	Kilfinichen, Mull
Donald McLean		Seaman	22	Kilfinichen, Mull
Ann McLean			24	Kilfinichen, Mull
Neil McKinnin	Torinbeg	Settler	30	Kilfinichen, Mull
Christina McLean, his wife			25	Kilfinichen, Mull
Catherine Campbell			50	Kilfinichen, Mull
Allan			infant	
Neil McKinnin	Glenbaire	Settler	45	Kilfinichen, Mull
Marjery McGilvra, his wife			40	Kilfinichen, Mull
Donald McKewen		Labourer	21	Kilfinichen, Mull
Allan McKewen			17	Kilfinichen, Mull
Angus McKewen			12	Kilfinichen, Mull
Mary McKewen			23	Kilfinichen, Mull
Isabella McKewen			14	Kilfinichen, Mull
Effie McKewen			12	Kilfinichen, Mull
Archibald McGilvera	Camberon Moy	Labourer	45	Torosay, Mull
Mary McLean, his wife			40	Torosay, Mull
Hugh McGilvera		Labourer	19	Torosay, Mull
John McGilvera		Settler	25	Torosay, Mull
Ann McGilvera			22	Torosay, Mull
Catherine McGilvera			20	Torosay, Mull
Hector McLean	Cambus	Settler	28	Kilfinichen, Mull
Margaret McInnis, his mother			45	Kilfinichen, Mull
Mary McLean, his sister			16	Kilfinichen, Mull
Alexander McLean		Labourer	24	Kilfinichen, Mull
John McLean			22	Kilfinichen, Mull
Hugh McLean			18	Kilfinichen, Mull
Mr McLean	Plus family including two servants. 8 in all.			
Archibald McLean	Kilbrianan	Wright, joiner	25	

* The majority of the Hudson's Bay Company workers were employed on three year contracts and were paid £20 per annum.
Source: NAC SP (C-1) 294, 558–61

APPENDIX E

| Names | Above 15 | | 8–15 | | Children |
	Men	Women	Boys	Girls	under 8
Mr. McLean, Wife, Maid & Plowman	2	2			5
Hector McLean, Hugh & sister	2	1			
Alexander McLean, Donald, mother and sister	2	2			
Jonathon McVicar Carpenter & wife	1	1			
Hector McEachern & wife	1	1			
Hector McDonald & wife servant to McLean	1	1			1
Angus McDonald, wife and 2 daughters and 2 sons	1	2	2		1
Neil McKinnon, wife, 3 sons and 3 daughters	2	3	1	1	1
Donald McMillan, Sailor	1				
Patrick McNulty & wife (Foxford)	1	1			
James Smith, wife and 3 children	1	1			3
Duncan McNaughton	1				
Donald Livingston & wife Ann McG		1	1		
Donald Livingston Jnr. & Jess	1	1			
Miles Livingston	1				
Thomas Mullourey, Senr. 30 (Newport)	1				
James Mahop 32–34 (Tireva)	1				
Joseph Cathers, 15, to be under Liv'n boy	1				
Michael Cryan, 20, Sailor Lt W (Erris)	1				
Thomas Corcoran 37 (Coolavin)	1				
Jno Conway 24–26 (Tubbercary Stis)	1				
Patt Clabby 30/34 (Sligo)	1				

174

| Names | Above 15 | | 8–15 | | Children |
	Men	Women	Boys	Girls	under 8
Jno Carson, 30, Cooper (Fermanagh)	1				
Peter Dunn, 24 (Sligo)	1				
Jno Flynn 18 Colloony	1				
James Golden got sick, 24/22 (Magheraken, Sligo)	1				
Austin Joyce, 22 (Westport)	1				
Joseph Kenny 20 (Westport)	1				
Mic Kilbride, 24 (Sligo)	1				
Peter Rutigan 40 (Stockster)	1				

Hudson's Bay Company Workers

George Holmes
Robert McVicar
Andrew McDermott
Jo Bowrke
Edward Castelo
John Warren
Charles Sweeny
James Heron, Oxf.
Fran Heron, Swn
Michael Haydon, Smith

Mic Kelley 23
M. Kilcool 22
Mic Kilkeny 23
Philip Leydon 20
James Quin 27
Philip Roony 22
Mic Roony 19
Hugh Swords 22
James Swords 19
Jo Somers 20
William Taylor 22
Andrew Tymon 24

Donald McDonald
Jo McIntyre
Hugh McLean

Bryan Gilgan 30
John Forbes 30
Patt McGovern 28
Thomas Mulberry Jnr 20
Jno Murrin 20
James Bruin 20
John Cunningham 18
James Davey 20
Fran Everard 20
Jo Feeny 17
Mich Gillan 18
James Gardiner 17
Henry Gilgan 22

Jno McMains, Sawyer (Granoid)
Edwards Bell, Donegall
Michael Boyle (Enniskillin)
Michael Hyland, Sawyer (Bally Shannon)
James Johnston
Thomas Sweeny
James Pinkman-Nailer

William Malone, 17 Moon†
James Brannen, 17 Moon
Patrick Flynn 16 Moon
Cornelius Hoye, 20 Moon
Joseph Kennedy, 15 Moon

Names		Above 15 Men	8–15 Women	Children Boys	Girls	under 8
Total Red River Settlement (R.R.S.)	71	37	18	4	1	11
		34	17	3	1	11
Johno Walsh & wife, 22 Sligo		1	1			
Jo Underwood (16–13)		1				
Francis Swords, 23, Longnd		1				
Patrick Swords 12		1				

11 boats	R.R.S. 37[m]	18[wm]	4[b]	1[g]	11[ch]
3 Canoes	Company	28			
		5 (ove)			
		[others]			
11[ch] x 6 =66		70 [m]			
3[wm] c 33[ch]		18 [wm]			
		16 [ch]			
		34			
		104			
		[total]			
11 [boats] 9 [people]		99			
3 [canoes] 4 [people]		12			
		111[total carrying capacity]			

Endorsed:-1812 O. Keveny's Return of men classed

* Source: SP (C-1) 560–62. Place names given in the listings are in Ireland.
† Probably Moone in Ireland.

APPENDIX F

RED RIVER INHABITANTS WHOSE NAMES APPEAR
IN A PETITION ASKING FOR PROTECTION FOLLOWING
THE SEVEN OAKS BATTLE OF 1816

Donald Livingstone (1812)
George McBeath (1815)
Angus Mathewson (1815)
Alex. Sutherland (1813)
George Ross (n/k)
Alex. Murray (1815)
James Murray (1815)
John Farquharson (n/k)
John McLean (1812)
John Bannerman (1815)
George MacKay (1815)
Alexander Polson (1815)
Hugh Polson (1815)
Robert McBeath (1815)
James Sutherland (1815)
James Sutherland (1815)
William Bannerman (1815)
Donald MacKay (1815)
John Flett (n/k)
John Bruce (1813)
Robert MacKay (1815)
William Bannerman, jun. (1815)
Roderick MacKay (1815)

Alex. McLean (1812)
George Adams (1815)
Martin Jordan (1811)
Robert MacKay (1815)
William MacKay (1815)
Alex. Mathewson (1815)
John McBeath (n/k)
John Sutherland (n/k)
Alex. McBeath (1815)
Christian Gunn (widow) (1815)
Alex. McKay (1815)
William Sutherland (1815)
Alex. Sutherland, son (1815)
Ebenezer Sutherland (1815)
Donald Bannerman (1815)
Hugh McLean (1812)
George Bannerman (1815)
Donald Sutherland (1815)
Beth Beathon (n/k)
John Matheson (1815)
George Sutherland (1813)
Margaret McLean (widow) (n/k)

Source: Martin, Archer, *The Hudson's Bay Company Land Tenures* (London: Wm. Cloves & Sons, 1898) 192–93] Departure years, shown in parentheses, have been taken from passenger and settler lists (Tables 5, 7, Appendices B, C, E)

177

NOTES

1   Words from a speech by Selkirk quoted in Reverend A.C. Garrioch, *First Furrows* (Winnipeg: Stovel Co. Ltd., 1924) 23.

2   A memorial plaque on Alexander Avenue, in present-day Winnipeg, marks the site of Fort Douglas, which was in use from 1812 to 1824.

3   Selkirk Papers (C-16) 17292: Journal of Miles MacDonell, 1817; John Morgan Gray, *Lord Selkirk of Red River* (London: Macmillan, 1963) 214, 234–5, 343.

4   Through the land surrender treaty, the chiefs of the Saulteaux and Cree Indians ceded to Lord Selkirk the lands of the Red River, within a two-mile settlement belt. In return, each tribe received 100 lbs. of tobacco which was paid annually.

5   Until Confederation in 1867, British North America consisted of separate self-governing colonies.

6   Jean is Jean Wedderburn-Colvile of Ochiltree and Crombie (Ayrshire). Jean was aged 21 and Selkirk was 36 at the time of their marriage.

7   SP (A-27) 1005: Lady Selkirk to Lady Katherine Halkett, 15 May, 1820.

8   J.M. Bumsted, "The Quest for a Usable Founder: Lord Selkirk and Manitoba Historians," *Manitoba History,* No. 2 (1981) 2–7.

9   The original Selkirk Papers were destroyed in a fire at St. Mary's Isle in 1940. Fortunately, transcripts were kept on microfilm and copies are held at the National Archives of Canada and the Provincial Archives in Manitoba and British Columbia. A separate correspondence file, containing Selkirk's letters to Alexander McDonald of Dalilia is to be found at Edinburgh University.

10   George Bryce, *Manitoba: Its Infancy and Growth and Present Condition* (London: 1882) 10–11.

11   Major scholarly studies on Selkirk's work include: George Bryce, *The Romantic Settlement of Lord Selkirk's Colonists.* Toronto: Musson Book Co, 1909; Chester Martin, *Lord Selkirk's Work in Canada,* Oxford Historical and Literary Studies, vol. 7. Oxford at the Clarendon Press, 1916; John Perry Pritchett, *The Red River Valley, 1811–1849.* New York: Russell & Russell, first published 1942 and reissued 1970; John Gray, *Lord Selkirk of Red River.* London: MacMillan, 1963.

12   J.M. Bumsted (ed.) *The Collected Writings of Lord Selkirk,* vol. i (1799–1809): *Observations on the Present State of the Highlands of Scotland, with a view of the causes and probable consequences of emigration,* (Winnipeg: The Manitoba Record Society, 1984) 102–3. Hereafter this source is referred to as *Selkirk's Observations*.

13   The Earldom of Selkirk was created in 1646 by Charles I. Selkirk inherited extensive prime agricultural land in Wigtownshire (whose annual rented value was over £5,000 by 1790), as well as over 10,000 acres in Kirkcudbrightshire.

14 St. Mary's Isle is today the peninsula formed by the main channel of the River Dee on the west and Kircudbright Bay on the east.

15 *DCB*, vol. v, 264–9.

16 *The Oxford Dictionary of Quotations* (London: Oxford University Press, 1959) 107.

17 Scotland produced a remarkable number of world-renowned intellectuals within decades of the Act of Union with England in 1707. They contributed greatly to diverse fields of study including science, law, philosophy, economics and medicine. The term "Scottish Enlightenment" was first introduced by William Robert Scott in 1900 to describe this extraordinary phenomenon.

18 Arthur Herman, *The Scottish Enlightenment, The Scots Invention of the Modern World* (London: Fourth Estate, 2001) 53–5, 64–5, 83–5, 188–91, 220–46.

19 Pritchett, *Red River Valley*, 17–21.

20 Eric Richards, *A History of the Highland Clearances: Emigration, Protest, Reasons* vol. 2 (London: Croom Helm, 1985) vol. 2, 477–503.

21 T.C. Smout, *A History of the Scottish People, 1560–1830* (London: Fontana Press, 1990) 321–37.

22 *Selkirk's Observations*, 102.

23 In 1794, Basil died of tuberculosis while Alexander died of yellow fever. In 1796, Dunbar also died of yellow fever. Both brothers became infected with the disease while in the Caribbean.

24 Gray, *Lord Selkirk*, 15.

25 John, Lord Daer, died of tuberculosis.

26 Pritchett, *Red River Valley*, 25–7.

27 *Ibid*, 37–52.

28 SP (A-27) 410: Lord Selkirk to Lady Selkirk, 23 April, 1817.

29 Thomas Douglas, 5th Earl of Selkirk, *A Sketch of the British fur trade in North America with observations relative to the North West Company of Montreal.* (London, 1816) 123–4.

CHAPTER 2 – EMIGRATION FRENZY IN THE HIGHLANDS AND ISLANDS

1 Scottish Record Office GD 9/166/23, 23A: Letter from Dr. William Porter to John MacKenzie, Secretary of the British Fisheries Society, 27 Dec. 1802. The American War of Independence began in 1775 and ended in 1783.

2 The British Fisheries Society had established fishing villages from the 1780s as a means of extending employment opportunities in the Highlands.

3 SRO GD 9/166/23, 23A.

4 SRO GD 9/166/2: Letter from Dr. William Porter, supervisor of the British Fisheries Society village at Lochbay, Skye to Sir William Pulteney, a director of the Society, 18 Jan. 1802

5 *Ibid.*

6 Structural changes had also occurred in the Lowlands but had caused little protest. The consolidation of farms into larger productive holdings required the tenantry to give up and replace subsistence farming on their own land, with the sale of their labour in the market place of either country or town. People generally had little difficulty in finding alternative work.

7 Kelp is burnt seaweed used in the manufacture of soap and glass. The seaweed

was kept burning with straw or heather for 4 to 8 hours. Once the weed was alight, it was raked and pounded with long-handled iron clubs. When cool, it was broken into lumps and loaded on ships for export. The industry declined in the 1820s with the availability of cheaper foreign equivalents.

8 The kelp industry was highly profitable from the late eighteenth century, reaching its high point around 1810. Landlords sought to maximize their profits from kelp production by encouraging their tenantry to live on ever smaller plots of land. This eventually created conditions of extreme congestion and overpopulation in regions which generally had very low soil productivity. J.M. Bumsted, *The People's Clearance: Highland Emigration to British North America 1770–1815* (Edinburgh: Edinburgh University Press, 1982) 41–3, 84–8.

9 Robert Brown, *Strictures and remarks on the Earl of Selkirk's observations on the present state of the Highlands* (Edinburgh, 1806) 94.

10 National Library of Scotland MS.9646 "On Emigration from the Scottish Highlands and Islands attributed to Edward S. Fraser of Inverness-shire" (1801–4) ff. 23,35,45.

11 Bumsted, *People's Clearance*, 83–5; T.M. Devine, *Exploring the Scottish Past: Themes in the History of Scottish Society* (East Linton: Tuckwell Press, 1995) 107–113; Eric Richards, "Varieties of Scottish Emigration in the Nineteenth Century," *Historical Studies*, vol. 21 (1985) 473–494.

12 Tacksmen were an elite class in the Scottish feudal system who acted as factors or farm managers under a laird. They usually sublet much of their own land to subtenants who did most of the work on the great Highland estates. With the introduction of improved farming methods in the 1770s, the tacksmen's role became increasingly obsolete and many reacted to the sweeping changes by promoting emigration within their local population and were highly influential in encouraging large numbers to emigrate.

13 Ian Adams and Meredyth Somerville, *Cargoes of Despair and Hope: Scottish Emigration to North America 1603–1803* (Edinburgh: John Donald, 1993) 91–7.

14 Specie is coin money as opposed to paper money. *SM* vol. xxxiv 515.

15 *Scots Magazine,* vol. xxxiii, 500.

16 James MacDonald, merchant of Portree, and Norman MacDonald, of Sleat, petitioned for themselves and on behalf of: Hugh Macdonald, Edmund Macqueen, John Betton, and Alexander Macqueen [all] of Sleat, and the Rev. Mr. William Macqueen and Alexander Macdonald [both] of Skye. *Colonial Records of North Carolina,* vol. viii, 620–1, vol. ix, 303–4.

17 Ian McGowan (ed.), *Samuel Johnson, A Journey to the Western Isles of Scotland* (Edinburgh: Canongate, 2001) 51.

18 In 1773, some 800 people from Skye and North Uist were intending to emigrate to America; NLS MS1306 ff.54, 55, 68: Delvine Papers, 1771–1773. McGowan, *Samuel Johnson,* 58. Adams and Somerville, *Cargoes of Despair and Hope,* 96.

19 Sir John Sinclair, *First Statistical Account of Scotland,* 21 vols. (Edinburgh, 1791–99) vol. xx, 160–61.

20 For example, in 1773 between 700 and 800 people sailed from Stornoway while 775 left from Stromness. *SM* vol. xxxv, 55. In September 1774, the *Marlborough* of Whitby called at Stromness to collect 55 Orkney Island emigrants. It sailed to

Georgia with about 80 emigrants in total, including 25 who embarked at Whitby. *SM* vol. xxxvi, 558.

21 National Library of Scotland, MS 6602, ff. 21–5: Letter, 1784 from George Dempster to Henry Dundas.

22 James Barron, *The Northern Highlands in the Nineteenth Century Newspaper Index and Annals*. 3 vols. (Inverness: R. Carruther & Sons, 1903–13) vol. III, 400.

23 *First Statistical Account of Scotland,* vol. xix 93–4. Initially, Orcadians went out to work for the Hudson's Bay Company as indentured servants, remaining for a minimum of three years, then returning home. But from 1821 onwards, many became permanent residents of the nearby Red River settlement, founded earlier by Lord Selkirk.

24 SRO RH 4/188/2: Prize essays and Transactions of the Highland Society of Scotland, vol. iii, 1802–03, 475–92. Report of the Committee on Emigration, Jan. 1802.

25 The 1803 Passenger Act stipulated the daily minimums of beef, bread, biscuit or oatmeal, molasses and water which was to be provided for each passenger. It also specified a minimum space requirement of one person for every two tons burthen (ship's tonnage), an allocation which far exceeded earlier limits. Bumsted, *The People's Clearance,* 142–3.

26 Some fares rose to as much as £12. Bumsted, *The People's Clearance*, 147–8.

27 SRO RH 4/188/2, 476.

28 *Ibid*, 531–35. The four ships from Port Glasgow and Greenock were the *Northern Friends* of Clyde which sailed to Sydney, Cape Breton, the *Neptune* of Greenock which sailed to Quebec, the *Elora* (probably the *Aurora*) which sailed to Quebec and the *Mennie* which sailed to Charlottetown, Prince Edward Island. The additional three ships which sailed from Fort William were the *Friends of John Saltcoats, Jean* of Irvine and the *Helen* of Irvine which went to Quebec. NLS MS 9646, ff. 21,23.

29 RH 4/188/2, 644–657. Third Report of the Committee on Emigration, 25th March, 1803.

30 *Selkirk's Observations*, 161–8.

31 SRO GD9/166/23A.

32 *Ibid.*

33 *SA*, vol. xx, 132.

34 They also included Roman Catholics from Barra, Eigg and west Inverness-shire. J.M. Bumsted, *Land Settlement and Politics on Eighteenth Century Prince Edward Island* (Kingston: McGill-Queen's University Press, 1987) 57–61.

35 Between 1790 and 1793 around 900 Catholic Highlanders, mostly from South Uist, Barra, Moidart and Morar had come to the Island on one of five vessels: the *Jane, Lucy, Mally, Queen* and *Argyle*. See J. Orlo and D. Fraser, "Those Elusive Immigrants, Part 1," *The Island Magazine* No. 16 (1984) 36–44.

36 Factors were employed by Scottish lairds to manage their estates.

37 The 1802 group sailed on the *Mennie* from Port Glasgow. RH 4/188/2, 534: Letter from Colin Campbell, Custom House, Greenock, 24 June, 1802.

38 SRO GD 9/166/23, 23A. J.M. Bumsted, "Settlement by Chance: Lord Selkirk and Prince Edward Island," *Canadian Historical Review*, lix (1978) 179–81. NLS MS.9646, 37.

39 Alexander Irvine, *An Enquiry into the Causes and Effects of Emigration from the Highlands and Western Isles of Scotland, with Observations on the Means Employed*

for Preventing It (Edinburgh, 1802) 19, 54, 64–67. Bumsted, *People's Clearance,* 119–22.

40   Bumsted, "Settlement by Chance," 178–82.

41   Selkirk used his ownership of land in Oswego County, New York, as a bargaining ploy. Pritchett, *Red River Valley,* 28–30.

42   Norman MacDonald, *Canada, Immigration and Settlement 1763–1841* (London: Longmans, 1939) 152–4.

43   Selkirk had additional holdings at lots 53 and 60. Andrew Hill Clark, *Three Centuries and the Island: A Historical Geography of Settlement and Agriculture in Prince Edward Island, Canada* (Toronto: University of Toronto Press, 1959) 264, 269.

44   *Selkirk's Observations,* 168.

45   Richards, *A History of the Highland Clearances,* 196–204; Malcolm Gray, *The Highland Economy 1750–1850* (Edinburgh: Oliver & Boyd, 1957) 86–104. Argyll lost many people to North Carolina while most Perthshire and Inverness-shire emigrants went to New York. See for example *SM,* vol. xxxv, 499, 557, vol. xxxvi, 446.

46   *SM,* vol. xxxiv, 395.

47   SP (C-13) 13845; Selkirk to Hobart, 30 Nov.,1802.

48   *Ibid,* 13845–46.

49   NLS Adv MS 73.2.15 f. 44 Royal Highland and Agricultural Society of Scotland Papers, Notes of Edwards Fraser of Reelig, 1803.

50   NLS Adv MS 35.6.18 ff. 13–14, Melville Papers, 1803.

51   Strathclyde Regional Archives, TD 219/12/3: Letter John MacNeill of Gigha to Ilay Campbell at Edinburgh, 2 May 1803. SRO GD 174/16/5: Letter from Hector McLean in Fort William to Murdoch McLean of Lochbuie, Mull, 14th December, 1803.

52   NLS Adv MS 35.6.18: *State of Emigration from the Highlands of Scotland its extent, causes and proposed remedy* (London, March 21, 1803).

53   SRO GD 46/17/23: Edward S. Fraser to Lord Seaforth, 30 April, 1803.

54   He recommended this approach when recruiting in 1811 for Red River. SP (A-27) 33. Lord Selkirk to Miles MacDonell, London, 29 June, 1811.

55   Prince Edward Island Genealogical Society, *From Scotland to Prince Edward Island: Scottish Emigrants to Prince Edward Island from Death and Obituary Notices in Prince Edward Island 1835–1910* (n.d.).

56   Rusty Bitterman, "Economic Stratification and Agrarian Settlement: Middle River in the early Nineteenth Century" in Kenneth Donovan (ed.) *The Island: New Perspectives on Cape Breton History* (Fredericton: Acadiensis, 1990) 71–95.

57   MacDonald, *Canada, 1763–1841,* 151–4.

58   Patrick Cecil Telford White, (ed.) *Lord Selkirk's Diary 1803–04; A journal of his travels through British North America and the Northeastern United States* (The Champlain Society, Toronto, 1958) 3–4. Hereafter this source is referred to as *Lord Selkirk's Diary.*

59   *Selkirk's Observations,* 169.

CHAPTER 3 – SUCCESS AT BELFAST, PRINCE EDWARD ISLAND

1   Selkirk Papers (C-14) 14899: James Williams to Governor Fanning, 4 Aug., 1805.

2   Ibid, 14900. By 1805 eleven of the 63 Skye families had moved out of the locations initially given to them.

3   Along with many of his other papers, Selkirk's original diary was destroyed in a fire, in 1940, at St. Mary's Isle. The copy of the transcript used by the Champlain Society, in their publication of his diary, is housed at the National Archives of Canada.

4   *Lord Selkirk's Diary*, 12.

5   *Dictionary of Canadian Biography*, vol. vi, 412–15. Having been engaged by Selkirk to recruit settlers from Skye for Belfast, Dr. MacAulay was disappointed not to have been given the job of managing Selkirk's business interests on the Island. The job went instead to James Williams, a businessman, who arrived on the *Oughton*.

6   *Lord Selkirk's Diary*, 17.

7   Mr. Shaw and Cameron were Selkirk's men in the sense of running errands and assisting him in his outings and dealings with settlers. The two MacDonalds were probably passengers.

8   *Lord Selkirk's Diary*, 3–4.

9   Having acquired lot 57 in the lottery (which determined the ownership of the Island's 67 townships), of 1767, Captain Smith had named it Belfast – after his native city, Belfast, in Ireland. There is, however, some confusion over the origin of Belfast. Selkirk clearly thought that it was the name of an old French village. However the *Gentlemen's Magazine*, London, 1771, credits its naming to Captain Smith. Alan Rayburn, *Geographical Names of Prince Edward Island; Toponymy Study* (Ottawa: Department of Energy, Mines and Resources, 1973) 21–2.

10   *Lord Selkirk's Diary*, 5.

11   *Ibid*; Dr. MacAulay was a Gaelic-speaking academic who had worked as a factor on Lord MacDonald's estate in Skye. A much respected local figure, he combined the roles of schoolmaster, lay preacher and physician until his death in 1827. Having been elected to the House of Assembly in Prince Edward Island, in 1806, he was speaker of the House in 1818.

12   *Lord Selkirk's Diary*, 5.

13   *Ibid*, 6. The *Dykes* was a 235 ton brig, built in 1798, in Maryport, with an "A1" rating (first class) from Lloyd's (*Lloyd's Shipping Register*).

14   The Stanhope settlement had been organized by Lord Advocate James Montgomery. L.H. Campey, *A Very Fine Class of Immigrants. Prince Edward Island's Scottish Pioneers, 1770–1850* (Toronto: Natural Heritage, 2001) 20–1, 136. Known as the Island of St John at the time, it was renamed Prince Edward Island in 1799.

15   The Malpeque Bay settlement was organized by the Stewart family, principally Lieutenant Colonel Robert Stewart. *Ibid*, 21–2, 136.

16   Lot 36 had been purchased from James Montgomery and the Scotchfort settlement had been organized by John MacDonald of Glenaladale. Campey, *Fine Class of Immigrants*, 23–29, 138.

17   *Lord Selkirk's Diary*, 7. J.M. Bumsted, *The Scottish Catholic Church and Prince Edward Island 1770–1810* (PAPEI no. 3846); *The Scottish Catholics in Prince Edward Island 1772–1922*, Memorial Volume (Summerside, PEI, 1922) 47–54.

18   *Lord Selkirk's Diary*, 6–7; The old Mr. Stewart was Peter Stewart. John and Charles Stewart were both members of the Island's House of Assembly. F.W.P. Bolger (ed.) *Canada's Smallest Province: A History of Prince Edward Island*, (Halifax: Nimbus, 1991) 66–9.

19   Clark, *Three Centuries and the Island,* 264–9.

20   Bolger, *Canada's Smallest Province,* 70–1.

21   Quit rents were used as a source of revenue by the Island's government. They were assessed at between two and six shillings per one hundred acres. Proprietors had to agree to settle their lands within ten years at the rate of 100 people per township. The Island's incoherent and chaotic land policies hindered its development and ability to attract immigrants. Thus, its population grew very slowly during the late eighteenth and early nineteen centuries. Clark, *Three Centuries and the Island,* 48–52; Bolger, *Canada's Smallest Province,* 38–42.

22   *Lord Selkirk's Diary,* 7. The leasehold system was only completely abolished in 1873 when Prince Edward Island entered the Canadian Confederation. Bumsted, *Land Settlement and Politics* 196–200; Clark, *Three Centuries and the Island,* 91–95.

23   SP (C-14), 15025–27. Copy Inventory of attested copies of land in Prince Edward Island purchased by the Earl of Selkirk and sent out by Mr. Stewart to be registered in the Island, May 1807. Selkirk must have obtained Charles Pearce's one-half share of lot 60 by 1803. The inventory makes no mention of this. He acquired the other half from William MacKinnon in 1805. He also purchased lot 32 but there is no record of it being used to accommodate his settlers; Martin, *Lord Selkirk's Work,* 177.

24   Selkirk was able to take advantage of new arrangements, introduced in 1802, which lessened the arrears liability in proportion to the number of settlers on each lot. SP (C-14) 14892, State of Quit Rents due on the Earl of Selkirk's Lands in Prince Edward Island, 1st May, 1808; Clark, *Three Centuries and the Island,* 46,47, 81; Bolger, *Canada's Smallest Province,* 73–4.

25   *Lord Selkirk's Diary,* 11. The computation of the number of "full passengers" was a way of dealing with children and infants. Thus, while the *Polly* carried 400 souls, it was cleared through customs as having the equivalent of 280 full passengers, with those aged under 16 being divided by a number to arrive at a final tally. The *Polly* was a 284 ton ship, which had been built in Whitby in 1762. It had an "E1" rating (second class) from Lloyd's (*Lloyd's Shipping Register*).

26   *Lord Selkirk's Diary,* 12.

27   Before leaving, Selkirk instructed McMillan and McFee to build a storehouse in 10 days. Paying them £5, they were to build "a log-house 25' x 16', roofed so as to stand this winter." *Ibid,* 16.

28   Nicholson's full name was Donald Nicholson of Stenscoll. (Duirinish parish, Skye).

29   *Ibid,* 15, 16, 29.

30   *Ibid,* 17–18.

31   The American War of Independence ended in 1783 with the defeat of the British and the establishment of independence for the citizens of the United States of America. Following the war, tens of thousands of civilians and former soldiers and officers, who had remained loyal to the British side during the war, fled from the United States and became relocated in British America. These people became known as United Empire Loyalists or simply, Loyalists.

32   Public Archives of Nova Scotia RG1 vol. 376, 78–93, 104–110. Land grants, made in 1784, to Loyalists and disbanded troops at Prince Edward Island and at Antigonish and Pictou, Nova Scotia. Among other places on the Island, grants were made

at Pownal Bay (lot 50), Belfast village (lot 57) and Pinette River (lot 58). Clark, *Three Centuries and the Island,* 57–8.

33 Selkirk acquired lots 57 and 58 from Samuel Smith, a merchant, and James Smith, a Captain in the Royal Navy. A group of 52 emigrants from Morayshire, whose expedition had been organized by Samuel Smith, arrived at lot 57, in 1775, just at the beginning of the American Rebellion. Demoralized by their remote location and horrendous problems of settlement, they did not stay. Lot 58, which Selkirk purchased from Joshua Mauger, had also previously housed settlers who, disillusioned with its prospects, had moved on. PAPEI Acc 2779/1: Chartering of *John* and *Elizabeth,* 1775. Campey, *Fine Class of Immigrants,* 29,30, 137. Clark, *Three Centuries and the Island,* 56.

34 *Lord Selkirk's Diary,* 28.

35 *Ibid.* Allen Cameron of Ardnamurchan, Argyll, who had arrived with Selkirk in 1803, may have been one of those to move on to Tryon (lots 28 and 29). He died at Augustine Cove (lot 28), near Tryon in 1870 (See PEI Gen. Soc., *Survey,* 5).

36 *Lord Selkirk's Diary,* 29.

37 *Ibid,* 29, 34.

38 *Ibid,* 29–30.

39 *Ibid,* 32; SP (C-14) 14865.

40 *Lord Selkirk's Diary,* 30. Nothing was given free of charge and those who could not pay were given assistance in the form of loans. His charges for land varied depending on the quality and location. He had originally proposed selling land at "1/2 dollar per acre for back lands, $1 for front lands, $2 for old, cleared land; and $5 for marsh or cleared land so far as can be given."

41 Settlers were being offered rates "scarcely amounting to one-half of the price usually demanded by other proprietors of the Island." *Selkirk's Observations,* 175.

42 The 1802 group sailed on the *Duke of Kent* of Greenock. NLS MS 9646 f. 23. Bumsted, *People's Clearance,* 147.

43 *Lord Selkirk's Diary,* 16, 30.

44 Donald Nicholson died on the Island in 1833, aged 96 (PEI Gen. Soc., *Survey,* 23). Roderick MacKenzie, from Lochalsh, moved to Cape Breton by 1811, where he helped to establish the Middle River settlement which attracted many others from his native Ross-shire. Bitterman, "Middle River in the early Nineteenth Century" in Kenneth Donovan (ed.) *The Island, New Perspectives in Cape Breton History,* 71–95.

45 SP (C-14) 14866.

46 *Lord Selkirk's Diary,* 30–33.

47 *Ibid,* 32–33.

48 *Ibid,* 29, 31. Selkirk used a modified version of Williamson's principle in "setting down the lots around a central point for a village." These methods had been pioneered by Charles Williamson who founded settlements in Genesee (New York).

49 *Ibid,* 33.

50 Originating from Ardnamurchen, Argyll, Father Angus MacEachern became Bishop of Charlottetown in 1831. Warburton, *History of Prince Edward Island,* 250. Campey, *Fine Class of Immigrants,* 27–8. Situated in the middle of the Gulf of St. Lawrence, the Magdelan Islands became a refuge for Acadians, who were deported from Nova Scotia in 1755.

51 *Lord Selkirk's Diary*, 23.

52 *Selkirk's Observations*, 177.

53 *A True Guide to Prince Edward Island, formerly S. John's, in the Gulph* [Gulf?] *of St. Lawrence, North America*, (Liverpool, 1808) 10–11.

54 *Selkirk's Observations*, 178.

55 *Lord Selkirk's Diary*, 22.

56 *Selkirk's Observations*, 178.

57 *Ibid.*

58 A. Shortt and A.G. Doughty (ed.), *Canada and its Provinces. A History of the Canadian people and their institutions by one hundred associates* (Toronto: Publishers Association of Canada, 1913–17) vol. xiii, 356–7. The diarist who wrote these words was Benjamin Chappell, the joiner and postmaster of Charlottetown. The *Oughton* was a 207 ton brig, built in 1787 at Leith; she had an "E2" rating, signifying that although she was seaworthy, some of her equipment was in a poor condition (*Lloyd's Shipping Register*).

59 *Lord Selkirk's Diary*, 35, 39, 351; SP (C-14) 14884. The *Oughton* had left Loch Boisdale with 229 3/8 "full passengers."

60 *Lord Selkirk's Diary*, 35–6.

61 *Ibid.*

62 Their principal request was to have credit arrangements for a longer period. *Ibid,* 37.

63 *Ibid,* 37–8.

64 *Ibid,* 38.

65 SP (C-14) 14940: James Williams to Lord Selkirk, 16 Nov. 1807. Settlers initially used marsh land as a natural water meadow. Because their part of lot 53 lacked marshes the South Uist settlers had no ready source of hay.

66 Tenants from Lord MacDonald's estate in Skye who were intending to emigrate c. 1802 (SRO GD 221/4433/1: Lord MacDonald papers.). The list is in Campey, *Fine Class of Immigrants*, 34. Most of the names in the c.1802 list can be found in the land sale records for lots 57, 58 and 60 appearing in SP (C-14) 14863-67. *Lord Selkirk's Diary* refers to the MacRaes, Mackenzies and Gillies of Ross-shire (e.g. 15, 32, 33); their names appear in the land records for lots 58 and 60. Data from tombstone inscriptions and death notices also reveals that lots 57 and 58 were primarily settled by Skye and Wester Ross settlers (PEI Gen. Soc., *Survey*).

67 SP (C-14) 14863-69: Lands sold upon the Earl of Selkirk's Estate, Prince Edward Island, 1807; SP (C-14) 14937-40: James Williams to Lord Selkirk, 16 Nov., 1807.

68 *Ibid.* For example, some Argyll settlers had taken up land in lot 28, while Sutherland people had gone to lots 20 and 21.

69 The 1784 arrivals were MacDonells from Glen Garry who had previously emigrated to the Mohawk Valley (New York). Their early success attracted others. Around 450 west Inverness-shire emigrants arrived at Glengarry in 1790, 1792 and 1793, while around 1,100 arrived in 1802. Marianne McLean, *People of Glengarry 1745–1820: Highlanders in Transition 1745–1820* (Montreal: McGill-Queen's University Press, 1991) 83, 102–14. Gray, *Lord Selkirk*, 32–3.

70 Gray, *Lord Selkirk*, 32–3.

71 Selkirk looked over his lands at Oswego County, New York, during his 1803 tour of the United States. The land had been purchased by an agent for the Selkirk

estate in 1794 and was later sold. Pritchett, *Red River Valley*, 23–24; Helen Cowan, "Selkirk's Work in Canada: An Early Chapter," *Canadian Historical Review*, vol. 9 (4) 1928, 299–308; *Lord Selkirk's Diary*, xxvii–xxvix.

72 *Lord Selkirk's Diary*, 345–52.

73 The six indentured servants were: Angus Frazer, Finlay Smith, Malcolm Buchanan, William Chisholm, Samuel Nicholson and Angus McSwain.

74 *Lord Selkirk's Diary*, 349. This was the same Donald Nicholson who acted as the principal spokesman for the Skye settlers in 1803.

75 *Ibid*, 351.

76 *Ibid*, 350.

77 Campey, *Fine Class of Immigrants*, 140; SP (C-14) 14867.

78 Nicholson paid 7s. 6d per acre for 300 acres. SP (C-14) 14939-40.

79 SP (C-14) 14945-46, 14867. The five families each got 100 acres.

80 MacDonald, *Canada, 1763–1841*, 154, Bumsted, *People's Clearance*, 194–5.

81 SP (C-14) 14982-83: John MacDonald of Glenaladale to Selkirk, 23 April, 1810.

82 SP (C-14) 15103: Selkirk to James Williams, 2 May, 1808.

83 NLS MS 11976 ff. 3–4: Comments in a Journal, July 1808, of Gilbert second Earl of Minto, recorded during a visit to Blair Atholl on extensive current emigration from the district to Prince Edward Island and its deliberate stimulation by emigration agents.

84 SP (C-14) 15103: Selkirk to James Williams, 2 May, 1808.

85 SP (C-14) 15121: James Williams to Selkirk, 28 Jan., 1809; The three ships were the: *Elizabeth, Mars* and *Clarendon* of Hull (Campey, *Fine Class of Immigrants*, 142).

86 Evidence from tombstone inscriptions and death notices shows that the Island experienced a major influx from Mull and Colonsay, between 1804 and 1808, with many settling at lots 31, 62 and 65 (PEI Gen. Soc. *Survey*).

87 Campey, *Fine Class of Immigrants*, 140–3.

88 Ibid, 48–65.

89 Later evidence shows that, in 1841, considerable numbers of landholders were squatters. Clark, *Three Centuries and the Island*, 95, 99.

90 D.C. Harvey, 'Early Settlement and Social Conditions in Prince Edward Island,' *Dalhousie Review*, vol. xi, no. 4 (1932) 458–9.

91 Selkirk's financial accounts were in a shambolic state by this time, due to the failings of his agent, James Williams. SP (C-13) 14149-53: Selkirk to Lord Grenville (Prime Minister), no date; SP (C-14) 14863-69: Lands sold upon the Earl of Selkirk's Estate, Prince Edward Island, 1807; *Lord Selkirk's Diary*, 348. J.M. Bumsted, 'Selkirk's Agents, A Tale of Three Settlements,' *The Beaver*, (33) June–July, 1992.

92 The multiplier of 50 probably underestimates present values. For example, Roy Jenkins used it in *Churchill* (Pan Books, 2001) to equate 1874 costs with modern day money (page 6).

93 SP (C-14) 14628-52: Plans and Undertakings for the Baldoon Settlement c. 1804.

94 His father was Basil Dunbar Hamilton (Douglas) of Baldoon. Gray, *Lord Selkirk*, 34–5.

CHAPTER 4 – INITIAL SETBACKS AT BALDOON, UPPER CANADA

1   National Archives of Canada MG24 I8, 61–2: Robert Innis to Alexander M. Sandwich, 25 Oct., 1804.
2   Selkirk Papers (C-14) 14637: Plans and Undertakings for the Baldoon Settlement, c. 1804.
3   *Selkirk's Diary*, 144.
4   Even by as late as 1939 the water level had never receded to the low level reached in 1804. George W. Mitchell, 'Lord Selkirk's Baldoon Settlement' in *Kentiana, The Story of the Settlement and Development of the County of Kent* (Chatham: Kent Historical Society, 1939) 37–40. Lloyd J. Clark, "The Baldoon Lands, the effect of changing drainage technology, 1804–1967" Masters Thesis, University of Western Ontario, 1970.
5   SP (C-13) 14130-36: Representations by the Earl of Selkirk, 25, 26 July, 1805.
6   The Gore of Chatham, an area of about 12 miles square, was previously known as Shawnee township. It had been purchased by the British Crown from Chippewa chiefs in 1797, for approximately £800 Quebec currency. Selkirk's Baldoon property abutted on its southern boundary, along the so-called 1790 purchase line, which had been established by an earlier Indian treaty. Shawnee township later became known as the Township of Sombra in Lambton County, A.E.D. MacKenzie, *Baldoon: Lord Selkirk's Settlement in Upper Canada*, (London, Ontario; Phelps Publishing Co. 1978) 52
7   Patterson, Gilbert, *Land Settlement in Upper Canada, 1783–1840* (Toronto: Ontario Archives, 1921) 197. The land chosen by Selkirk at the Falls of St. Mary secured access from Lake Superior to Lake Huron and on to Lake Erie. It was a strategically-placed pass which provided a vital link between the northwest and the eastern provinces. The site thus had great military and commercial importance.
8   SP (C-13) 13931.
9   MacKenzie, *Baldoon: Lord Selkirk's settlement in Upper Canada*, 26.
10 SP (C-13) 13930-31: Selkirk's 'Suggestions Respecting Canada,' 27 March, 1806.
11 SP (C-13) 13919-26: "Outline of a Plan for the Settlement and Security of Canada," 29 July, 1805.
12 Helen Cowan, *British Emigration to British North America; The First Hundred Years* (Toronto: University of Toronto Press, 1961) 7–12.
13 Gray, *Lord Selkirk*, 26–27.
14 Although the original group consisted of 15 families, initially only 14 families qualified for lots. However, in the end, Selkirk got land for 15 families. MG24 I8 vol. 1, 143–5, vol. 13.
15 Born in Fort Augustus, (Inverness-shire) McDonell, a Roman Catholic, had first moved with his family to New York in 1773 and later moved to Kingston. Gray, *Lord Selkirk*, 32–3; *DCB*, vol. VII, 554–5.
16 Peter Hunter was Lieutenant-Governor of Upper Canada from August 1799 to September 1805, replacing Peter Russell who had been "acting" in that role after the departure of John Graves Simcoe in 1796.
17 *Selkirk's Diary,* 341.
18 Alexander Brown, a shepherd, had been hired to assist Burn. Selkirk would later have a number of merino rams and ewes sent from Scotland and Denmark to add to his North American flocks. MacKenzie, *Baldoon*, 36, 38. Victor Lauriston, *Romantic Kent, More Than Three Centuries of History, 1626–1952* (Chatham, n.p., 1952) 50.

19 Alexander Brown also herded some of the flock but took them by a different route. Lauriston, *Romantic Kent,* 50, 54.

20 Bumsted, "A Tale of Three Settlements," 37, 40.

21 SP (C14) 14617: Selkirk to Thomas Clark, 21 Dec., 1809.

22 NAC MG24 I8 vol. 12 1–2.

23 SP (C-14) 14643: Plans and Undertakings for the Baldoon Settlement, c. 1804.

24 Fred Coyne Hamil, *The Valley of the Lower Thames, 1640–1850,* (Toronto: University of Toronto Press, 1951) 46, 48.

25 NAC MG 24 I8, vol. 1, 20–1: Robert McQueen to Alexander MacDonnell, 29 Sept., 1804.

26 NAC MG24 I8 vol. 4., 104, 298, 299.

27 Description of Baldoon Farm in James Soutar's *Almanac,* 1882, taken from Donna Jean Cornelius, *History of Wallaceburg, Part Two* (Wallaceburg Research and Information Study, 1974) 38.

28 Fourteen houses were needed since one log house had already been built for Peter MacDonald, who was in charge of the fifteen families. Hamil, *Lower Thames,* 48–9. *Selkirk's Diary,* 330. MacKenzie, *Baldoon,* 36, 38.

29 *Dictionary of Canadian Biography*, vol. vii, 554–5.

30 The Glengarry lads would each get 100 acres, free, or 200 acres "at the government fees." SP (C-14) 14643. Having originated from west Inverness-shire, they had previously settled in the Mohawk Valley, New York. "A list of the names of the inhabitants from Corriesbush" (Corry's Bush in the Mohawk Valley) had been prepared for Lord Selkirk by George Chisholm in February 1804 (NAC MG24 I8 vol. 4, 1). It can be presumed that these were further immigrant Scots who were intersted lin relocating to Baldoon but there is no evidence to show that any actually did. The list of 16 names included 6 McIntoshs, 3 Campbells and 2 McMillans.

31 *Selkirk's Diary,* 336. The group which arrived at Quebec in late June from Prince Edward Island was led by John MacDonnell [MacDonald]. *QG,* 28 June.

32 NAC MG24 I8 vol. 4, 105–8: Passengers and Labourers to the Earl of Selkirk's Settlements in North America. This appears as Table 3.

33 *Batteaux* were the light river boats used on the Great Lakes and rivers.

34 *Selkirk's Diary,* 331.

35 Also joining them was Lionel Johnson and his family. Johnson, born in Wooler, Northumberland, had moved to Albany, New York, where he was engaged as a shepherd in 1803 by Selkirk during his visit there. George W. Mitchell, "Lord Selkirk's Baldoon Settlement," *Kent Historical Society Papers and Addresses*, vol. 1, 14–5; Lauriston, *Romantic Kent*, 50.

36 NAC MG 24 I8 vol. 4, 105–8.

37 *Ibid,* vol. 1, 145.

38 Letter sent by John MacDougald of Baldoon to his brother, Hugh in Mull, dated 29th April, 1806. The original letter is in the possession of Barb Thornton of Wallaceburg, who is a descendant of this family. A copy appears in SP (C-14) 14739-40. The MacLean tombstone can be found at Riverview Cemetery, Wallaceburg. The inscription is for Hector MacLean of Tyree, born 25 December, 1794. Marilyn Wild, "Natives of Scotland who Emigrated to Kent County, Ontario, Canada," *Central*

Scotland Family History Society Bulletin, No. 12, Spring, 1996, 28; Mitchell, "Lord Selkirk's Baldoon Settlement" (Kent Hist. Soc.) 20.

39 Duane Meyer, *The Highland Scots of North Carolina* (Durham: University of Carolina Press, 1961), 27, 67, 79, 86.

40 *SA,* vol. xx, 375, 380.

41 *Ibid,* 278, 302.

42 Tenants from Murdoch MacLean of Lochbuie's estate were enquiring about a ship crossing to Pictou. SRO GD 174/16/5.

43 Evidence from tombstone inscriptions and death notices reveals that the Island experienced an influx of Mull and Colonsay immigrants from 1804 (PEI Gen. Soc., *Survey*).

44 MacKenzie, *Baldoon,* 38–9.

45 All but Allan MacLean were indentured servants. During their meeting with Selkirk at Kingston, Peter MacDonald, the group's spokesman had requested that time spent there should be offset against their indenture period, but this was refused. *Selkirk's Diary,* 331; MacKenzie, *Baldoon,* 40.

46 SP (C-14) 14628-52: Plans and Undertakings for the Baldoon settlement, c. 1804.

47 *Ibid,* 14637-8, 14644.

48 *Ibid,* 14638-9.

49 MacKenzie, *Baldoon,* 45.

50 Sheep scab is a disease caused by the presence of small mites which bite the sheep. It causes extreme itching, loss of performance and, if left untreated, the condition will result in death. MacKenzie, *Baldoon,* 45.

51 Donald MacCallum had also died by this time.

52 MacKenzie, *Baldoon,* 46, 48; Hamil, *Valley of the Lower Thames,* 49–50.

53 Robert Gourlay, *Statistical Account of Upper Canada complied with a view to a grand system of emigration* (London: Simpkin & Marshall, 1822), 298–9. However, a later list produced by Alexander MacDonell in 1809 (Table 4) indicates that the total death toll was around 22. Many more daughters die than sons.

54 SP (C-14) 14540-42: Selkirk to McDonell, 1 Feb., 1805. Selkirk advised that the settlers should be given loans, not "gratuitous gifts," in order "not to encourage too much dependence."

55 Selkirk's petitioned for land in Shawnee township on 25/26 July, 1805 (SP (C-13) 14130-36).

56 Hamil, *Valley of the Lower Thames,* 50.

57 SP (C-14) 14347: McDonell to Selkirk 28 July, 1805.

58 *Ibid,* 14546: Selkirk to McDonell, 2 Nov., 1805; McKenzie, *Baldoon,* 53, Gray, *Lord Selkirk of Red River,* 41.

59 SP (C-14) 14556: Selkirk to McDonell 31 Jan., 1806

60 John MacDougald to Hugh MacDougald, Mull, 29 April, 1806.

61 *Ibid*

62 SP (C-14) 14557: Selkirk to McDonell, 31 Jan., 1806; *Ibid* 14407, McDonell to Selkirk, 30 June, 1807.

63 Hamil, *Valley of the Lower Thames,* 51.

64 SP (C-14) 14407: McDonell to Selkirk, 30 June, 1807.

65 SP (C-14) 14616: Selkirk to Thomas Clark, 21 Dec., 1809.

66 Hamil, *Valley of the Lower Thames,* 52.

67 SP (C-14) 14464: McDonell to Selkirk, 20th April, 1809.

68 NAC MG24 I8 vol. 5, 272–4. Hamil, *Valley of the Lower Thames,* 52–3.

69 NAC MG24 I8 vol. 2,167–71, vol 13.

70 *Ibid,* vol. 2, 167–71. McDonell tried unsuccessfully to exchange these lots for others, even though he had been instructed by Selkirk to keep them, realizing that, once drained, they would be valuable holdings.

71 SP (C-14) 14590-1: List of the Baldoon settlers in 1809 produced by Alexander McDonell.

72 NAC MG24 I8 vol. 2, 167–71, vol. 13. List C in Volume 13 shows land allocations which were probably made in around 1809. By then, there were the following additional names: James Carfrae (weaver), Samuel Crayble (millwright), Joseph Miller, George Sweener (blacksmith), Robert Albin, Nicholas Cornwall, Gerrard Linsley, William Caldwell, James Burns, Elijah Bassett, Charles Fisher, Mathias Crow and Alexander Brown.

73 *Wallaceburg Old Boys' and Girls' Reunion* (Wallaceburg, 1936) 5. McKenzie, *Baldoon,* 62.

74 SP (C-14) 14494-14501, McDonell to Selkirk, 15 Jan., 1810. Hamil, *Valley of the Lower Thames,* 52–3.

75 Some of the men at the settlement actually joined the local Militia and fought in the War. Mitchell, "Lord Selkirk's Baldoon Settlement," 17.

76 NAC NMC-47842-410 – Thames – 1815. An 1815 map shows dwellings immediately to the south of Baldoon Farm on Big Bear Creek.

77 "Dover Parish Census – 1817, the Baldoon Settlement," *Ontario Genealogical Society Bulletin,* Kent Branch, vol. 9 (3) 1986, 55. Gourlay stated that there were only 9 or 10 families at Baldoon at the time, but the numbers were clearly higher. Gourlay, *Statistical Account, Upper Canada,* 299.

78 SP (C-4) 3668-9: William Jones to Selkirk, 4 July, 1817.

79 Patterson, *Land Settlement in Upper Canada,* 197–8; SP (C-4) 4389: Selkirk to Samuel Smith, 24th Jan., 1818.

80 SP (C-14) 14611-20: Selkirk to Thomas Clark, 21 Dec., 1809.

81 Selkirk had lots 1 and 2 in Concession I, Township of Chatham, Kent County and lot 24 in Concession I, Township of Dover, Kent County. MG24 I8 vol.1, pp. 143–5. In 1818 they were sold at $4.00 per acre. SP (C-4) 4467-8: Thomas Clark to Lord Selkirk, 2 Feb., 1818.

82 William Smith, of Sandwich, was Under-Sheriff for the Western District of Upper Canada.

83 SP (A-27) 1009-10: Thomas Clark to Andrew Colvile, 1 July, 1820; George Bryce, *The Makers of Canada: MacKenzie, Selkirk and Simpson* (Toronto: Morang, 1905) 134. This other holding, valued at between £3,000 and £4,000, was originally given the name of Wedderburn township. More than half of Moulton was swampy and it was sold at a considerable loss shortly after Selkirk's death (MG24 I8 vol. 3, 249).

84 NAC MG24 I8 vol. 3, Receipts for land in 1820.

85 The 1822 Census for Little Bear Creek and Township of Sombra appears in *Wallaceburg Old Boys' and Girls' Reunion,* 23.

86 Alan Mann and Frank Mann, *Settlement on the Sydenham: The Story of Wallaceburg* (Wallaceburg: Mann Historical Files, 1984); *Historical Atlas of Essex and Kent Counties, Ontario, 1880–1* (Toronto: H. Belden & Co., 1973) 57–58.

87　McKenzie, *Baldoon,* 62–74. Neil T. MacDonald, *The Baldoon Mystery* (Wallace-burg: Standard Press, 1986) 74.

88　Bumsted, "Tale of Three Settlements," 39; *DCB,* vol. vii, 554–5.

89　*Selkirk's Obervations,* 178.

90　NAC MG24 I8 vol. 2, 76–8: John Sims to Alexander McDonell, 9 Aug., 1808.

91　SP (C-14) 14651. MacDonald, *Baldoon Mystery,* 6. John MacDonald was the son of Donald MacDonald of Tyree.

92　Evelyn Glendinning and Alan Mann, *Trinity, History of the Methodist and United Church in Wallaceburg, 1842–1942* (Wallaceburg: Standard Press, 1992) 1. The schoolhouse was located at the corner of Kilbride Road and Bluewater Road (Topographic Map Sheet 40 J/9 814156). The timber-framed Methodist Church, constructed in 1881–1882, was later moved to Whitebread which lies on the east bank of the Chenal Ecarté River, at the northwest extremity of Kent County.

93　For instance, Angus MacDonald of Kirkland had been a printer while Donald MacDonald of Tyree had been a tailor. MG24 I8 vol. 5, 293–4.

94　*Selkirk's Diary,* 331.

95　NAC MG24 I8 vol. 1, 108: Alexander McDonell to John MacDonald, Baldoon, 1 Oct., 1805.

96　SP (C-14) 15148: List of payments 20 June, 1805. See footnotes †, ‡, and § in Table 4.

CHAPTER 5 – EARLY CONFLICT AT RED RIVER

1　SP (A-27) 29–30: Simon McGillivray to the wintering partners of the North West Company, Fort William, 9 April, 1812. Simon's brother, William, was head of the North West Company.

2　The fur trade territories of the Hudson's Bay Company were known as Rupert's Land.

3　Edinburgh University, Laing Manuscripts (Letters, Lord Selkirk to Alexander McDonald of Dalilia, Callander, 14th Aug. 1811–6th March, 1815) La.II.202/1: 14th Aug, 1811.

4　*Ibid.* Letter SP (A-27) 14: Memorandum by Selkirk, 1811. He would have to pay a penalty of £10 for each vacancy on his recruitment list of 200.

5　E.E. Rich, *Journal of Occurrences in the Athabaska Department by George Simpson 1820 and 1821* (Toronto: Champlain Society, 1938) xix–xxvi. Later Sir George Simpson, he was Governor of Rupert's Land from 1821 to 1860.

6　Bumsted, *People's Clearance,* 114–5.

7　The wintering partners supervised the fur trade in the interior while the Company's merchants, who were based in Montreal, raised capital, hired workers, purchased goods and sold the furs. They all met each year at their headquarters in Fort William.

8　SP (A-27) 405: Lord Selkirk to Lady Selkirk, 23 April, 1817.

9　Bryce, *Makers of Canada,* 145–7. Alexander MacKenzie, John Inglis and Edward Ellice had also bought £2,500 worth of Hudson's Bay Company shares at this time, in the hope of gaining influence for the rival North West Company. Selkirk and his supporters obtained about one third of the total shareholding interest. Selkirk's influence far exceeded that of any other individual or group and gave him control over the company.

10 *Ibid,* 57–8.

11 Edinburgh University La.II.202/38: 26 Feb., 1814.

12 Selkirk, *A Sketch of the British fur trade,* 123–4.

13 John Halkett, *Statement respecting the Earl of Selkirk's Settlement in North America* (London, June, 1817) vii.

14 The boundaries of the district of Assiniboia were defined in a deed reprinted in Pritchett, *The Red River Valley, 1811–1849* (New York: Russell & Russell, first published 1942 and reissued 1970) 45.

15 "Lord Selkirk's Advertisement and Prospectus of the New Colony" in *Ibid,* 49–52.

16 EU La.202.II/7, 8th Nov., 1811. SP (C-1) 119–20: List of people receiving gratuitously the number of townships opposite their names, 8 Nov., 1811, 7 Jan., 1812.

17 There has been considerable debate over the meaning and appropriateness of the terms, Métis, métis," mixed-blood" and "half-breed." The term Métis is used throughout this book to signify people with mixed Indian and European ancestry.

18 DCB vol. vi, 440–4; Gray, *Lord Selkirk,* 32. Coming to New York as a boy, Miles MacDonell later moved to Glengarry in the Loyalist migration. He became a soldier and rose to the rank of Captain in the Canadian Volunteers.

19 Gray, *Lord Selkirk,* 32–3, 56–7.

20 SP (A-27) 33: Selkirk to MacDonell, 29 June, 1811.

21 Roderick McDonald promised the men collected at Glasgow higher wages and better accommodation on board ship than MacDonell was prepared to provide. This caused great discontent and resentment.

22 Men were employed as indentured servants, usually on three year contracts. The Orkney Islands had provided the Hudson's Bay Company with most of its overseas workforce from the eighteenth century.

23 PAC MG 19, E4 Letterbook of Capt. Miles MacDonell to the Rt. Hon Earl of Selkirk, 1769–1828, clxxxviii. Pritchett, *Red River Valley,* 57–63.

24 *Inverness Journal,* 19 April, 21 July, 1811.

25 Letterbook, Miles MacDonell, clxxxviii–ix.

26 The *Prince of Wales* was a 342 ton ship built in 1793 and had an "E1" rating (second class) from Lloyd's; The *Eddystone* was a 245 ton ship built in 1802 with an "A1" (first class) rating while the *Edward and Anne* was a 238 ton ship with an "E1" rating (*Lloyd's Shipping Register*).

27 Bumsted, *People's Clearance,* 204–7.

28 Letterbook, Miles MacDonell, cxcii–iii. Numbers coming forward were lower than expected. For example, it had been hoped to recruit 70 in Ireland.

29 *Ibid,* cxcii.; SRO E.504/33/3.

30 Bumsted, "The Affair at Stornoway," *The Beaver,* Spring 1982, 53–8. There were long delays at Stornoway in clearing passengers through customs. York Factory was the main depot of the Hudson's Bay Company. Harold A. Innes, *The Fur Trade in Canada* (Toronto: University of Toronto Press, 1962) 158–65.

31 Miles MacDonell Papers, NAC MG18 E4 vol. 1, 145. The men selected by Miles MacDonell to go to the Red River Settlement, and those who were in Seal Islands, near York Factory, in October 1811, appears in Appendix B. The list gives 39 names with 3 that were crossed out.

32 Pritchett, *Red River Valley*, 67–74.

33 *Ibid.* 151. A list of the first arrivals at the Red River settlement, who came in August 1812, appears in Appendix C. They were about half of the number which had initially been selected by MacDonell.

34 Bryce, *Lord Selkirk's Colonists*, 84.

35 George Bryce, *Manitoba: It's Infancy, Growth and Present Condition* (London, 1882) 160–3. Recollections of John Polson, farmer, who arrived in 1815. He remembered that "Fort Douglas stood on the north side of the creek, this side, north of Alexander Logan's house, in the city of Winnipeg...near the bank of the Red River."

36 SP (A-27) 30. *IJ* 7 Feb. 1812.

37 SP (C-1) 712: Selkirk to MacDonell, 20 June, 1812.

38 SP (C-1) 521.

39 EU La.II.202/13,15: 10 March, 1812, 6 May, 1812. "Young MacDonald" was Archibald, who at Selkirk's expense, had been studying medicine in London in the winter of 1812–1813. Pritchett, *Red River Valley,* 122.

40 A 330 ton ship, the *Robert Taylor* had an "A1" classification (*Lloyds Shipping Register*). She had been built in 1803.

41 SP (C-1) 712–17: Selkirk to MacDonell, 20 June, 1812.

42 EU La.II.202/15, 22: 6 May, 1812, 6 Jan., 1813. The list of people recruited, in 1812, in Mull for the Red River Settlement and the Hudson's Bay Company by Charles McLean appears in Appendix D (SP (C-1) 294, 558–61). Pritchett, *Red River Valley*, 95–100.

43 Owen Keveny's list of the settlers and Hudson's Bay Company employees who sailed on the *Robert Taylor* from Sligo in June 1812, appears as Appendix E. (SP (C-1) 560-2).

44 Daer was the title held by the heir to the Selkirk earldom.

45 SP (A-27) 97–8: Selkirk to Miles MacDonell, 12 June, 1813. Kildonan people reacted angrily to the plan to have them moved in 1813 from their homes in the interior to the coast. There were riots in some areas.

46 *Ibid,* 99–100.

47 EU La.II.202/23: 23 Jan., 1813.

48 R.J. Adam (ed.) *Papers on Sutherland Estate Management* (Edinburgh: Scottish Historical Society, 1972) vol. 2, 192–4.

49 EU La.II.202/31: 8 May, 1813.

50 SRO GD 268/216/18: Lady Stafford to James Loch 1813. Eric Richards, *Patrick Sellar and the Highland Clearances* (Edinburgh: Polygon, 1999) 103–5. Lady Stafford's husband, the Marquess of Stafford, became the Duke of Sutherland in 1833. She had succeeded to the earldom of Sutherland in her own right. Selkirk hoped to lease land from Lord Stafford to accommodate the men's families temporarily. NLS SP Dep 313 1128/28: William Young to Earl Gower, 3 May, 1813.

51 Bumsted, *People's Clearance*, 208–10.

52 NLS SP Dep 313/1128/29,31: William Young to Earl Gower, May 1813.

53 EU La.II, 202/30: 30 April, 1813.

54 SP (C-1) 654-5.

55 EU La.II, 202/ 32/35, 29 May, 21 June, 1813.

56 SP (A-27) 101: Selkirk to MacDonell, 12 June, 1813.

57 NAC Miles MacDonell Papers, MG19 E4 vol 1, 165–8.

58   Pritchett, *Red River Valley*, 118–21. During the Napoleonic Wars (1803–1815) ships normally sailed in convoy. One of the ships in this group was a government naval ship.

59   *Ibid*, 122–4.

60   EU La.II.202/37: 6 Nov., 1813.

61   Chester Martin, *Red River Settlement, Papers in the Canadian Archives Relating to the Pioneers* (Ottawa: Public Archives of Canada, 1910) 3.

62   He was the same Archibald McDonald who had been sent out by Selkirk to investigate Archibald Mason. The *Prince of Wales* arrived at Churchill on August 18, 1813.

63   SP (C-2), 1172: McDonald to Selkirk, 24 July, 1814. Grant MacEwan, *Cornerstone Colony: Selkirk's Contribution to the Canadian West* (Saskatoon: Prairie Books, 1977) 74–80.

64   SP (A-27) 194–5: MacDonell to Selkirk, 25 July, 1814.

65   SP (C-2) 1292–3.

66   SP (C-2) 2026, 2028, 2033. Gray, *Lord Selkirk*, 105–11.

67   SP (C-2) 1548–9: John Pritchard to Selkirk, 20 June, 1815.

68   Extracts of a letter from a gentleman of Red River to his wife in London, 6th Aug., 1815, printed in *DGC*, 23 Jan., 1816.

69   John D. Diefenbaker, *One Canada, Memoirs of the Rt. Hon. John Diefenbaker* (Toronto: Macmillan, 1975) 4–5.

70   SP (C-2) 1868: Simon McGillivray to Archibald McGillivray, 2 July, 1815.

71   SP (C-2) 1542-6: "List of Families and Servants carried off from the Red River Settlement by the North West Company, 1815."

72   PRO CO 42/165: List of men, showing the amount each owed for clothing and provisions given to them and their families by Lord Selkirk (exclusive of other claims against them when they left Red River in June, 1815).

73   Forty-two men left for Red River in 1811 (Appendix C); seventy-one in 1812 (Appendix E); ninety-six in 1813 (Table 5) and fourteen in 1814. Bryce, in *Lord's Selkirk's Colonists* (104), states that 13 families and from 40 to 60 people remained behind. Archibald MacDonald who had accompanied the group, reported that there were "about sixty persons." SP (C-15) 16497-8: Narrative respecting the destruction of the Earl of Selkirk's settlement upon Red River by Archibald Mac-Donald, March 1816. Hugh MacLean wrote to Selkirk in June 1815 on behalf of those who had remained and his list included 23 company men. SP (C-2) 1559. John MacLeod was also known to be present taking the total to 24.

74   SP (C-2) 1559.

75   SP (C-15) 16498.

76   SP (C-2) 1593-5: John MacLeod to Selkirk, 3 Aug., 1815.

77   *Ibid*.

78   SP (C-16) 17368: Colin Robertson's Journal, 7 Aug., 1815; SP (C-2) 2005: Evidence of John Murray, Feb., 1816; NAC MG 29 C73; SP (C-2) 1560: Hugh MacLean to Selkirk, June, 1815.

79   The places of origin have been taken from the passenger and servant/labourer lists produced in 1811, 1812 and 1813 (Table 5, Appendices B,C,D,E).

80   SP (C-9) 9736: Red River and Colonial Register, 1815. Affidavit of Hector McEachern in *Correspondence in the years, 1817, 1818 and 1819 between Earl Bathurst and*

John Halkett esq. on the subject of Lord Selkirk's settlement at Red River in North America (London, 1819) 146–54.

81 SP (C-2) 1971-3: MacDonell to Selkirk, 1 Jan., 1816.

82 Colin Read, *The Rising in Western Upper Canada 1837–8, the Duncombe Revolt and After* (Toronto: University of Toronto Press, 1982) 16–31.

83 Bryce, *Lord Selkirk's Colonists*, 103.

84 *DGC*, 23 Jan., 1816.

85 SP (C-16) 17368: Colin Robertson's Journal, 7 Aug., 1815.

86 The *IC* (28 June, 1816) reported that 216 people left Thurso in 1815.

87 EU La.II.202/22: 6 June, 1813.

88 SP (C-2) 1659-61: Passenger List, 1815 crossing of *Prince of Wales* from Thurso.

89 SP (C-19) 20183-6: Robert Semple to Selkirk, 20 June, 1815.

90 Having suffered a breakdown in the summer of 1814, Miles MacDonell had written to Selkirk asking to be relieved of his duties.

91 SRO E.504/26/8. The *Hadlow* also carried the Orcadian men engaged that year as company workers. The *Eddystone* sailed with the *Prince of Wales* and *Hadlow*. Donald Gunn and Charles R. Tuttle, *History of Manitoba from the earliest settlements to 1835 and from 1835 to the admission of the province into the Dominion* (Ottawa: Malcolm Roger & Co., 1880) 131–3.

92 Pritchett, *Red River Valley*, 163–4.

93 SP (A-27) 238: Governor of Hudson's Bay Company to Lord Bathurst, 20 Dec., 1815.

94 EU La.II.202/44: 8 Sept., 1815.

95 Pritchett, *Red River Valley*, 164–7.

96 Gray, *Lord Selkirk*, 123. These settlers would acquire land in West Gwillimbury in 1819.

97 Dr. John Strachan, *A Letter to the Rt. Hon. Earl of Selkirk on his Settlement at the Red River near Hudson Bay* (London: Longman, 1816). He was Rector of York, Upper Canada.

98 Gunn, *History of Manitoba*, 120.

99 Gray, *Lord Selkirk*, 130, 127, 274.

100 Having been taken as a prisoner to Montreal in 1815, MacDonell was now free. While he retained the title of Governor, he was to act under Colin Robertson in Assiniboia. Pritchett, *Red River Valley*, 181–3.

101 The gunfight in 1816 between the Métis and the Red River settlers, at Seven Oaks, became known as the "massacre of Seven Oaks." Twenty-one colonists, the Governor and one Métis warrior were killed in the battle.

102 Gray, *Lord Selkirk*, 150–1; Charles Ermatinger's house, on Queen Street, Sault Ste. Marie, has been restored and is now a Heritage Site open to the public.

103 SP (C-3) 2528: Peter Fidler's Narrative of the Destruction of the Colony, 1815–1816.

104 *A Narrative of Occurrences in the Indian Countries of North America, since the connexion of the Right Hon. the Earl of Selkirk with the Hudson's Bay Company, and his Attempt to establish a Colony on the Red River; with a detailed Account of His Lordship's Military Expedition to, and Subsequent Proceedings at, Fort William, in Upper Canada.* (London, 1817) 67.

105 The arrested partners were sent off in three canoes to Montreal to stand trial. Papers taken by Selkirk, during his occupation of Fort William, formed part of

his evidence against them. But, having friends in government and in the judi-ciary, the partners were later released on bail and escaped punishment. Jean Morrison, *Superior Rendezvous-Place, Fort William in the Canadian Fur Trade,* (Toronto: Natural Heritage, 2001) 91–100.

106   SP (A-27) 811A: MacDonell to Capt. Roderick MacDonald, 25 June, 1818.

CHAPTER 6 – THE SILVER CHIEF ARRIVES

1   SP (A-27) 1051, 1052A: Peguis to Andrew Colvile, 12 June, 1821.

2   *DCB* vol. ix, 626–7. Peguis carried a testimonial with him from Lord Selkirk which stated that he "has been a steady friend of the settlement ever since its first estab-lishment and has never deserted its cause in its greatest reverses."

3   Bryce, *Lord Selkirk's Colonists*, 146.

4   SP (A-27) 1014J, 1051, 1052A: Alexander MacDonell to Andrew Colvile, 8 Aug, 1820; Peguis to Andrew Colvile, 12 June, 1821.

5   SP (A-27) 811A: Miles MacDonell to Captain Roderick MacDonald, 25 June, 1818; Gray, *Lord Selkirk,* 234–5.

6   There were also "Canadians in canoes" who brought "some ammunition, a little tobacco and spirits." SP (C-16) 17294: Journal of Miles MacDonell, 1817; Archer Martin, *The Hudson's Bay Company's Land Tenures and the Occupation of Assini-boia by Lord Selkirk's Settlers* (London: Wm. Cloves & Sons, 1898) 13.

7   SP (C-4) 3293: H. Forrest to Selkirk, 19 March, 1817.

8   SP (C-4) 3250-1: MacDonell to Selkirk, 6 March, 1817.

9   Cuthbert Grant (1793–1854) led his Métis warriors (known as "Bois-Brulés") in an attack on the Red River settlement in 1816 and dispersed the colonist (Battle of Seven Oaks). The son of a North West Company trader and a Métis woman, he was educated in Montreal, and possibly also in Scotland. He was one of the greatest of the early Métis leaders. Following the merger of the Hudson's Bay and North West companies in 1821, Grant would, along with many others in the Métis population, settle at White Horse Plains, to the west of the Red River set-tlement (Figure 7). Devoting his energies to farming, he was granted his land by the Hudson's Bay Company, who also named him "Warden of the Plains." He served as a magistrate and on the Council of Assiniboia, the local government of the settlement.

10   SP (A-27) 1277-8: Letter from Peguis, written 1857 (enclosed with a letter from the Secretary of the Aborigines Protection Society to the Rt. Hon. Henry Labouchère, Chairman of the Parliamentary Committee). Cuthbert Grant had led the Métis attack on the settlement on June 19, 1816. The Battle of Seven Oaks left 23 dead of which only one was from Grant's side. Governor Robert Semple and 21 colonists accounted for the other 22 deaths.

11   SP (A-27) 811A.

12   SP (C-15) 16296: Affidavit of James McDonell, 5 Dec., 1815.

13   SP (C-2) 1723: Extract of a speech by Peguis, n.d.; SP (C-4) 4428-36: Draft peti-tion from Red River Settler Scots to the Prince of Wales, Regent of G.B., about wrongs experienced and requesting protection, n.d.. In 1835, Peguis received an annuity of £5 per annum from the Hudson's Bay Company in recognition of his support and help.

14 SP (C-16) 17292: Miles MacDonell Journal, 16 June–10 Oct., 1815.

15 SP (C-16) 17294: Journal of Miles MacDonell, 1817.

16 The Ojibwe, who came into the region from Sault Ste. Marie, were known in Red River as the Saulteaux.

17 SP (C-4) 3813: Coltman to Selkirk, 17 July, 1817.

18 SP (C-16) 17295.

19 George Bryce, *The Remarkable History of the Hudson's Bay Company, including that of the French traders of north-western Canada and of the North-West, XY and Astor fur companies* (Toronto: W. Briggs 1900) 248–9. The Bois Brûlés (or "charcoal faces") were Métis. The names given, in the treaty, for the five Indian Chiefs were their French names: Le Sonnant, La Robe Noir, Peguis, L'Homme Noir and Grandes Oreilles.

20 *Ibid*, 17301–2, 17317.

21 In addition, three circles, each of six miles radius were granted around Fort Douglas, Fort Daer and Grand Forks. SP (A-27) 1035A: Text of treaty negotiated 18 July, 1817.

22 Bryce, *Lord Selkirk's Colonists,* 147. While there were doubts about the validity of the treaty thus agreed, the Hudson's Bay Company continued to honour it over many years. They paid the annual quit rent of tobacco at the appointed time and only made grants to settlers within the two mile "settlement belt."

23 *Ibid.* The other settlers could purchase tracts of 100 acres at 5 s. per acre, payable in produce.

24 Selkirk also made plans for a mill and bridge to be built. SP (C-2) 1492: Selkirk to MacDonell; Bryce, *Manitoba,* 257; Alexander Ross, *The Red River Settlement; its rise, progress and present state* (London, 1856) 42–44; Pritchett, *Red River Valley,* 196–7.

25 SP (A-27) 811A: MacDonell to Roderick MacDonald, 25 June, 1818; EU La.II.202/32, 34, 35: 29 May, 3 June, 21 June, 1813. Bryce, *Lord Selkirk's Colonists,* 146.

26 Pritchett, *Red River Valley,* 191–2; Gray, *Lord Selkirk,* 200–2.

27 Extract from "Colin Robertson's Correspondence Book" cited in Morrison, *Superior Rendezvous*, 71–2.

28 Pritchett, *Red River Valley,* 205,206, 209.

29 SP (A-27) 398M, 398M2: Lady Selkirk to Lord Selkirk, 7 May, 1817.

30 Bryce, *Lord Selkirk's Colonists,* 149.

31 Gray, *Lord Selkirk,* 259–77.

32 *DGC,* 10 Nov., 1818.

33 Selkirk's letter was published in London in 1819 under the title, *A Letter to the Earl of Liverpool from the Earl of Selkirk.*

34 *Papers relating to the Red River Settlement, 1815–1819,* House of Commons No. 584.

35 Martin, *Selkirk's Work,* 164–5.

36 SP (A-27) 923: Selkirk to James Wedderburn, 1819.

37 SP (A-27) 966D-E: Selkirk to Andrew Colvile, 11 Dec., 1819.

38 Morrison, *Superior Rendezvous,* 114.

39 SP (A-27) 1005: Lady Selkirk to Katherine Halkett, 1 April, 1820.

40 *Montreal Gazette* 7 June, 1820.

41 *The Scotsman,* 29 April, 1820.

42 SP (A-27) 1028A: George Simpson to Andrew Colvile, 5 Sept., 1821.

CHAPTER 7 — THE SCOTTISH SETTLERS OF RED RIVER

1 George Bryce, *The Old Settlers of Red River* (Winnipeg: Manitoba Daily Free Press 1885) 8.

2 SP (A-27) 41: Selkirk to MacDonell 29 June, 1811.

3 Bryce, *Lord Selkirk's Colonists,* 171.

4 Robert J. Coutts, *The Road to the Rapids, Nineteenth century Church and society at St. Andrew's Parish, Red River* (Calgary: University of Calgary Press, 2000) 1–8.

5 Pritchett, *Red River Valley*, 223–6.

6 Reverend John West commented on their unsuitability as colonists in his report of 1823. UBSC C C1 O 72/5.

7 The French-Canadian voyageurs were renowned for their ability to paddle canoes at great speed over long periods.

8 Thomas Flanagan, *Métis Lands in Manitoba* (Calgary: University of Calgary Press, 1991) 13–27.

9 Some Orcadians worked for the North West Company, while the Hudson's Bay Company also employed Canadians. Elaine Allan Mitchell, "The Scot in the Fur Trade" in W. Stanford Reid (ed.), *The Scottish Tradition in Canada* (Toronto: McClelland & Stewart, 1976) 27–49.

10 SP (A-27) 56: Selkirk to MacDonell, 23 Dec, 1811.

11 SP (C-1) 725: Selkirk to MacDonell, 20 June, 1812.

12 Lewis Thomas, (ed.) The *Prairie West to 1905*. Toronto: Oxford University Press, 1975.

13 Edith I. Burley, *Servants of the Honourable Company, Work Discipline and Conflict in the Hudson's Bay Company, 1770–1879* (Toronto: Oxford University Press, 1997) 68–71; John, W. Groundwater Shearer and J.D. Mackay (eds.) *The New Orkney Book* (Edinburgh: Nelson Printers, 1966) 63–9.

14 By the time of the merger in 1821, Orcadians accounted for less than forty per cent of the total workforce. John Nicks, "Orkneymen in the HBC 1780–1821" in Carol M. Judd and Arthur J. Ray, *Old Trails and New Directions: Papers of the third North American Fur Trade Conference* (Toronto: University of Toronto Press, 1980) 102–3.

15 *IJ* 21 Feb. 1812. A feu was a perpetual lease at a fixed rent.

16 EU La.II.202/ 26A: Selkirk to Charles McLean, Feb 20, 1813.

17 SP (A-27) 10: Memorandum from Selkirk n/d.

18 OLA D31/21/5: Orkneymen in HBC Service in Peace River, Athabasca and the west of Canada. D31/22/1: Biographical details, Orkneymen in HBC.

19 OLA Y1: James Sutherland to his brother John, 24 Aug., 1817. The originals of this collection are stored at the Glenbow Foundation, Calgary, Alberta.

20 OLA D15/3/4: Halcro-Johnston Papers, Letter to John Johnston, Stromness, from John Purrs, Quebec 16 May, 1801.

21 *Ibid,* 166.

22 *SA*, vol. xix, 246.

23 *Ibid,* 249.

24 *Ibid*, 93–4.

25 Nicks, *Orkneymen in the HBC*, 115; NAC (C-2170): Red River Census, 1831, 1834–1835.
26 Bryce, *Old Settlers of Red River*, 7.
27 SP (A-27) 827-8: Captain Matthey to Selkirk, 30 Aug, 1818. Population figures for Métis and Native Peoples were not recorded.
28 Ross, *Red River Settlement*, 50.
29 SP (A-27) 952: Samuel Gale to Lady Selkirk, 10 Sept., 1819.
30 Fort Daer, the Hudson's Bay Company post, was at Pembina.
31 SP (C-4) 4245-8: Selkirk, Miscellaneous Letters, 22 Dec., 1817; Pritchett, *Red River Valley*, 226–8.
32 Ross, *Red River Settlement*, 51, *IC*, 1 July, 1819; Bryce, *Lord Selkirk's Colonists* 167.
33 Ross, *Ibid*, 63–4.
34 *IC* 1 July, 1819; SP (A-27) 991: Andrew Colvile to Samuel Gale, 23 Feb., 1820.
35 Sir George Simpson became Governor of the Hudson's Bay Company following the merger of 1821. He had been a former clerk and accountant in Andrew Colvile's sugar-importing firm. SP (A-27) 1028A: George Simpson to Andrew Colvile, 5 Sept., 1821.
36 Bryce, *Lord Selkirk's Colonists,* 165.
37 In addition to Colvile and Halkett, Selkirk's other executors included: Sir James Montgomery, husband of Elizabeth, his sister, and James Wedderburn, his wife's brother, who was Solicitor-General for Scotland, and Professor Dugald Stewart. Bryce, *Lord Selkirk's Colonists*, 164; SP (A-27) 700. Selkirk's wife, Jean had two brothers: Andrew Colvile, who was based in London, and James Wedderburn, who lived in Edinburgh.
38 SP (A-27) 1084-5: John Halkett to Andrew Colvile, 9 Feb., 1822.
39 Governor George Simpson and Selkirk's representatives had power jointly to grant and sell land.
40 Alexander MacDonell became acting Governor of Red River from 1816. He was replaced in 1822 by Captain Bulger, who was followed by Donald MacKenzie. SP (A-27) 1028H, 1072-3: George Simpson to Andrew Colvile, 5 Sept., 1821; John Halkett to Andrew Colvile, 22 Nov., 1821.
41 SP (A-27) 1097C, F: Capt. Bulger to Andrew Colvile, Aug 4, 1822.
42 For example, in 1822, Rev. John West accompanied "a Director of the Hudson's Bay Company and one of the executors of the late Earl of Selkirk" to Pembina, to investigate concerns that too many people were settling "at this distant and extreme point of the Colony from the Stores." UBSC C C1 o 72/5, 23.
43 Their land grants varied from 30 to 200 acres and all had river frontages. The new arrivals could buy their land outright, but if it was leased, they had to provide labour for the upkeep of the Colony's roads and bridges. Gerhard J. Ens, *Homeland to Hinterland, The changing world of the Métis in the nineteenth century* (Toronto: University of Toronto Press, 1996) 30–5.
44 Although sometimes the Kildonans had to turn to hunting to supplement their food supplies.
45 Coutts, *Road to Rapids*, 4, 66–72.
46 EU.La.II.202/43: Selkirk to Alexander McDonald, 6 March, 1815; Gray, *Lord Selkirk,* 270.

47 George Bryce and C.N. Bell, *Original Letters and other Documents relating to the Selkirk Settlement*, Historical and Scientific Society of Manitoba, 1889, Transaction no 33. Many of the settlers spoke Gaelic.

48 SP (A-27) 1209-10: George Simpson to Andrew Colvile, 15 May, 1833.

49 OLA D31/21/6/3: Reminiscences of Sheriff Colin Inkster, c. 1960.

50 The Glasgow Colonial Society was established in 1825 to promote the Presbyterian faith in British North America. Its work was concentrated in the Maritimes and in Upper and Lower Canada. Bryce, *Lord Selkirk's Colonists,* 168.

51 SP (A-27) 1115: George Simpson to Andrew Colvile, 8 Sept., 1823.

52 *DCB*, vol. 8, 765–8.

53 OLA D31/21/5; Coutts, *Road to Rapids,* 101–3. The Swan River is to the west of Lake Winnipeg.

54 OLA Y1: James Sutherland to his brother John Sutherland, 10 Aug., 1828.

55 *Ibid*: 8 Aug., 1831.

56 Bryce, *Red River Colonists*, 184.

57 Shortt and Doughty, *Canada and its Provinces*, vol. 20, p. 421.

58 SP (A-27) 1139-41: George Simpson to Andrew Colvile, 31 May, 1824.

59 Agriculture did not become firmly established in the new Colony until 1827, the year after the great flood, and even then progress in cultivating land moved ahead very slowly. Ens, *Homeland to Hinterland,* 30–7.

60 SRO GD 46/1/530: Letter from Alexander Stewart to Mrs. Stewart MacKenzie, 26 June, 1832.

61 From 1830 to 1890, some 500 men would come to Rupert's Land to work for the company. Philip Goldring, "Lewis and the Hudson's Bay Company in the Nineteenth Century," *The Journal of the School of Scottish Studies* (University of Edinburgh) vol. 22, 1978, 23–41; Burley, *Servants of the Honourable Company,* 96–7.

62 SP (A-27) 1280.

63 NAC (C-2170): Red River Census Returns, 1834–1835.

64 UBSC C C1 037/24: Subscription List for the Church Missionary Society, 1827.N.

65 NAC (C-2170): Red River Census Returns, 1834–1835.

66 Ross, *Red River Settlement*, 110–1.

67 In 1813, when he was recruiting settlers in Sutherland, he was disappointed that no extra ship was being "sent out for a cargo of timber," thus restricting passenger accommodation to the space available on "the Company's regular ships," which, in any case, would largely be "taken up with their own servants." EU.La.II.202/26A: Selkirk to Charles McLean, 20 Feb., 1813.

68 Alexander Sutherland appears in the passenger list for the *Prince of Wales* crossing of 1815 (Table 7). Catherine McPherson's name is in the passenger list for the 1813 crossing (Table 5); W.J. Healy, *Women of Red River, being a book written from the recollections of women surviving from the Red River Era* (Winnipeg: Peguis Publishers Ltd., 1987) 53–5.

69 NAC MG29 C73 10-1, 14-5, 19-20,31-33: Letters to Alexander Sutherland from Eppy Sutherland and William McPherson 1823, 1828, 1831.

70 John West was unable to adapt to the realities of a fur trade society and was replaced in 1823 by Reverend David Jones.

71 Coutts, *Road to Rapids*, 7, 24, 26–30.

72 Garrioch, *First Furrows*, 70.

73 *Ibid,* 72.

74 *Ibid*, 46–9. Peguis Memorial at St. Peter's Church.

75 A great many of the Scottish settlers contributed funds to the 1827 appeal. UBSC C C1 037/24.

76 PAM HBCA D.5/11: Petition of the Presbyterian Inhabitants of the Red River Settlement, 10 June, 1844. The petition listed 36 names: Alexander Rose, Robert Logan, James Sinclair, Alexander McBeath, John McBeath, Alexander Polson, Alexander Matheson, Angus Matheson, John Sutherland, John Matheson, John Gunn, George Munrow, Alexander Matheson, Angus Matheson, Hugh Matheson, William Gunn, Alexander Sutherland, Hugh Polson, James McKay, Robert McKay, John Polson, Donald Bannerman, George Sutherland, Robert McBeath, William McDonald, Donald Matheson, Roderick McBeath, John Fraser, Morrison McBeath, Donald McDonald, John Matheson, Hugh Cameron, Hugh Matheson, Neil Livingstone, Alexander Sutherland and Donald McDonald. Before organizing petitions, Ross complained to the Church Missionary Society that Scots at Red River were not getting the recognition they deserved. UBSC C1/Co/8/2: Letter, 10 Aug., 1829.

77 PAM HBCA D.5/11.

78 PAM MG2 C14/24: Eden Colvile to Alexander Ross, 16 April, 1851.

79 Bryce, *Red River Colonists*, 266.

80 Dr. John Black was born in Dumfriesshire. Founded in 1871, Manitoba College was one of the colleges which later federated with the University of Manitoba. The Reverend George Bryce and Dr. Black were its first teachers. *DCB*, vol. 11, 79–80. George Bryce, *John Black, the Apostle of the Red River or How the blue banner was unfurled on the Manitoba Prairies* (Montreal: William Briggs, 1898) 52–65, 114–29.

81 The fur trade had brought French-Canadian women to the West well before the arrival of the Selkirk settlers.

82 Observed by Catherine Sutherland, granddaughter of Alexander. She became Mrs. W.R. Black. Healy, *Women of Red River,* 76.

83 Frits Pannekoek, 'The Anglican Church and Disintegration of Red River Society' in R. Douglas Francis and Howard Palmer (eds.) *The Prairie West, Historical Readings* (Edmonton: Pica Pica Press, 1985) 103–5.

84 OLA Y1: James Sutherland to his brother John Sutherland, 10 Aug., 1842.

85 *Ibid,* 10 Aug., 1840.

86 James Ross was the principal spokesman for the English-speaking settlers during the Red River Uprisings of 1869–70. Coutts, *Road to the Rapids,* 99.

87 Healy, *Women of Red River,* 68, 86–7.

88 Her father was John Sutherland. *Ibid,* 59–61.

89 *Ibid,* 212–13. Irene M. Spry "The Métis and Mixed-Bloods of Rupert's Land before 1870" in Jacqueline Paterson and Jennifer S.H. Brown (eds.) *The New Peoples, being and becoming Métis in North America* (Winnipeg: University of Manitoba Press, 1985) 97–118.

90 SP (A-27) 1280.

91 Gerald Friesen, *The Canadian Prairies, A History* (Toronto: University of Toronto Press, 1984) 91–128.

92 Ens, *Homeland to Hinterland,* 172–5.

93 SP (A-27) 1278-9: Lord Selkirk (6th Earl) to his mother, 30 June, 1863. Dunbar James Douglas, who had succeeded his father as Earl in 1820, died in 1885. He married Cecely Louisa Grey Egerton, but there were no children. After the 6th Earl's death, the Selkirk Estate was transferred to his sister, Lady Isabella Helen Hope.

94 The reconveyance took place on 4 May, 1836. Martin, *Lord Selkirk's Work*, 175, 223.

CHAPTER 8 – LATER DEVELOPMENTS AT BELFAST, BALDOON AND RED RIVER

1 *Selkirk's Observations*, 161.

2 The adverse effects of the government's land policies on the development of settlement in the colonies, are discussed in MacDonald, *Canada, 1763–1841*, 512–24.

3 *Selkirk's Observations*, 162–5.

4 *Ibid*, 165.

5 Thomas Talbot, of Anglo-Irish descent, had gained his knowledge of North America by serving in the army.

6 *Selkirk's Observations*, 168–85.

7 MacAulay's letter, which first appeared in a London newspaper and later in the *Charlottetown Weekly Recorder*, is reprinted in *The Recaller*, Belfast Historical Society, April, 2001; SP (C-14) 14982-4: MacDonald to Selkirk, 23 April, 1810. Dr. MacAulay fought a long-running battle with James Williams, with each heading rival groups on the Island.

8 SP (C-6) 6456-62: Johnston to Selkirk, 28 Aug, 1819.

9 Walter Johnstone, *Travels in Prince Edward Island, Gulf of St. Lawrence, North America in the years 1820–1821, undertaken with a design to establish Sabbath Schools* (Edinburgh, 1823) 55.

10 Campey, *Fine Class of Immigrants*, 80–9.

11 There were widespread clearances in Skye from the mid-1820s, as well as in later decades. Those who emigrated in 1839–1841 received financial assistance from Lord MacDonald and the Edinburgh and Glasgow Relief Committees (SRO GD 221/4434/1: Lord MacDonald papers).

12 Evidence from tombstones and death notices indicates where many settled (PEI Gen. Soc., *Survey*). Most were former tenants of Lord MacDonald who originated from Kilmuir, Snizort and Portree in the northeast of Skye.

13 The government had attempted to curtail immigration to Cape Breton until 1817, restricting land to all but Loyalists, ex-soldiers and fish merchants. However, these measures proved to be futile since, from as early as 1790, a great many Scottish families simply took land on Cape Breton by squatting.

14 MacAulay would have gained 1000 acres of land for himself if successful. Rusty Bittermann, "Economic Stratification and Agrarian Settlement: Middle River in the early Nineteenth Century" in Kenneth Donovan (ed.) *The Island, New Perspectives on Cape Breton History* (Cape Breton, 1990) 71–95; Rusty Bittermann, Robert A. MacKinnon and Graeme Wynne "Of Equality and Interdependence in the Nova Scotian Countryside 1850–70," *Canadian Historical Review* vol. lxxiv (1993) 5–12.

15 For example, Chester Martin, in *Lord Selkirk's Work*, claimed that Baldoon had "scarcely passed beyond the stage of a straggling pioneer village" (p. 24). Gray, in *Lord Selkirk,* believed that Selkirk "had all but given up, in dismay at its lack of success and ruinous cost" (p. 49).

16 Marilyn Wild's "Natives of Scotland who emigrated to Kent County" shows that 31% originated from Argyll, the largest single, identifiable group (*Central Scotland FHS Bulletin*, No. 9 (1994); No. 10,11 (1995); No. 12,13, (1996).

17 Malcolm Wallace, "Pioneers of the Scotch Settlement on the Shore of Lake St. Clair," *Ontario Historical Society,* vol. xli, 1949 173–200.

18 Cowan, *British Emigration to British North America,* 115–8; Hamil, *Valley of the Lower Thames,* 111–8.

19 For example, see SP (C-13) 13919-26: "Communications with Government in relation to America," Selkirk to Lord Hobart, 1805–1807.

20 Talbot offered each settler a free grant of 50 acres, conditional on the building of a house, the sowing of 10 acres within three years and the completion of half of the road. If the settler met the conditions he could buy additional land; if not, he was forced to vacate.

21 A great many were Baptists. Donald E. Meek, "Evangelicalism and Emigration: Aspects of the role of dissenting evangelicalism in Highland emigration to Canada" in Gordon MacLennan (ed.) *Proceedings of the First North American Congress of Celtic Studies* (1986) 15–37. Scottish settlers living at Dunwich and Aldborough in 1820 are listed in Wilfrid Campbell, *The Scotsman in Canada* vol. ii (London: Sampson Low & Co., 1911) 211–3. They included: George and William Bannerman, Angus McKay, Alexander, Donald and George Sutherland, Alexander, Angus and Donald Gunn.

22 They were joined in the following year by James and Angus Sutherland, Andrew McBeth, George Ross and "one Murray." The initial group also included Robert Sutherland, Robert and Donald MacKay, John Matthewson, Arthur Campbell and George Bannerman. *Illustrated Historical Atlas, County of Simcoe, Ontario, 1881* (Port Elgin: Cumming Atlas Reprints, 1975) 12, 30.

23 Andrew F. Hunter, *A History of Simcoe County* (Barrie: Historical Committee of Simcoe County, 1948) 21–2, 311–2. Five more Red River colonists are said to have arrived at Holland River in 1816, coming by way of Parry Sound and Orillia.

24 A.G. Brunger, 'The Distribution of Scots and Irish in Upper Canada 1851–71,' *Canadian Geographer,* vol. 34 (1990) 250–58. Grey County Scots were mainly concentrated in an L-shaped band of townships comprised of Osprey (bordering on Nottawasaga in Simcoe County), Artemesia, Glenelg and Egremont.

25 NAC MG29 C73 37-41: Alexander MacPherson to Alexander Sutherland, 18 April, 1843; Donald MacPherson to Alexander Sutherland, 5 April, 1844.

26 In 1913, 30 families from the Duke of Sutherland's estate settled on land that he had acquired in an area north of Brooks, Alberta. However, it is unlikely that was related to the much earlier exodus to Red River. Norma J. Milton, "The Scots in Alberta," in Howard and Tamara Palmer (eds.) *Peoples of Alberta: Portrait of Cultural Diversity* (Saskatoon: Western Prairie Books, 1985) 109–22.

27 W.L. Morton, *Manitoba, A History* (Toronto: University of Toronto Press, 1967) 151.

28 PAM MG2 C14/203: Letter dated 7 March, 1857; Coutts, *Road to the Rapids,* 107–9.

29 William Kennedy was the son of Aggathas (Cree) and Alexander Kennedy (Orca-
    dian), a Chief Factor of the Hudson's Bay Company. The petition appears in Lewis
    G. Thomas, (ed.) *The Prairie West to 1905* (Toronto: Oxford University Press, 1975)
    59–61.

30 Louis Riel and his followers organized a "National Committee" and formed a pro-
    visional government to negotiate directly with Canada. J.M. Bumsted, *The Peoples
    of Canada, a Pre-Confederation History,* vol. 1 (Toronto: University of Oxford Press,
    1992) 371–6.

31 Riel fled to the United States in 1870. He led the Métis in the North West Rebel-
    lion of 1885 and, following defeat, was hanged for treason.

32 Martin, *Lord Selkirk's Work,* 180–4.

33 By 1886, Manitoba's population had soared to 109,000, with the Métis, both French
    and English-speaking, representing only seven per cent of the total. Coutts, *Road
    to the Rapids,* 110.

34 R.C. Russell, *Carleton Trail: The broad highway into the Saskatchewan country from
    the Red River settlement, 1840–80* (Saskatoon: Modern Press, 1965) 16–23.

35 Land companies were established to promote settlement in the prairies. Twenty-
    seven companies had been formed by 1882. A.N. Lalonde, "Colonization
    Companies in the 1880s" *Saskatchewan History,* vol. xxiv No. 3 (1971) 101–14. The
    Dawson route, linking Canada with Red River, which opened in 1868, was built
    by a Scottish-born engineer, Simon Dawson.

36 Ernest W. Marwick, "Stromness and the Hudson Bay Trade, the last twenty years,"
    The Orkney Herald, 15 July, 1952.

37 Details of families from the Outer Hebrides who emigrated to the Prairies can be
    found in Bill Lawson, *A Register of Emigrants from the Western Isles of Scotland
    1750–1900,* 2 vols. Island of Harris, Scotland: self-published, 1992.

38 OLA D31/21/1/6: "From Orkney to Orkney." The York Colonization Company
    was an Ontario Land Company.

39 OLA D31/21/1/8: Binscarth – "This Farm in the Cleft of the Hill." *DCB* vol. xiii,
    929–31. Binscarth was known initially as "Colony Farm." The site was moved
    following the arrival of the North West Railroad in 1886.

40 James MacKinnon, "A Short History of the Pioneer Scotch Settlers, St. Andrews,
    Saskatchewan," *The Courier,* Regina, 1921; Wayne Norton, *Help us to a Better Land,
    Crofter Colonies in the Prairie West* (Regina: University of Regina, 1994) 1, 23–29,
    84–6; Turner, 'Scottish Settlement of the West' in Reid, *Scottish Tradition in Canada,*
    82–3.

41 Scots from Ayrshire, Perthshire, Aberdeenshire and the Lothians came to Moffat
    over the next twenty years; almost half originated from Buchan in Aberdeenshire.
    Kay Parley, "Moffat, Assiniboia, North-West Territories" *Saskatchewan History,* vol.
    xx, No. 1 (1967) 32–6.

CHAPTER 9 – SELKIRK AND HIS SETTLERS

1 Garrioch, *First Furrows,* 21.
2 *Selkirk's Observations,* 150.
3 SP (C-13) 13903-6: Dugald Stewart to Selkirk, 1802.
4 Lord Selkirk wrote *Observations on a proposal for forming a Society for the Civilization*

and Improvement of the North American Indians within the British Boundary in 1807.

5   SP (A-27) 390H, 390J: Lady Selkirk to Lord Selkirk, Montreal, Hogmanay, 1816.

6   SP (A-27) 700: Samuel Gale to Lady Selkirk, Oct. 1817.

7   SP (C-3) 2530: Peter Fidler's "Narrative of the Destruction of the Colony," 1816.

8   Martin, *Lord Selkirk's Work in Canada,* 191.

9   The shares sold for £100, 000 in 1863.

10 Martin, *Lord Selkirk's Work in Canada,* 186–7 (Martin's quotes Selkirk in the *Selkirk Papers,* 6009).

11 Strachan, *Letter to Selkirk on his settlement at Red River,* 10.

12 William Wallace (ed.) *Documents relating to the North West Company* (Toronto: Champlain Society, 1934) 36.

13 SP (C-4) 1723: Speech by Peguis, n.d.

14 Bryce, *Manitoba,* 269–70.

15 *Selkirk's Observations,* 168.

16 In 1813, Selkirk had proposed the raising of "a corps for service in America," on the understanding that, at the end of their service, its men would be settled at Red River at government expense. Although his proposal was not supported, at the time, the government used his arguments and ideas in the creation of the Upper Canada military settlements, which were founded from 1815. Bumsted, *Peoples' Clearance,* 218–9.

17 Cowan, *British Emigration,* 40–45.

18 *Selkirk's Diary,* 29; Cowan, "Selkirk's Work," 305–8.

19 SP (A-27) 60: Miles MacDonell to Selkirk, 29 May, 1812.

20 Pritchett, *Red River Valley,* 70.

21 *Selkirk's Diary,* 12, 33.

22 SP (C-14) 14739-40.

23 SP (C-2) 1593-5: John MacLeod to Selkirk, 3 Aug., 1815.

24 Pritchett, *Red River Valley,* 97.

25 Healy, *Women of Red River,* 53–4.

26 For example see, Hugh Miller, *Sutherland as it was and is: How a country may be ruined.* Edinburgh: John Johnstone, 1843.

27 Bryce, *Manitoba,* 364.

28 In "The Scots Monument Booklet," St. Andrew's Society of Winnipeg, n.d.,

BIBLIOGRAPHY

PRIMARY SOURCES (MANUSCRIPTS)

Edinburgh University Special Collections (EU)

La.II.202 Laing Manuscripts, Selkirk to Alexander McDonald of Dalilia, Callander, 1811–1815.

Hudson's Bay Company Archives (HBC)

HBCA D.5/11, ff. 294–5 Petition of the Presbyterian Inhabitants of the Red River Settlement, 10 June, 1844.

National Archives of Canada (NAC)

C-2170 Red River Settlement Census Returns, 1831–1846 (Microfilm).
MG19 E4 Miles MacDonell Papers.
MG 19 E4 Letterbook, to the Rt. Hon Earl of Selkirk, 1769–1828, published as "Selkirk Settlement; letter book of Captain Miles MacDonell...," PAC, *Report*, 1886, pp. clxxxvii–ccxxvi.
MG24 I8 Alexander McDonell Papers.
MG29 C73 Alexander Sutherland Papers.
NMC-47842–410-Thames-1815, 1815 map of Baldoon.
NMC-6067 Red River Land Treaty, 1817.
Selkirk Papers (Microfilm Reels): A-27, C-1, C-2, C-3, C-4, C-6, C-9, C-13, C-14, C-15, C-16.

National Library of Scotland (NLS)

Adv MS 73.2.15, f. 44 Royal Highland and Agricultural Society of Scotland Papers, Notes of Edwards Fraser of Reelig, 1803.
MS1306 Delvine Papers, 1771–1773.
Adv MS 35.6.18, ff. 8 –15, Melville Papers, State of Emigration from the Highlands of Scotland, its extent, causes and proposed remedy, London, March 21, 1803.
MS 6602, ff. 21–5 George Dempster to Henry Dundas, 1784.
MS 9646 "On Emigration from the Scottish Highlands and Islands attributed to Edward S. Fraser of Inverness-shire" (1801–04).

MS 11976 ff. 3–4. Minto Papers, Journal concerning Emigration from Blair Atholl to Prince Edward Island, 1808.

SP Dep 313/1128/28, 29, 31 Sutherland Papers, William Young to Earl Gower, May 1813.

Orkney Library and Archives (OLA)

D15/3/4 Halcro-Johnston Papers.

D31/21/5 and D31/22/1 Orkneymen in Hudson's Bay Company.

D31/21/6/3 Reminiscences of Sheriff Colin Inkster, c. 1960.

D31/21/1/6 "From Orkney to Orkney."

D31/21/1/8 Binscarth – "This Farm in the Cleft of the Hill."

Y1 Copies of letters from James Sutherland of Red River to his brother in South Ronaldshay, 1814–1842.

Public Archives of Manitoba (PAM)

MG2 C14 Alexander Ross Papers.

Public Archives of Nova Scotia (PANS)

RG1 vol. 376 pp. 78–93, 104–110. Land grants, 1784, to Loyalists and disbanded troops at Prince Edward Island and at Antigonish and Pictou, Nova Scotia.

Public Archives of Prince Edward Island (PAPEI)

Acc 2779/1 Chartering of *John and Elizabeth*, 1775.

Public Record Office, London (PRO)

CO 42 Colonial Office, Correspondence, Canada.

Scottish Record Office (SRO)

E.504 Customs Records, 1776–1830.

GD 9/166/2 Dr. William Porter to Sir William Pulteney, 18 Jan. 1802.

GD 9/166/23, 23A Dr. William Porter to John MacKenzie, 27 Dec. 1802.

GD 46/1/530 Alexander Stewart to Mrs. Stewart MacKenzie, 26 June 1832.

GD 46/17/23 Edward S. Fraser to Lord Seaforth, 30 April 1803.

GD 174/16/5 Hector McLean to Murdoch McLean, 14th Dec. 1803.

GD 221/4433/1, GD 221/4434/1 Lord MacDonald Papers.

GD 268/216/18 Lady Stafford to James Loch, 1813.

RH 4/188/2 Prize essays and Transactions of the Highland Society of Scotland, vol. iii, 1802–03, 475–657. Reports of the Committees on Emigration, 1802–1803.

Strathclyde Regional Archives (SRA)

TD 219/12/3 John MacNeill to Ilay Campbell, 2 May 1803.

University of Birmingham Special Collections (UBSC)

Church Missionary Society Papers.
C C1 o 72/1-8 Rev. John West (1822–1823).
C C1 o 37/1-70 Rev. David T. Jones (1823–1839).
C C1 o 16/1-163 Rev. William Cockran (1825–1865).
C C1 o 26/1-7 Rev. William Garrioch (1825–1830).
C C1 o 63/1-66 Rev. John Smithurst (1839–1851).
C1/Co/8/2 Alexander Ross, 1829.

Wallaceburg and District Museum

Baldoon Indentures, Hugh MacCallum and John MacDonald, Piper, 11th July 1807, Baldoon.
Brown Family, Genealogy.

In Private Hands

Letter, John MacDougald of Baldoon to his brother, Hugh, in Mull, 29 April 1806.

PRINTED PRIMARY SOURCES AND CONTEMPORARY PUBLICATIONS

Brown, Robert, *Strictures and remarks on the Earl of Selkirk's observations on the present state of the Highlands* (Edinburgh: 1806).
Bryce, George, *John Black, the Apostle of the Red River or How the blue banner was unfurled on the Manitoba Prairies* (Montreal: William Briggs, 1898).
_____, *Manitoba: Its Infancy and Growth and Present Condition* (London: 1882).
Bryce, George and Charles N. Bell, *Original Letters and other Documents relating to the Selkirk Settlement*, Transaction No. 33 (Historical and Scientific Society of Manitoba, 1889).
Bryce, George, *The Makers of Canada: MacKenzie, Selkirk and Simpson* (Toronto: Morang, 1905).
_____, "The Old Settlers of Red River" (Winnipeg: *Manitoba Daily Free Press*, 1885).
_____, *The Remarkable History of the Hudson's Bay Company, including that of the French traders of north-western Canada and of the North-West, XY and Astor fur companies* (Toronto: W. Briggs, 1900).
_____, *The Romantic Settlement of Lord Selkirk's Colonists* (Toronto: Musson Book Co., 1909).
Colonial Records of North Carolina (ed.) William L. Saunders (Raleigh, 1886–90) vols. viii, ix.
Douglas, Thomas, 5th Earl of Selkirk, *Observations on a proposal for forming a Society for the Civilzation and Improvement of the North American Indians within the British Boundary* (London: 1807).
_____, *A Letter to the Earl of Liverpool accompanied by correspondence with the Colonial Department in the years 1817–1819, on the subject of the Red River Settlement in North America* (London: 1819).
_____, *Observations on the Present State of the Highlands of Scotland, with a view of the*

causes and probable consequences of emigration (London: 1805; 2nd edition, London and Edinburgh: 1806).

_____, *A Sketch of the British fur trade in North America with observations relative to the North West Company of Montreal* (London: 1816).

Gourlay, Robert, *Statistical Account of Upper Canada compiled with a view to a grand system of emigration* (London: Simpkin & Marshall, 1822).

Gunn, Donald and Charles R. Tuttle, *History of Manitoba from the earliest settlements to 1835 and from 1835 to the admission of the province into the Dominion* (Ottawa: Malcolm Roger & Co., 1880).

Historical Atlas of Essex and Kent Counties, Ontario, 1880–1 (Toronto: H. Belden & Co., 1973).

Illustrated Historical Atlas, County of Simcoe, Ontario, 1881 (Port Elgin: Cumming Atlas Reprints, 1975).

Halkett, John, *Statement respecting the Earl of Selkirk's Settlement in North America* (London: June 1817).

Irvine, Alexander, *An Enquiry into the Causes and Effects of Emigration from the Highlands and Western Isles of Scotland with Observations on the Means Employed for Preventing it* (Edinburgh: 1802).

Johnstone, Walter, *Travels in Prince Edward Island, Gulf of St. Lawrence, North America in the years 1820–1821, undertaken with a design to establish Sabbath Schools* (Edinburgh: 1823).

Martin, Archer, *The Hudson's Bay Company's Land Tenures and the Occupation of Assiniboia by Lord Selkirk's Settlers* (London: Wm. Cloves & Sons, 1898).

Miller, Hugh, *Sutherland as it was and is: How a country may be ruined* (Edinburgh: John Johnstone, 1843).

A Narrative of Occurrences in the Indian Countries of North America, since the connexion of the Right Hon. the Earl of Selkirk with the Hudson's Bay Company, and his Attempt to establish a Colony on the Red River; with a detailed Account of His Lordship's Military Expedition to, and Subsequent Proceedings at, Fort William, in Upper Canada (London: 1817).

Ross, Alexander, *The Red River Settlement; its rise, progress and present state* (London: 1856).

Sinclair, Sir John, *First Statistical Account of Scotland*, 21 vols. (Edinburgh: 1791–99).

Strachan, Dr. John, *A Letter to the Rt. Hon. Earl of Selkirk on his Settlement at the Red River near Hudson Bay* (London: Longman, 1816).

A True Guide to Prince Edward Island, formerly St. John's, in the Gulph [sic] of St. Lawrence, North America (Liverpool: 1808).

BRITISH PARLIAMENTARY PAPERS

Papers relating to the Red River Settlement, 1815–1819, House of Commons, No. 584.

NEWSPAPERS AND PERIODICALS

Dumfries and Galloway Courier and Herald
Inverness Courier
Inverness Journal
Lloyd's Shipping Register 1798–1815

Montreal Gazette
Orkney Herald
Quebec Gazette
Scots Magazine
The Scotsman

SECONDARY SOURCES

Adam, R.J. (ed.) *Papers on Sutherland Estate Management* (Edinburgh: Scottish Historical Society, 1972).

Adams, Ian, and Meredyth Somerville, *Cargoes of Despair and Hope: Scottish emigration to North America 1603–1803* (Edinburgh: John Donald, 1993).

Barron, James, *The Northern Highlands in the Nineteenth Century Newspaper Index and Annals*, 3 vols. (Inverness: R. Carruthers & Sons, 1903–13).

Belfast Historical Society, *The Recaller*, Apr. 2001.

Bitterman, Rusty, "Economic Stratification and Agrarian Settlement: Middle River in the early Nineteenth Century" in Kenneth Donovan (ed.) *The Island, New Perspectives on Cape Breton History* (Fredericton: Acadiensis, 1990) 71–95.

Bittermann, Rusty, Robert A. MacKinnon and Graeme Wynne, "Of Equality and Interdependence in the Nova Scotian Countryside 1850–70," *Canadian Historical Review* vol. lxxiv (1993) 1–43.

Bolger, F.W.P. (ed.) *Canada's Smallest Province: A History of Prince Edward Island* (Halifax: Nimbus, 1991).

Brunger, A.G., "The Distribution of Scots and Irish in Upper Canada 1851–71," *Canadian Geographer*, vol. 34 (1990) 250–58.

Bumsted, J.M., *Land Settlement and Politics on Eighteenth Century Prince Edward Island* (Kingston: McGill-Queen's University Press, 1987).

_____, "Selkirk's Agents, A Tale of Three Settlements," *The Beaver*, (33) June–July 1992, 33–41.

_____, "The Quest for a Usable Founder: Lord Selkirk and Manitoba Historians," *Manitoba History*, No. 2 (1981) 2–7.

_____, (ed.) *The Collected Writings of Lord Selkirk*, vols. I (1799–1809), II (1810–1820) (Winnipeg: The Manitoba Record Society, 1984, 1987).

_____, *The Peoples of Canada, a Pre-Confederation History*, vol. 1 (Toronto: Oxford University Press, 1992).

_____, "Settlement by Chance: Lord Selkirk and Prince Edward Island," *Canadian Historical Review*, lix (1978) 179–82.

_____, "The Affair at Stornoway, 1811," *The Beaver*, Spring 1982, 53–8.

_____, *The People's Clearance: Highland Emigration to British North America 1770–1815* (Edinburgh: Edinburgh University Press, 1982).

_____, *The Scottish Catholic Church and Prince Edward Island 1770–1810* (PAPEI no. 3846).

Burley, Edith I., *Servants of the Honourable Company, Work Discipline and Conflict in the Hudson's Bay Company, 1770–1879* (Toronto: Oxford University Press, 1997).

Campbell, Wilfrid, *The Scotsman in Canada*, vol. ii (London: Sampson Law & Co., 1911).

Campey, Lucille H., *"A Very Fine Class of Immigrants": Prince Edward Island's Scottish Pioneers 1770–1850* (Toronto: Natural Heritage Books, 2001).

Clark, Andrew Hill, *Three Centuries and the Island: A Historical Geography of settlement and agriculture in Prince Edward Island, Canada* (Toronto: University of Toronto Press, 1959).

Clark, Lloyd, J. "The Baldoon Lands, the effect of changing drainage technology, 1804–1967" (Masters Thesis, University of Western Ontario, 1970).

Cornelius, Donna Jean, *History of Wallaceburg, Part Two* (Wallaceburg Research and Information Study, 1974).

Coutts, Robert J., *The Road to the Rapids, Nineteenth century Church and society at St. Andrew's Parish, Red River* (Calgary: University of Calgary Press, 2000).

Cowan, Helen, *British Emigration to British North America: The First Hundred Years* (Toronto: University of Toronto Press, 1961).

———, "Selkirk's Work in Canada: An Early Chapter," *Canadian Historical Review,* vol. 9 (4) 1928, 299–308.

Devine, T.M., *Exploring the Scottish Past: Themes in the History of Scottish Society* (East Linton: Tuckwell Press, 1995).

Dictionary of Canadian Biography, vols. v–xiii (Toronto: 1979–85).

Diefenbaker, John D., *One Canada, Memoirs of the Rt. Hon. John Diefenbaker* (Toronto: Macmillan, 1975).

"Dover Parish Census – 1817, the Baldoon Settlement," *Ontario Genealogical Society Bulletin,* Kent Branch, vol. 9 (3) 1986, 55.

Ens, Gerhard J., *Homeland to Hinterland: The Changing World of the Métis in the Nineteenth Century* (Toronto: University of Toronto Press, 1996).

Flanagan, Thomas, *Métis Lands in Manitoba* (Calgary: University of Calgary Press, 1991).

Friesen, Gerald, *The Canadian Prairies: A History* (Toronto: University of Toronto Press, 1984).

Garrioch, Rev. A.C, *First Furrows* (Winnipeg: Stovel Co. Ltd., 1924).

Glendinning, Evelyn and Alan Mann, *Trinity: History of the Methodist and United Church in Wallaceburg, 1842–1942* (Wallaceburg: Standard Press, 1992).

Goldring, Philip, "Lewis and the Hudson's Bay Company in the Nineteenth Century," *The Journal of the School of Scottish Studies* (University of Edinburgh) vol. 22, 1978, 23–41.

Gray, John Morgan, *Lord Selkirk of Red River* (London: Macmillan, 1963).

Gray, Malcolm, *The Highland Economy 1750–1850* (Edinburgh: Oliver & Boyd, 1957).

Guillet, Edwin, *Early Life in Upper Canada* (Toronto: Ontario Publishing Co., 1933).

Hamil, Fred Coyne, *The Valley of the Lower Thames, 1640–1850* (Toronto: University of Toronto Press, 1951).

Harvey D.C., "Early Settlements and Social Conditions in Prince Edward Island," *Dalhousie Review*, vol. xi, no. 4 (1932) 458–9.

Healy, W.J., *Women of Red River, being a book written from the recollections of women surviving from the Red River Era* (Winnipeg: Peguis Publishers Ltd., 1987).

Herman, Arthur, *The Scottish Enlightenment: The Scots Invention of the Modern World* (London: Fourth Estate, 2001).

Hornby, Susan (ed.) *Belfast People: An Oral History of Belfast, Prince Edward Island* (Charlottetown: Tea Hill Press, 1992).

Hunter, Andrew F., *A History of Simcoe County* (Barrie: Historical Committee of Simcoe County, 1948).

Innes, Harold A., *The Fur Trade in Canada* (Toronto: University of Toronto Press, 1962).

Lalonde, A.N., "Colonization Companies in the 1880s," *Saskatchewan History,* vol. xxiv No. 3 (1971) 101–14.

Lauriston, Victor, *Romantic Kent: More Than Three Centuries of History, 1626–1952* (Chatham, n.p., 1952).

Lawson, Bill, *A Register of Emigrants from the Western Isles of Scotland 1750–1900,* 2 vols. (Harris, 1992).

MacDonald, Neil T., *The Baldoon Mystery* (Wallaceburg: Standard Press, 1986).

MacDonald, Norman, *Canada: Immigration and Settlement 1763–1841* (London: Longmans, 1939).

MacEwan, Grant, *Cornerstone Colony: Selkirk's Contribution to the Canadian West* (Saskatoon: Prairie Books, 1977).

MacKenzie, A.E.D., *Baldoon: Lord Selkirk's settlement in Upper Canada* (London, Ont., Phelps Publishing Co., 1978).

MacKinnon, James, "A Short History of the Pioneer Scotch Settlers, St. Andrews, Saskatchewan," *The Courier,* Regina, 1921.

Mann, Alan and Frank Mann, *Settlement on the Sydenham: The Story of Wallaceburg* (Wallaceburg: Mann Historical Files, 1984).

Martin, Chester, *Lord Selkirk's Work in Canada,* Oxford Historical and Literary Studies, vol. 7 (Oxford at the Clarendon Press, 1916).

_____, *Red River Settlement, Papers in the Canadian Archives Relating to the Pioneers* (Ottawa: Public Archives of Canada, 1910).

Marwick, Ernest W., "Stromness and the Hudson Bay Trade, the last twenty years," *The Orkney Herald,* 15 July 1952.

McGowan, Ian (ed.), *Samuel Johnson, A Journey to the Western Isles of Scotland* (Edinburgh: Canongate, 2001).

McLean, Marianne, *People of Glengarry 1745–1820: Highlanders in Transition* (Montreal: McGill-Queen's University Press, 1991).

Meek, Donald E., "Evangelicalism and Emigration: Aspects of the role of dissenting evangelicalism in Highland emigration to Canada" in Gordon MacLennan (ed.) *Proceedings of the First North American Congress of Celtic Studies* (1986) 15–37.

Meyer, Duane, *The Highland Scots of North Carolina* (Durham: University of North Carolina Press, 1961).

Milton, Norma J., "The Scots in Alberta," in Howard and Tamara Palmer (eds.) *Peoples of Alberta: Portrait of Cultural Diversity* (Saskatoon: Western Prairie Books, 1985) 102–22.

Mitchell, Elaine Allan "The Scot in the Fur Trade" in W. Stanford Reid (ed.), *The Scottish Tradition in Canada* (Toronto: McClelland & Stewart, 1976) 27–49.

Mitchell, George W., "Lord Selkirk's Baldoon Settlement" in *Kentiana, The Story of the Settlement and Development of the County of Kent* (Chatham: Kent Historical Society, 1939) 37–40.

_____, "Lord Selkirk's Baldoon Settlement," *Kent Historical Society Papers and Addresses,* vol. 1, 12–21.

Morrison, Jean, *Superior Rendezvous-Place: Fort William in the Canadian Fur Trade* (Toronto: Natural Heritage Books, 2001).

Morton, W.L., *Manitoba: A History* (Toronto: University of Toronto Press, 1967).

Nicks, John, "Orkneymen in the HBC 1780–1821" in Carol M. Judd and Arthur J. Ray, *Old Trails and New Directions: Papers of the third North American Fur Trade Conference*

(Toronto: University of Toronto Press, 1980) 102–26.

Norton, Wayne, *Help us to a Better Land: Crofter Colonies in the Prairie West* (Regina: University of Regina Press, 1994).

Orlo, J. and D. Fraser, "Those Elusive Immigrants, Part 1," *The Island Magazine*, No. 16 (1984) 36–44.

Owran, Doug, *Promise of Eden: The Canadian Expansionist Movement and the idea of the West, 1856–1900* (Toronto: University of Toronto Press, 1980).

The Oxford Dictionary of Quotations (London: Oxford University Press, 1959).

Pannekoek, Frits, "The Anglican Church and Disintegration of Red River Society" in R. Douglas Francis and Howard Palmer (eds.) *The Prairie West: Historical Readings* (Edmonton: Pica Pica Press, 1985) 100–6.

Parley, Kay, "Moffat, Assiniboia, North-West Territories" *Saskatchewan History,* vol. xx, No. 1 (1967) 32–6.

Patterson, Gilbert, *Land Settlement in Upper Canada, 1783–1840* (Toronto: Ontario Archives, 1921).

Prince Edward Island Genealogical Society, *From Scotland to Prince Edward Island: Scottish emigrants to Prince Edward Island from death and obituary notices in Prince Edward Island 1835–1910* (n.d.).

Pritchett, John Perry, *The Red River Valley, 1811–1849* (New York: Russell & Russell, first published 1942 and reissued 1970).

Rayburn, Alan, *Geographical Names of Prince Edward Island; Toponymy Study* (Ottawa: Department of Energy, Mines and Resources, 1973).

Read, Colin, *The Rising in Western Upper Canada 1837–8: The Duncombe Revolt and After* (Toronto: 1982).

Reid, W. Stanford (ed.), *The Scottish Tradition in Canada* (Toronto: McClelland & Stewart, 1976).

Rich, E.E., *Journal of Occurrences in the Athabaska Department by George Simpson 1820 and 1821* (Toronto: Champlain Society, 1938).

Richards, Eric, *A History of the Highland Clearances: Emigration, Protest, Reasons* (London: Croom Helm, 1985).

_____, *Patrick Sellar and the Highland Clearances* (Edinburgh: Polygon, 1999).

_____, "Varieties of Scottish Emigration in the Nineteenth Century," *Historical Studies*, vol. 21 (1985) 473–94.

Russell, R.C., *Carleton Trail: The broad highway into the Saskatchewan country from the Red River settlement, 1840–80* (Saskatoon: Modern Press, 1965).

The Scottish Catholics in Prince Edward Island 1772–1922, Memorial Volume (Summerside, PEI: 1922) 47–54.

St. Andrew's Society of Winnipeg, *The Scots Monument*, Monument Booklet, P.O. Box 595, Winnipeg, Manitoba, R3C 2J3.

Shearer, John, W. Groundwater and J.D. Mackay (eds.) *The New Orkney Book* (Edinburgh: Nelson Printers, 1966).

Shortt, A. and A.G. Doughty (eds.), *Canada and its Provinces: A History of the Canadian people and their institutions, by one hundred associates* (Toronto: Publishers Association of Canada, 1913–17).

Smout, T.C., *A History of the Scottish People, 1560–1830* (London: Fontana Press, 1990).

Spry, Irene M., "The Métis and Mixed-Bloods of Rupert's Land before 1870 in Jacqueline Paterson and Jennifer S.H. Brown (eds.) *The New Peoples, being and becoming*

214

Métis in North America (Winnipeg: University of Manitoba Press, 1985) 97–106.

Stuart, Kent, "The Scottish Crofter Colony, Saltcoats 1889–1904," *Saskatchewan History*, vol. xxiv(2) 1971, 41–50.

Thomas, Lewis G. (ed.) *The Prairie West to 1905* (Toronto: Oxford University Press, 1975).

Wallace, Malcolm, "Pioneers of the Scotch Settlement on the Shore of Lake St. Clair," *Ontario Historical Society*, vol. xli, 1949, 173–200.

Wallace, William Stewart (ed.) *Documents relating to the North West Company* (Toronto: Champlain Society, 1934).

Wallaceburg Old Boys' and Girls' Reunion (Wallaceburg: 1936).

Thomas, Lewis (ed.) The *Prairie West to 1905* (Toronto: Oxford University Press, 1975).

Turner, Alan R., "Scottish Settlement of the West" in W. Stanford Reid (ed.), *The Scottish Tradition in Canada* (Toronto: McClelland & Stewart, 1976) 76–91.

White, Patrick Cecil Telford (ed.) *Lord Selkirk's Diary 1803–04: A journal of his travels through British North America and the Northeastern United States* (Toronto: The Champlain Society, 1958).

Wild, Marilyn, "Natives of Scotland who Emigrated to Kent County Ontario, Canada," *Central Scotland Family History Society Bulletin,* No. 9 (1994); No. 10,11 (1995); No. 12,13, (1996).

INDEX

COVER CREDITS

Front cover: Photograph of a portrait of Thomas Douglas, Fifth Earl of Selkirk, believed to be by Sir Henry Raeburn. *Toronto Reference Library, J. Ross Robertson Collection.*
Back cover: *Short Stay Among the Orkney Islands*, June 3, 1821, a painting by Peter Rindisbacher. It shows a ship off the Orkney Islands, possibly waiting to collect passengers for British North America. Born in Switzerland in 1806, Rindisbacher emigrated with his family to Red River in 1821. He lived in Red River for seven years, painting scenes that he witnessed. He died in St. Louis, Missouri, aged 28. *National Archives of Canada, C-001902.*

ABOUT THE AUTHOR

Dr. Lucille Campey is a Canadian, living in Britain, with over thirty years of experience as a researcher and author. It was her father's Scottish roots and love of history which first stimulated her interest in the early exodus of people from Scotland to Canada. She is the great-great-granddaughter of William Thomson, who left Morayshire, on the northeast coast of Scotland in the early 1800s to begin a new life with his family, first near Digby then in Antigonish, Nova Scotia. He is described in D. Whidden's *History of the Town of Antigonish* simply as "William, Pioneer" and is commemorated in the St. James Church and Cemetery at Antigonish. Lucille was awarded a Ph.D. by Aberdeen University in 1998 for her researches into Scottish emigration to Canada in the period 1770-1850.

This is Lucille's third book on the subject of emigrant Scots. Described by PEI's *The Guardian* as "indispensable to Islanders of Scottish ancestry," her first book, *"A Very Fine Class of Immigrants": Prince Edward Island's Scottish Pioneers 1770-1850* (Natural Heritage, 2001), gives the most comprehensive account to date of the Scottish influx to the Island. Her second book, *"Fast Sailing and Copper-Bottomed": Aberdeen Sailing Ships and the Emigrant Scots They Carried to Canada 1774-1855* (Natural Heritage, 2002), gives a gripping account of emigrant shipping from the north of Scotland to Canada in the sailing ship era.

A Chemistry graduate of Ottawa University, Lucille worked initially in the fields of science and computing. After marrying her English husband she moved to the north of England, where she became interested in medieval monasteries and acquired a Master of Philosophy Degree (on

240

the subject of medieval settlement patterns) from Leeds University. Having lived for five years in Easter Ross, in the north of Scotland, while she completed her doctoral thesis, she and Geoff returned to England, and now live near Salisbury in Wiltshire. Lucille's fourth book will concentrate on the Scottish pioneers of Nova Scotia and Cape Breton.